How I Built An INTEGRATED RESORT

Daniel Cheng

Contents

PREFACE

one Actors 1

two Foundation... 20

three The glass slipper 37

four The Herfindahl-Hirschman principle...................... 49

five Let the numbers do the talking 61

six Urban master plan 76

seven X marks the spot.................................... 91

eight Destination resort? 110

nine Iconicity.. 121

ten "KYC" 132

eleven Rise of the digital-natives.................... 147

twelve That's entertainment............................ 160

thirteen Rejuvenation.................................... 182

fourteen Convention-al wisdom 197

fifteen A room with a view.............................. 210

sixteen Primum non nocere 219

seventeen Integrated 232

eighteen Till...do us part 246

nineteen The "matchmaker" 260

Index.. 279

PREFACE

"Integrated resorts" are the new "casino resorts."

The Singapore government has said integrated resorts (IR) represent a new industry paradigm and should be called leisure, entertainment, and business zones. In their definition, an IR will have "all kinds of amenities - hotels, restaurants, shopping, convention space, even theaters, museums, and theme parks. They attract hundreds of thousands of visitors per year. The great majority will not be there to gamble. They may be tourists, executives, or businessmen, who go to enjoy the resort or attend conventions or conferences. But within this large development and slew of activities, there is one small but essential part which offers gaming and which helps make the entire project financially viable."

This raises an interesting comparison. Some might argue that the described IR model sounds remarkably similar to what already exists in established gambling destinations like Las Vegas, with iconic resorts like Bellagio and the Mirage offering similar combinations of amenities alongside casinos. Is "integrated resort" just a glorified moniker for modern casino resorts and all for namesake purposes? While Las Vegas prioritizes entertainment through expansive casinos, Singapore-styled integrated resorts take a distinct approach, positioning the casino as a smaller, less prominent element. This aligns with Asian cultural sensibilities, where casino gambling often carries a social stigma and is viewed differently from the Western perspective of entertainment. Yet, even that is not where the true substance of what represents an integrated resort lies. While formal definitions and classifications can provide a starting point, they offer a limited perspective on the essence of integrated resorts. These resorts extend beyond static concepts and rigid templates, instead evolving with each new project. The pioneering Singaporean developments serve as significant early examples of this dynamism, with Marina Bay Sands often regarded as a leading example. However, even this shouldn't be considered a fixed benchmark. The core concept of an integrated resort lies in its integration, representing a dynamic framework that continuously adapts and pushes the boundaries of the hospitality experience.

This book aims to correct widespread misconceptions about integrated resorts by providing a detailed analysis of their core "integrative characteristics." Through the lens of the author's firsthand experience in the industry's formative years, particularly in Asia, 'How I Built an Integrated Resort' deconstructs the IR model, delving into the "who, what, why, and how" involved in its planning, design, and development. Presented as a series of building blocks, the book serves as a valuable resource not just for IR operators but also for government policymakers, developers, investors, academics, and other stakeholders seeking to navigate the dynamic IR industry.

one
ACTORS

Operators, investors, legislators, regulators.
NGOs, lobbyists, agents, enterprises.
Financiers, lawyers, consultants, builders.
Administrators, denizens, suppliers, customers.

The creation of an integrated resort involves a confluence of various actors that enter the scene in one of the following stages of its formation:

1. Ideation
2. Legislation
3. Licensing
4. Construction
5. Operation

Building an integrated resort isn't a solo act. It's a grand orchestral performance, with diverse players entering the stage at different moments. Forget Hollywood stars; these "actors" are composed of visionaries, regulators, and operators, shaping this complex world of integrated resorts. Each troupe member joins the dance at a specific point: from the initial flicker of a bold idea (ideation) to the intricate steps of securing approval (legislation) and licenses (licensing), then onto the bricks-and-mortar construction (construction) and finally, the grand opening and ongoing performance (operation). But in this show, not every player shares the same spotlight. Some are fleeting silhouettes during the early rehearsals, while others take center stage throughout the run. Still others hold crucial backstage roles, their unseen actions steering the entire production, even determining its success or curtain call. Each party harbors unique motivations, driving their participation. These don't always harmonize; occasionally, conflicting melodies disrupt the rhythm. This book aims to be the maestro, harmonizing these diverse voices. By understanding the perspectives and goals of every actor, we can orchestrate the smoothest performance possible, ensuring the triumphant finale of the integrated resort. The curtain rises on the integrated resort, not with a flourish, but with a cacophony of voices vying for attention. This opening act is a symphony of motivations, a chorus of players with dreams to chase and dollars to clutch. Governments, strapped by economic woes, see integrated resorts as the glittering aria that can revive their fortunes. Tourism, a siren with a glittering song, promises a surge of visitors and a blossoming hospitality sector. But beneath the alluring melodies lurks the basso profundo of the business community, their instruments the clinking of coins and the rustle of banknotes. Large corporations, their pockets heavy with investment capital, conduct elaborate solos, offering access and influence in exchange for a favorable legislative score. Smaller businesses, banding together in associations, raise a collective mezzo-soprano, hoping to sway political agendas and elections. But not all voices harmonize. In many Asian nations, the spotlight on corporate funding raises concerns about corruption, silencing their solo acts. Lobbying firms, the deft conductors, then take center stage, navigating the intricate corridors of power on behalf of their business clients. In Japan, marketing agencies become the bridge, blending lobbying with public relations, whispering policy suggestions, and shaping public opinion.

Yet, the stage demands more than just influence. It craves expertise, and there, veterans from the Las Vegas stage stand poised. Casino gaming consultancies, the virtuosos of market analysis, deliver compelling recitals of feasibility studies and financial forecasts. Their reports, like persuasive concertos, convince governments and lenders of the harmony integrated resorts promise to bring. Some, like Spectrum Gaming, have pirouetted across multiple stages, from Singapore's cautious waltz to Thailand's hopeful tap dance to Japan's intricate ballet. Others remain discreet, the unseen puppeteers shaping the production from the wings. But this intricate dance isn't confined to suits and spreadsheets. Academia, often a muted oboe, occasionally rises to a powerful crescendo. In Japan, Osaka Commerce University emerged as a passionate chorus, its research and advocacy playing a crucial role in advancing integrated resort legislation. This, then, is the captivating cacophony of Stage 1, a diverse ensemble whose every note, harmonious or discordant, shapes the future of the integrated resort symphony.

The ideation stage of integrated resort development is fertile ground for a diverse array of stakeholders, particularly those within the private sector. At the forefront are casino operators and their key investors, local real estate and construction companies, and their army of consultants, lawyers, and lobbyists. American companies are particularly adept at navigating this stage, having honed their expertise in their established home market. Las Vegas Sands, a prime example, leveraged its extensive experience and influential network to achieve significant successes, not only in its domestic market but also internationally. Whispers of their persuasive abilities reaching the highest echelons of power in Macau during the casino license bidding process offer a testament to their prowess. They were said to have secured a high-level sponsor in the mayor of Busan City in South Korea though that effort to convince the national government to designate the port city for an integrated resort fell short. In Japan, they had hired a seasoned government bureaucrat as their key person on the ground and the company was the leading contender for an IR license until they abandoned the pursuit on the cusp of the collapse of Yokohama City's IR ambition. The Malaysian Genting Group adopted a similar approach, employing strategic lobbying efforts to secure a racino license in New York City. Local players also bring crucial expertise and influence to the table. In Japan, for instance, major real estate developers and construction firms played a pivotal role in advancing the integrated resort legislation. Their deep understanding of the local market and established relationships with key stakeholders proved invaluable in navigating the complex policy landscape. ORIX Corporation, a leading real estate giant, exemplifies this strategic collaboration, securing a significant stake in the first Japanese IR project alongside construction powerhouses like Obayashi and Takenaka.

Driven by the enticing lure of substantial debt generation for their portfolios, financial institutions become avid participants in the integrated resort ideation phase. They often align themselves with pro-casino lobbies, lending influential support to deregulation efforts and partnering closely with casino companies to advance this agenda. This intricate relationship between the financial sector and the casino industry, despite the latter's "junk bond" classification, extends beyond a simple one-way street. Casinos offer a continuous stream of opportunities for financial institutions, encompassing diverse areas from funding construction and renovations to supporting daily operations. Investment banking divisions within banks play a crucial role in helping casinos raise capital through IPOs, bond issuances, and lucrative mergers and acquisitions. Casino properties and assets, with their inherent stability, also serve as valuable collateral for loans, further bolstering capital reserves. This was particularly evident when casino-REITs (real estate investment trusts) gained traction. Notably, financial giants like The Blackstone Group, Apollo Global, and TPG Group have gone beyond mere partnerships and actively ventured into casino ownership themselves, further solidifying the intertwined interests of these sectors.

Unlike the external influence and private-sector lobbying often associated with integrated resort developments, Singapore's approach stands as a model of government-driven initiative. In the early 2000s, facing a struggling tourism sector, the government strategically identified integrated resorts as a key component of its national economic revitalization plan. This deliberate decision bypassed the pitfalls of external pressure and ushered in a multi-ministry task force tasked with meticulously assessing the feasibility, form, and scale of this new endeavor. At this crucial juncture, public officials assumed the pivotal role of transforming the envisioned integrated resort into a formally structured proposal for legislative consideration. This stage presented a critical turning point, with the potential for the vision to gain momentum, stall in uncertainty, or face outright rejection – a fate witnessed in Taiwan and multiple earlier attempts in Thailand. Even the normally-efficient Japan, mired in legislative quicksand for over two decades, demonstrated the precariousness of this phase. South Korea, in its haste to secure passage, compromised its framework, resulting in a suboptimal outcome that failed to attract significant investment. Singapore, however, navigated these potential pitfalls with characteristic rigor through a comprehensive due diligence process. This multifaceted approach transcended mere economic considerations, encompassing carefully balanced assessments of social and security aspects. While conducting in-depth market research, the government actively engaged the industry through a formal Request for Concepts exercise. This transparent initiative ensured diverse perspectives informed the final market framework, upon which international tenders were issued to solicit bids for partnership.

The journey from envisioning an opulent integrated resort to enshrining its existence in law is rarely a straightforward sprint. Instead, it often resembles a perilous trek through a political labyrinth, riddled with pitfalls and guarded by formidable adversaries. The inherently divisive nature of the casino industry casts a long shadow over this path, transforming legislation into a potent political weapon, a lucrative bargaining chip, or a career-ending gamble. Japan serves as a poignant illustration of this precarious dance. The Japan IR Bill, in spite of all its alluring promise of economic rejuvenation, became embroiled in the treacherous currents of political maneuvering. Lawmakers, blinded by the mirage of wealth and power concentrated in casino licenses, engage in high-stakes games of "pork-barreling," each desperately vying to secure licenses and shower their constituencies with the promised bounty of job creation and financial prosperity. However, beneath this surface shimmered a chilling reality:

most lawmakers harbor a deep-seated aversion to gambling legislation, a reluctance fueled by the specter of public censure and the risk of political decimation. The meteoric rise and downfall of Yokohama's once-unbeatable mayor, Fumiko Hayashi, stands as a stark testament to this fear. Her unwavering advocacy for casinos swiftly led to her electoral demise, a fate mirrored in the short-lived premiership of Yoshihide Suga, whose association with the IR bill cast a long shadow of doubt over his leadership.

The complexities extend beyond individual ambitions. Politicians, often entangled in a web of competing interests, can unwittingly become pawns in the hands of powerful entities. Established legal gambling businesses, jealously guarding their market monopolies, discreetly operate in the shadows, wielding their influence to torpedo rival casino legislation. Conversely, anti-gambling lobbies, driven by an unwavering moral conviction, can launch formidable campaigns, effectively portraying casinos as harbingers of societal and economic collapse. In the United States, this battle has kept commercial casinos out of Florida, while Native American hopes for expanded gaming operations in Massachusetts remain perpetually dashed on the rocks of political opposition. It is amidst this landscape of political quagmires that a beacon of hope flickers in Thailand. The kingdom's bipartisan support for casino legalization stands as a stark contrast to the entrenched opposition and internal wrangling often witnessed elsewhere. This rare alignment of opposing forces hints at the possibility of Thailand finally overcoming obstacles to casino legislation and unlocking its economic potential.

The cast of characters thickens as new players step onto the stage when legislative approval draws near. This is the moment when most casino companies, seduced by the irresistible allure of tangible business prospects, finally take center stage. Some might perceive them as latecomers to the party, arriving when the early trailblazers have already staked their claims and set the agenda in motion. After all, as the adage goes, "the early bird catches the worm." In the hyper-competitive world of casino investments, timely information and first-mover advantage are prized possessions. While not all who arrive early emerge victorious, that initial head start can prove invaluable. However, even for those who arrive after the initial fanfare, the door to success isn't necessarily shut. By crafting a compelling and strategically sound bidding concept, latecomers can still carve their niche in the competitive landscape. Nowhere is this more evident than in tightly controlled, high-stakes license bidding scenarios such as Singapore's. Here, a perfectly sculpted proposal that fulfills all the desired criteria, even at a later stage, can still clinch the coveted prize.

Yet, a proactive approach remains the wiser strategy. It gives early entrants a longer runway to decipher the complexities of local dynamics, forge crucial relationships, and build trust with stakeholders. Most importantly, it presents the opportunity to shape the narrative in their favor, swaying public opinion and influencing policy discussions. MGM Resorts and ORIX Corporation stand as prime illustrations of this principle. Deeply ingrained in the Japanese IR journey from its nascent stages, these companies weathered the political turbulence and ups and downs of the legislative process. Their unwavering dedication fostered grassroots support from local communities and instilled confidence in political leaders. Ultimately, their patient and persistent efforts culminated in securing the first IR license in Japan, a testament to the power of long-term commitment and strategic positioning. Similarly, Hard Rock International, owned by the Seminole Tribe of Florida, boldly established its presence in Hokkaido, a Japanese region overlooked by other major players. Their early commitment and unwavering support for the area garnered significant local backing. However, their endeavor was unfortunately thwarted by a political stalemate that froze the prefectural government's participation in the IR bid, highlighting the delicate interplay between business acumen and the unpredictable tides of political will.

Making casinos a reality involves traversing the intricate labyrinth of the legislative process, a complex landscape governed by established procedures and punctuated by pivotal moments of influence. Within this framework, the path to fruition commences with a spark – the formal introduction of a motion or proposal within the designated legislative body, such as a national assembly or parliament. In some democratic systems, the citizenry themselves can ignite this spark by directly submitting a drafted bill. Once launched, the bill embarks on a convoluted and multifaceted odyssey. It may be referred to dedicated committees for deeper analysis, where constructive feedback can refine and reshape its core tenets. Then comes the moment of public scrutiny, as the bill ascends the legislative floor for passionate debates that influence its trajectory with every vote. In bicameral systems like the United States, Japan, and Thailand, this journey often transcends a single chamber, demanding assent from both houses before reaching the head of state for final approval. However, before this legislative crescendo plays out, the bill exists in a state of relative malleability. It's during this formative phase, encompassing drafting and inception, that the seeds of influence are sown. Here, early advocates possess a distinct advantage, wielding the power to "influence the specifications" and nudge the legislation toward their preferred vision. This is where lobbyists and consultants come into their own, navigating the maze-like corridors of power and shaping the bill's nascent form with strategic acumen. Nowhere is this delicate interplay between vision and reality more evident than in the protracted saga of the Japan IR Bill. For over two decades, this legislation endured a tortuous birthing process, weathering countless revisions and parliamentary hurdles. Stakeholders from diverse sectors engaged in spirited debates, clashing over the number of licenses, their locations, the tax rate, and other critical parameters. It was during this protracted struggle that the casino lobby secured a pivotal victory, successfully advocating for the removal of the absolute floor area limit for casino facilities within integrated resorts, demonstrating the tangible impact of strategic advocacy within the legislative framework.

To effectively govern integrated resort development, the legislation should comprehensively address, and not be limited to, the following essential elements:

1. Regulatory Framework: Define the regulatory authority responsible for overseeing the industry and its supervisory powers and responsibilities.

2. Licensing and Permits: Outline the licensing process, criteria, and requirements for businesses and individuals to operate within the industry. This should include background checks, safety standards, and operational procedures.

3. Industry Standards: Establish the industry-specific standards for operational, safety, ethical, and financial

best practices. These standards cover standard operating procedures, approvals for casino marketing and promotions, access restrictions, safety and security, environmental impact, AMLA CTF compliance, and other relevant aspects.

4. Taxation: Define the casino tax regime for both businesses and consumers.

5. Zoning and Location: Address zoning regulations, taking into account factors like proximity to residential areas, environmental concerns, and the scale of the facility.

6. Safety and Security: Include provisions for the safety and security of workers, customers, and the general public.

7. Market Competition: Define the market structure to prevent monopolies, and anticompetitive practices, and ensure a level playing field for businesses. If applicable, specify any exclusivity period.

8. Casino Dispute Resolution: Define mechanisms for dispute resolution, arbitration, and legal recourse.

9. Reporting and Accountability: Establish auditing and reporting requirements, including financial disclosures, operational data, and compliance with regulations.

10. Fees and Penalties: Specify fees, fines, or penalties for violations of industry regulations and describe how they will be enforced.

Crafting a robust piece of integrated resort legislation is a crucial first step, but its power truly lies in its effective implementation and enforcement. As the saying goes, "laws are cobwebs that only catch the small flies." This stark reality was laid bare in Australia, where what many lauded as some of the world's most stringent casino laws ultimately proved woefully insufficient. The case in point: the shocking downfall of two major casino operators, prompting a cabinet minister to declare their operations a "cesspit of dishonesty, tax evasion, junkets, money laundering, and substantial infiltration by organized crime." The facade of Australia's highly praised state gaming commissions crumbled with the 2020 Bergin Inquiry, revealing a landscape of widespread illicit activities within casinos left to "self-regulate" under the indulgent eye of state regulators. This cautionary tale underscores the critical need for robust enforcement mechanisms alongside stringent legal frameworks. While Japan's IR Law appears stricter than Singapore's Casino Control Act, particularly regarding its citizen-oriented regulations aimed at preventing problem gambling, it leaves a crucial gap in specifying its execution. By delegating implementation to the discretion of individual prefectural authorities, the law introduces an element of variability and vulnerability to lax oversight or undue influence.

The pursuit of integrated resorts is rarely a unilateral endeavor. While proponents champion the economic and social benefits of these complex destinations, a diverse array of stakeholders often emerges to express reservations or outright opposition. This chorus of dissent can encompass various actors, including:

Rival political factions: Politicians with competing economic or ideological agendas may view IRs as detrimental to their interests or societal values.

Threatened business interests: Existing entertainment or hospitality sectors may perceive IRs as a threat to their market share and profitability.

Civil society groups: Organizations representing diverse social concerns, such as public health, religious values, or environmental protection, may express concerns about the potential negative impacts of IRs.

Individual stakeholders: Individuals with personal objections to gambling or specific anxieties about the social implications of IRs may voice their opposition.

The case of Japan serves as a stark illustration of the importance of acknowledging and engaging with these diverse perspectives. The protracted saga of the IR legislation in Japan was significantly influenced by the vocal opposition of civil society and non-governmental organizations (NGOs). Their concerns regarding problem gambling, social disruption, and organized crime infiltration resonated with a large segment of the population and ultimately led to a more cautious and measured approach to IR development. Thailand, as it contemplates its own IR ambitions, should heed the lessons learned from Japan. A competent government must prioritize understanding and addressing the full spectrum of public sentiment surrounding IRs. This goes beyond simply gauging market interest; it necessitates active engagement with diverse stakeholders, including civil society groups, labor unions, and community associations. Transparency and genuine dialogue are paramount in this process. Authorities that resort to superficial public consultations or insincere theatrics risk not only jeopardizing the success of their IR plans but also eroding public trust. Yokohama's failed attempt, a cautionary Icarus flying too close to the sun, reminds us of the perils of insincerity in this arena. However, the public landscape surrounding IRs is not always a monolith of opposition. Labor unions, for instance, may advocate for robust labor standards and responsible development practices within IR projects. Similarly, advocacy and civil rights NGOs may lend their support if IRs align with their agendas for social progress or promote equal employment opportunities for marginalized groups.

The order of magnitude of an integrated resort's scale results in a gestation period typically exceeding three years from approval to opening. This extended timeframe inherently harbors uncertainty and potential pitfalls. For stakeholders invested in the success of an IR, proactive measures are crucial to navigate through unforeseen headwinds. As experienced by Las Vegas Sands during the construction of Marina Bay Sands, financial hurdles can arise mid-construction, potentially jeopardizing the entire project. Singapore, with its foresight, had the cushion of additional competitive bids for its Marina Bay and Sentosa sites. This provided a contingency plan if Las Vegas Sands or Genting Singapore encountered insurmountable difficulties. Regardless of such readily available alternatives, new jurisdictions should consider incorporating other safeguard measures to mitigate such risks. These measures can take various forms:

Performance bonds or guarantees: Reliable financial institutions can backstop IR developers, ensuring project completion even if the developer faces financial headwinds.

Guaranteed completion clauses: Penalties or financial consequences for delays incentivize developers to adhere to timelines and prevent project stagnation.

Mandatory escrow accounts: Pre-construction funds deposited and released based on project milestones guarantee funding availability and mitigate potential cash flow problems.

These safeguards, combined with comprehensive financial due diligence during bid evaluation, provide a robust safety net for both the government and project stakeholders. Osaka's IR project illustrates the downside of lacking such safeguards. Their single-bid scenario leaves them vulnerable to delays or unforeseen obstacles faced by the sole consortium, ORIX-MGM Resorts. Unlike Singapore, they lack the luxury of readily available alternative contenders if their chosen developer falters. The path from envisioning an integrated resort to witnessing its grand opening can be unexpectedly long and winding. This was particularly evident in Japan, where two decades separated the initial conception and the first license award. During this protracted timeframe, the gaming landscape experienced a seismic shift. Influential figures moved on, new markets burst onto the scene, and established ones underwent dramatic transformations. The Japanese IR Bill, initially drafted with an optimistic view of a robust market fueled by unfettered Chinese junket operations, found itself adrift in a changed reality. By the time the first license was granted, the very foundation of the legislation – the vibrant junket sector – had vanished under the weight of a Chinese government anti-corruption crackdown. This confluence of bureaucratic inertia and an inability to adapt the legislative framework to the new market realities has cast a long shadow over the fledgling Japanese IR industry. Consequently, the IR process remains in a state of stasis, with policymakers grappling with how to recalibrate before issuing further licenses. This episode serves as a stark reminder for jurisdictions contemplating IR development: the market is a dynamic creature, and IR frameworks must be conceived as living documents, subject to periodic review and recalibration, especially in the face of prolonged timelines. Even if it necessitates scaling back ambitions or slowing down the overall pace, such agility is far preferable to clinging to outdated assumptions in a rapidly evolving landscape. While adaptability to dynamic market forces is crucial, ensuring investor confidence and market stability requires a judicious balance between policy agility and regulatory certainty. Frequent and unpredictable policy shifts pose a serious threat to IR investments. For foreign businesses, such volatility creates an environment of uncertainty that erodes confidence in the jurisdiction and discourages long-term commitment. These eddies of change can manifest in various ways, impacting investor confidence and market stability:

Increased Compliance Costs: Businesses grappling with new regulations or shifting legal interpretations incur additional expenses, diverting resources from productive activities and impacting competitiveness.

Inefficient Resource Allocation: Resources that could be channeled towards innovation and growth are instead directed towards adapting to new requirements, leading to suboptimal allocation and potentially hindering overall progress.

Market Instability: Constant policy adjustments breed uncertainty, potentially impacting investor confidence and dampening market enthusiasm for IR development.

To attract and retain foreign investments, jurisdictions must prioritize stability and predictability within the legal and regulatory framework governing IRs. This breeds an environment of trust and exhibits long-term vision, attracting the expertise and financial resources needed to bring these complex projects to fruition. Some key navigational tools may include:

Well-Considered and Transparent Policy Changes: Any future adjustments have to follow a clear and transparent process involving stakeholders like businesses, experts, and the public. Open communication and a consultative approach ensure that changes are informed and consider their long-term impact.

Gradual Transition Periods: Implementing new policies in phases allows businesses to adapt and adjust their operations in order to minimize disruptions and protect investments.

Commitment to a Stable Regulatory Framework: Setting an exclusivity period, similar to Singapore's approach, where core policies remain unchanged for a predefined period, provides investors with the confidence to commit to long-term plans and navigate the initial development phase without fear of sudden shifts.

By prioritizing predictability and fostering a climate of stability, jurisdictions can create an environment that attracts investors and fuels the full potential of IR developments. Embarking on this journey with a well-defined regulatory map translates to:

Enhanced Market Competitiveness: Attracting top-tier operators and the influx of international expertise and resources.

Sustainable Growth: Creating an environment for long-term investment and sustained economic development.

Reduced Regulatory Burden: Streamlined and predictable regulations allow businesses to focus on generating positive economic impact.

The success of Singapore's IRs stands as a testament to

the power of this approach. Their commitment to policy stability, coupled with a transparent and consultative process for future adjustments, instilled investor confidence and played a crucial role in making their IR vision a reality.

The grand opening of an integrated resort is the culmination of a long-term effort, transforming a vision into a welcoming reality for guests. However, this is not merely the endpoint; it signifies the genesis of a new market ecosystem. This nascent environment thrives on the intricate interplay between three key stakeholders: the licensed IR operator, the discerning consumer base, and the vigilant regulatory entity. The relationship between the regulator and operator is characterized by inherent ambivalence. While their common interest lies in the success of the IR, their motivations diverge. The regulator, entrusted with the public welfare, diligently balances fostering a thriving IR with safeguarding societal well-being. This often impinges on the profit-maximizing objectives of the operator, whose primary duty lies toward shareholders. This inherent tension necessitates dialogue and compromise, navigating the realm between economic prosperity and responsible governance. This balancing act becomes particularly pronounced when considering the core tenet of the IR model: diversification beyond traditional casino offerings. Casino operators, steeped in maximizing gambling floor space, may initially struggle to adapt to this paradigm. Las Vegas Sands' Marina Bay Sands is a powerful embodiment of the IR model's potential, achieving phenomenal success through a well-curated blend of non-gaming experiences. Yet, the grand opening is merely the initial act in a multi-phased performance. Commercial success does not guarantee equitable distribution of benefits or enduring viability. Winning a license is not a guaranteed path to long-term prosperity; rigorous evaluation and ongoing regulatory oversight are crucial to ensure that operators adhere to their commitments. Both operator and regulator can fall prey to complacency once initial targets are met, overlooking the true test of sustained excellence. Comprehending the intricate dynamics between these stakeholders is fundamental to crafting truly successful IRs. The government lays the bedrock framework, the operator orchestrates its activation, and the customer adjudicates its efficacy. The magic lies in the finely calibrated details, and this book delves into the key ingredients for this complex endeavor. The subsequent chapters serve as a comprehensive roadmap for all involved actors in the IR journey, encompassing the conceptualization, legislative framework, development, and operational intricacies of an IR. This dynamic guide navigates the exhilarating yet demanding path toward creating an integrated resort that resonates with all stakeholders, achieving both fiscal and social objectives.

two

FOUNDATION

The vision for a new integrated resort doesn't begin with a casino entrepreneur such as Sheldon Adelson or Steve Wynn, nor does it originate solely from an architect's pencil sketch on a blank canvas. Before casino magnates passionately describe their grandiose dreams and before an architectural firm transforms those aspirations into conceptual renderings on paper, a wireframe is carefully engineered to establish the foundational ground rules and boundaries. These parameters don't just define the physical attributes of the structure, such as its form and dimensions, but also encompass the principles behind every intricate detail of the design. The objective is to optimize its business potential while adhering to the regulatory requirements of the land. In the world of casino regulations, there is no room for exceptions, and any breach can lead to severe consequences, including monetary fines, business suspension, revocation of licenses, and even criminal charges. These regulations encompass both quantitative and qualitative directives and mandates, which serve as the bedrock of what an integrated resort business represents and how it operates. They set the baseline that every integrated resort must adhere to operationally.

The most effective regulations are crafted with the industry's greatest success in mind. Conversely, an integrated resort strikes a perfect equilibrium between compliance and profitability when every aspect, from design to operation, is driven by a cooperative spirit. The alignment between the regulator and the operator should be willing and not adversarial. When authoring regulations, a government must strike a balance between its objectives and the goals of businesses. Crafting a set of rules that heavily favors the government while imposing unrealistic demands on the industry may discourage interested parties or attract unsuitable candidates. In the case of Singapore, the casino tax regime was structured with tiered rates considerably lower than those in competing casino jurisdictions in the Asian region, aiming to attract high-value and quality investments. The tax formula was designed to encourage investors to develop blueprints for integrated resorts where casino gambling is centered around the premium segment, offering both the lowest casino tax and the highest net return for the business. This market strategy aligns well with Singapore's macroeconomic status, where the nation serves as a global financial hub, boasting one of the world's busiest international gateways, and is home to a predominantly middle-class population with substantial disposable income. The efficacy of every facet of these policies hinges on their suitability to the local context. For instance, the same Singapore IR framework would be ill-suited for a place like Thailand, where the majority of the population consists of the blue-collar working-class. Considering Thailand's larger population and geographic scale, a duopoly industry would inadequately serve the market, especially when accounting for the fact that Thailand attracts more than twice the number of tourists compared to Singapore.

The Philippines adopted Singapore's tiered casino tax structure but did not adopt the island's strict casino policies that impose restrictions on locals and require stringent due diligence on all individuals and business entities involved in casino gambling. This more lenient casino regime restricts local access by age only and allows for third-party VIP rooms and proxy gambling within integrated resorts. Proxy gambling is a practice where a high-stakes gambler or a VIP player is not physically present at the casino and authorizes another individual to place bets on their behalf. The dominance of Chinese junket operators in VIP rooms and proxy gambling, coupled with their suspected triad links, poses a serious regulatory issue for authorities seeking to ensure transparency and compliance in the casino industry. These practices often exist in a grey area in gaming regulations and were eventually banned in Macau, their birthplace. The interdiction on proxy gambling came in 2016, while junket VIP rooms were outlawed in 2021. The Philippine regulatory framework proved attractive to investors and operators with no qualms about doing business with the junkets, but companies operating in stricter gaming jurisdictions had no choice but to forego the market. For instance, the big American operators were unable to participate in the Philippines because it would create compliance issues for their gaming licenses in Nevada and Atlantic City.

The Philippine integrated resort market entered the industry at a time when the regulatory screws were gradually being tightened in Macau. The Manila integrated resorts were built to welcome Chinese players, and as the grey segments were being purged out of Macau, more and more found a haven in the Philippines, turning what was a moderately attractive market into a great success. It had the national gambling regulatory body, PAGCOR, optimistic that they could even exceed the much-heralded Singapore market within the next few years. The big question, though, is whether the spillover from Macau will continue to give or if it will be a mid-term capitalization of a market correction situation that is more happenstance than strategic. The embrace of the Chinese junket exiles has begun losing some of its warmth as they infiltrated the Philippine online gambling space and turned it into their own giant money laundering apparatus. They thrived under the cover of the hot-and-cold Sino-Philippine diplomatic relationship during the presidency of Rodrigo Duterte but began to fray when "Bongbong" Marcos took office and engaged in a more conciliatory relationship with China. The presence of Chinese junkets in the Philippines is also discrepant with the new president's aspiration to take his nation off the "grey list" of the global anti-money laundering watchdog, the Financial Action Task Force (FATF). It had looked inevitable to all except PAGCOR that their jurisdiction might be headed for a regulatory reset should the combination of pressure from the Chinese government and diminishing support in the Philippine congress force the junkets again to take flight further south to seek other friendly havens in Southeast Asia. But at least, the present PAGCOR administration is doing something right in its plans to shed its Janusian head to sell off its self-operated gaming businesses to become solely a regulator.

The foundation of the Philippine casino regulatory regime may be rough around the edges, but it gets the job done. The same cannot be said for South Korea when the country tried to emulate the successes in Macau, Singapore, and the Philippines. Being a powerhouse among the Asian tiger economies, it is not hard for them to believe that if their lesser regional neighbors can do it, then so could they, if not better. With the Hallyu Wave spreading Korean culture and influencing trends in music, fashion, and entertainment far and wide, South

Korean soft power is undeniably at its peak. As it turned out, it was a case of tunnel vision, with the faulty belief that the combination of growing inbound tourism and supersizing its existing foreigner-only casino framework was sufficient to create a robust integrated resort industry. The critical flaw lies in excluding investors from the vital local market while expecting them to invest billions of dollars. It doesn't take the bean counters in the casino companies to see that the math doesn't add up without a stable local customer base. The South Korean government's high minimum investment and development criteria clash with the limitations of a tourist-only market. One by one, interest from major casino operators waned as Las Vegas Sands, Seminole Hard Rock, and Galaxy Entertainment decided to pass, and Caesars abandoned its South Korean IR consortium. Eventually, the Native American gaming operator, Mohegan Gaming, emerged as the sole savior. The Connecticut tribe takes a big gamble with its most expensive venture yet, the Inspire Entertainment Resort. The resort hinges on a risky strategy: either luring the high-rollers from Macau's dismantled junket system or a long-shot policy change in South Korea allowing casino gambling for its citizens.

It appeared that lightning might have struck twice in Asia when Japan found itself with a single credible investor in its recently established integrated resort sector. After decades of stops and starts, MGM Resorts finally emerged as the operator for Japan's first integrated resort, set to open in Osaka in 2030. Two Japanese IR licenses remained unclaimed due to a lack of suitable suitors, as all other major casino operators withdrew after repeated uncertainties from the Japanese government. The Japanese integrated resort market has always been seen as fundamentally attractive, to the extent that it became a victim of its potential, leading to an over-exaggeration of the market. Despite bureaucratic red tape and less-than-polished policies in the Japanese IR Promotion and Implementation Law, the market fundamentals remain sound, even if not as inflated as at the peak of its hype. Opportunities still exist if integrated resorts are permitted in Tokyo, Fukuoka, Hokkaido, Nagoya, and other international tourism gateways in Japan that have all the essential characteristics for successful integrated resort development. By embracing these opportunities, Japan could establish its integrated resorts as a major local industry and a formidable regional competitor to Macau and Singapore.

The rationale behind legalizing integrated resorts is primarily economic, aiming to induce capital investment, generate tax, and create employment opportunities. Regulating gambling also serves as a means to counter illegal activities like underground casino dens that perpetuate fraud and money laundering while preventing the outflow of gambling revenue to other regions. Legalized casinos empower governments to implement harm reduction programs, allocating resources for public awareness campaigns, treatment facilities, and support services to address the negative impacts of gambling addiction. Integrated resorts not only boost tourism but also catalyze the development of the entertainment and hospitality industries, stimulating local businesses and enhancing overall economic well-being. The fiscal contributions from these resorts can be channeled into funding public services, infrastructure projects, or community initiatives. In some jurisdictions, gambling revenue is earmarked for specific social causes like education, healthcare, and addiction rehabilitative programs, directing funds toward addressing societal needs. While there is a strong basis for economic benefits, they come with a range of negative consequences, including addiction, social issues, and criminal activity associated with gambling. Balancing these benefits and drawbacks is crucial for making informed decisions regarding the legalization of integrated resorts.

Fiscal allure reigns supreme when it comes to legalizing casino gambling, particularly in regions grappling with economic hardship or lagging development. Unlike their multi-billion-dollar IR counterparts, "garden-variety" casino resorts present an easily attainable prospect. Requiring minimal infrastructure and a less-skilled workforce, these establishments function as efficient yet stripped-down hospitality options, catering solely to patrons seeking the thrill of the gamble. This translates to a much lower upfront investment while still generating substantial returns compared to traditional hotels. In essence, this strategy prioritizes maximizing short-term returns with minimal resources. Cambodia leverages this strategy to good effect. Lacking the infrastructure for a full-fledged integrated resort industry, it compensates with an alluring low flat casino tax and relaxed regulations, lowering the bar for qualifying investors. Conversely, Macau has historically leaned heavily on casino tax revenue, morphing it into a crutch for a government hesitant to diversify its economy. This reliance is further amplified by the continuous influx of wealth from mainland China, making it increasingly difficult to break free. However, focusing solely on tax revenue as the primary justification for legalizing casinos carries severe drawbacks. Not only does it neglect fostering other positive aspects, but it can also exacerbate social and security concerns within society. Recognizing this, the Chinese government is guiding Macau's gaming industry towards a more sustainable model, promoting long-term diversification into broader economic sectors while simultaneously combating entrenched criminal elements.

Recognizing the threat from neighboring resurgent tourism economies, both Singapore and Japan embarked on strategic endeavors to revitalize their respective tourist sectors. However, their approaches diverged considerably, reflecting unique contextual considerations and visions. For Singapore, nestled amidst the ascendant Asian metropolises, its cosmopolitan charm masked an aging skyline that necessitated a bold stroke to maintain regional tourism relevance. While the alluring fiscal prospects of the Macau model, heavily reliant on Chinese visitors and substantial casino tax levies, presented a tempting option, Singapore charted a more nuanced and sustainable course. Eschewing the immediate financial gains promised by exorbitant casino taxes, Singapore opted for a multifaceted strategy of brand reinvention and targeted tourism growth. This calculated gamble yielded profound results. While Singapore's casino tax revenue remains dwarfed by Macau's, its tourism sector has undergone a remarkable renaissance. Tourist arrivals have more than doubled since the first integrated resort opened in 2010, generating significant economic benefits across diverse sectors.

While Singapore embarked on a calculated tourism diversification strategy, Japan faced a different set of challenges. A confluence of factors – economic downturn, the SARS outbreak, and natural disasters – dealt a severe blow to Japan's tourism sector in the early 2000s. This decline was further exacerbated by the contrasting success of South Korea, whose "Hallyu wave" of K-pop and K-dramas ignited international interest and fueled a tourism boom. Recognizing the need for a revitalization strategy, Japanese lawmakers initially envisioned large-scale casinos, later evolving towards the integrated resort model inspired by Singapore's success. However, the protracted legislative process for the IR Bill coincided with an unexpected recovery in Japanese tourism, fueled by a surge of Chinese visitors. This unforeseen development rendered the original vision of the IR Bill somewhat obsolete, transforming it into a solution searching for a problem. Despite this shift in tourism dynamics, the Japanese government remained committed to pushing through the IR legislation. However, the focus shifted from general tourism revival to specifically targeting the meetings and conventions (MICE) sector. This pivot exposed a lack of clear vision and coherent guiding principles within the legislation. The absence of a well-defined roadmap has manifested in a tumultuous implementation process riddled with controversy and delays, raising concerns about the overall effectiveness and long-term viability of the IR project.

Integrated resorts transcend their role as opulent hospitality and entertainment destinations, unleashing a cascade of positive economic impacts that permeate the very fabric of a host destination. Singapore's vibrant tourism scene, boasting integrated resorts and the prestigious Formula 1 race, helped it score a major win by being the only Southeast Asian stop on Taylor Swift's record-breaking Eras tour. IRs act as powerful magnets, attracting millions of visitors and generating an enormous ripple effect that revitalizes the entire hospitality and tourism ecosystem. Hotels witness robust occupancy rates, restaurants hum with vibrant activity, and local attractions bask in the glow of increased foot traffic. This translates to enhanced employment opportunities, augmented revenue streams, and a flourishing tourism landscape buzzing with potential. The broader retail sector is experiencing a retail renaissance thanks to the influx of discerning visitors with a penchant for premium experiences fueling retail sales and injecting dynamism into the local commerce landscape. IRs act as potent catalysts, triggering a multiplier effect that reverberates throughout the broader economy. Lavish events, captivating concerts, and painstakingly choreographed productions hosted within IRs serve as a springboard for the wider entertainment industry, empowering performers, event organizers, and countless ancillary businesses. State-of-the-art conference and meeting facilities within IRs act as magnets for business travelers and event organizers, fostering the growth of the lucrative meetings and conventions industry. This not only benefits the IRs themselves but also generates substantial revenue for hotels, airlines, and other travel-related businesses, solidifying the destination's position as a premier MICE hub.

IRs are also fertile ground for local suppliers and producers. The sheer size of their operations translates to a significant boost for the local economy. They unlock opportunities for local businesses, fostering a surge in entrepreneurial ventures and creating new jobs. As visitor influx increases, the transportation sector receives a proportional boost. Taxis, ride-sharing services, public transportation networks, and even car rental companies witness a surge in demand, necessitating infrastructure improvements and job creation to cater to the burgeoning needs of the region. Property values often escalate due to the enhanced desirability of the location, benefiting homeowners, commercial property owners, and the overall real estate sector. This appreciation in value unlocks new investment opportunities and contributes to the overall economic dynamism of the region.

The allure of integrated resorts in regions grappling with high unemployment rates is undeniable. From the transformative landscapes of Macau and Singapore to the burgeoning developments in the Philippines, these projects offer the potential to generate tens of thousands of new jobs. Unbridled enthusiasm for job creation, however, can lead to unintended consequences and societal strains, as seen in Macau. The rapid deregulation of Macau's casino industry generated a surge in employment but simultaneously revealed the shortcomings in its domestic workforce. Companies grapple with adhering to local hiring policies while facing a shortage of skilled residents to meet employment quotas. The resulting reliance on overseas recruitment to fill the gap led to a rapid influx of foreign residents, drastically altering the demographic landscape. This population shift, while intended to address the immediate workforce gap, led to unanticipated and far-reaching repercussions. The once idyllic enclave became a frenetic hub plagued by traffic congestion and an infrastructure struggling to keep pace with the population boom. Daily necessities experienced price inflation, and property values soared beyond the reach of the average Macanese resident, fundamentally disrupting the social fabric of the community. This highlights the need for a proactive and multifaceted approach to workforce planning when developing IRs.

Singapore's proactive workforce planning is a counterpoint to Macau's approach. Compared to the latter's reactive approach to labor needs, Singapore's integrated resort development was underpinned by a comprehensive workforce plan embedded within the government's broader economic growth strategy. This foresight proved invaluable in navigating the considerable manpower demands associated with the 2010 launch of two major IRs, simultaneously creating over 20,000 new jobs. The workforce plan was precisely calibrated to match the projected growth trajectory of the IR sector, ensuring a readily available talent pool. Recognizing the limitations of its domestic workforce, Singapore embraced a supplementary migrant workforce strategy involving a tiered approach. Employment Passes are issued to eligible skilled professionals with specialized expertise not readily available locally, allowing them to spearhead growth initiatives and contribute their unique knowledge to the IR industry. Mid-level skilled workers who possess valuable technical or vocational skills are given S-Passes which bridges the gap between highly specialized roles and entry-level positions. Work Permits address the demand for lower-skilled labor, particularly in construction where local interest is traditionally low. To safeguard local employment opportunities, Singapore implemented a system of quotas, levies, and stringent criteria for hiring foreign workers. This ensured a balanced approach, prioritizing opportunities for Singaporean citizens while addressing critical skill gaps. This proactive and multi-pronged strategy yielded several benefits. The forward-thinking workforce strategy ensured a smooth transition when the IRs opened, avoiding the disruption experienced by Macau due to an unplanned influx of foreign workers. The tiered approach guaranteed access to both highly skilled professionals and essential manual labor, fostering operational efficiency and competitiveness. Safeguards prevented the displacement of local workers, fostering public support for the IR project and promoting social cohesion. While Japan presents fertile ground for the burgeoning integrated resort industry, its notoriously restrictive labor market casts a long shadow on its ambitions. Unlike Singapore's meticulously planned workforce strategy, the Japanese government has yet to articulate a clear path forward for addressing the high manpower demands of this nascent sector. Historically, Japan has maintained a cautious stance towards immigration, fostering a highly homogeneous local workforce. Recognizing the demographic challenges posed by an aging population and declining workforce, the government has implemented targeted initiatives, such as industry-specific visas and an agricultural work program. However, these efforts remain underpinned by a cautious approach that prioritizes social cohesion and careful management of foreign labor integration. This conservative approach presents a high hurdle for the Japanese IR industry. A substantial portion of its job openings necessitate foreign expertise, particularly considering the limited foreign language proficiency of many Japanese workers when compared to the demands of international tourism. This deficiency may be overlooked by investors drawn by the prospect of surpassing established IR hubs like Macau and Singapore. Adding to the complexities, the Japanese Ministry of Health, Labor, and Welfare has been conspicuously silent on the possibility of exemptions to its immigration policies for the IR industry. This lack of transparency will create operational complexities and uncertainties for the ORIX-MGM consortium, tasked with filling the extensive staffing needs of its planned Osaka IR slated for a 2030 opening date.

The substantial employment opportunities generated by integrated resorts can act as a big stimulus for rural economies, countering the prevalent trend of human capital migration from smaller communities to larger cities. This strategy has been widely employed to revitalize economies in remote locations. However, the investment potential is inherently linked to proximity to major commercial and population centers. Expecting billions of dollars for an integrated resort in an isolated site with a small local population and limited accessibility is unrealistic compared to metropolitan cities. While rural economic rejuvenation was emphasized in Japan's integrated resorts plan, this focus didn't translate into the actual legislation and policies outlined in the IR Bill. The legislation failed to differentiate adequately between metropolitan and regional locations, showing a clear bias toward the former. This made it nearly impossible for investors to financially justify applying the same development criteria to, for example, a Hokkaido integrated resort compared to one in Tokyo.

While often associated with bustling urban centers, integrated resorts can also serve as catalysts for revitalizing struggling rural economies. By carefully locating IRs away from major population hubs, policymakers can harness the dual benefit of economic stimulation while employing physical distance as a deterrent for problem gamblers. A prime example of this approach is the Kangwon Land Resort in South Korea, situated a four-hour train journey from Seoul. This distance acts as a natural deterrent, attracting only those with a stronger commitment to gambling, while simultaneously injecting much-needed economic activity into the previously declining mining town of Jeongseon. However, prioritizing economic gains cannot come at the expense of social well-being.

Regulatory frameworks governing IRs must strike a delicate balance between fostering economic prosperity and mitigating the likely downsides associated with gambling. Singapore, geographically constrained and unable to replicate the distance-based approach of Kangwon Land, implemented a unique solution: a casino entry fee for residents. This measure aims to curb impulsive gambling behavior by introducing a financial barrier to entry. Furthermore, the very concept of IRs emerged from a desire to move beyond the Las Vegas model, notorious for its central focus on casinos. To mitigate potential risks and promote a safe environment, integrated resorts prioritize responsible gambling while offering a variety of entertainment, leisure, and hospitality options alongside casinos. Singapore further bolstered this commitment by enacting robust social safeguards. These include:

Casino entry fee and minimum age barrier: Serving as deterrents to casual or underage gambling, the latter more common than the former.

Casino exclusion and visit limits program: Allowing individuals or their family members concerned about their gambling habits to be excluded from entering the casino or set spending limits.

Vulnerable individuals proactively enrolled in exclusion program: Protecting those deemed at risk, such as bankrupts and welfare recipients.

Restrictions on casino marketing: Preventing aggressive advertising that could exacerbate gambling problems.

Duty of care requirements for IR operators: Mandating operators to provide responsible gambling resources and implement measures to identify and assist problem gamblers.

For Japan, navigating the complexities of its integrated resort legislation proved akin to wrestling with a jumbo shrimp. To secure passage of the IR Law, the government made substantial compromises to its ruling coalition partner, resulting in stringent restrictions on casino access for Japanese citizens. While these restrictions surpassed even Singapore's measures in apparent rigor, they lacked substance in their implementation details. The subsequent IR Basic Policy meant to flesh out these safeguards and security protocols, fell woefully short of expectations.

No matter how prudently constructed a law's foundation may be, inflexibility in the face of evolving market realities can spell trouble. While the gaming sector may not experience the lightning-fast transformations of the tech sector, they remain subject to dynamic shifts. Over its two-decade lifespan, the Japanese IR Bill has seen its initial vision for a domestic casino industry become outdated due to significant shifts in the tourism landscape and the Asian gaming market. Additionally, the ever-shifting geopolitical landscape, particularly in Sino-U.S. relations, introduced unforeseen risks for investors. Prioritizing swift passage over adaptability to current realities resulted in two major shortcomings: an ineffective rollout characterized by ambiguity and a lukewarm response from the industry itself.

The essence of an integrated resort legislation cannot be fully captured within legal texts alone. Visions of desired outcomes require careful translation into specific policies, gaining acceptance from both investors and operators. Regulating them effectively, however, remains a complex task. This difficulty may arise from the inherent nature of the vision itself or from the inability of either the government or operators to fulfill their intentions. What can be effectively regulated are finite and quantifiable parameters, some of which can indirectly influence qualitative objectives. Singapore's tiered casino tax system illustrates this concept vividly. It acts as both an incentive and a deterrent: it encourages operators to focus on the premium gaming segment through tax breaks (the carrot) while preventing them from overstepping boundaries through progressive taxation (the stick). Ultimately, regulations serve as the blueprint, determining the architecture of the industry it begets and the businesses it draws in.

three
THE GLASS SLIPPER

In the intricate world of global business, the maxim "if the shoe fits" takes on profound significance when companies embark on the strategic quest of choosing markets to invest in. It's not merely about finding any market; it's about discovering the one where the regulatory framework fits seamlessly with the business DNA and where the market potential aligns harmoniously with the company's strengths. Much like an individual discerningly selecting shoes that not only match their style but also provide the right support and comfort, businesses scrutinize markets for a snug fit with their operational DNA. Regulatory frameworks act as the tailored structure that holds the business in place, ensuring a comfortable stride forward. A market with regulations that resonate with a company's ethos facilitates smoother operations, fostering an environment where the business can flourish without unnecessary constraints. Effective business practices look beyond regulations. They seek market opportunities that match the company's capabilities, ensuring a good fit.

Choosing the right market is akin to shoes that not only complement one's style but also ensure comfort during the journey. For businesses, this means identifying markets where their strengths are not only valued but also present fertile ground for their success. A market that aligns with a company's strengths becomes the stage where it can perform at its best, leveraging its core competencies to capitalize on the opportunities presented.

However, much like individuals periodically reassessing their footwear for wear and tear, businesses must continually evaluate the fit of their chosen markets. Regulatory landscapes evolve, and market dynamics shift. The "if the shoe fits" principle reminds businesses that the perfect fit today may require adjustments or a reevaluation in the future. It embodies the quest for markets where regulations and market demand align seamlessly with a company's DNA, ensuring not only a comfortable fit today but also the flexibility to adapt and thrive in the dynamic landscapes of tomorrow. Just as the right pair of shoes propel an individual forward with confidence, the right market empowers businesses to stride boldly toward success, grounded in regulatory harmony and fortified by the alignment of strengths with market potential.

Casino operators assessing new gaming jurisdictions cannot gauge the market's potential in a vacuum. For example, integrated resorts in the Philippines operate within a regulatory framework misaligned with standards in Las Vegas and Atlantic City, effectively disqualifying operators like Las Vegas Sands, Wynn Resorts, and MGM Resorts from participating in Manila's Entertainment City. On that yardstick, Indochina does not even fall into their radar, despite a glimmer of hope a few years back that Vietnam might tighten its gaming regime and piqued a little interest from Sands, Caesars, and Seminole Hard Rock. Conversely, Chinese junket companies traversing the fringes of traditional regulatory frameworks, with activities less transparent and subject to legal ambiguities, know better than to attempt operating in highly regulated jurisdictions like Singapore. Regulatory alignment aside, each company has a sweet spot where its strengths intersect with market demand to create the most favorable conditions for growth and profitability. This is when the target market complements their brand and DNA to maximize brand resonance and lead to increased engagement. In the global gaming market, market leaders assert dominance in their specific niches, leveraging their expertise and resources to establish a formidable presence. For example, Las Vegas Sands in conventions and Wynn Resorts in the premium market. These leaders have powerfully shaped their territories, setting high industry standards to command large shares in the market. Meanwhile, other players strategically settle into their niches, recognizing where their strengths align, such as the Genting Group in the mass market and MGM Resorts in entertainment. In this diverse market landscape, each participant finds its place, contributing to a balanced and competitive industry ecosystem. When new jurisdictions open up, companies have to make an honest evaluation if the market conditions suit their strengths. Cinderella won't be able to dance properly at the ball if the glass slipper doesn't fit.

The Flamingo, the Golden Nugget, the Sands, and the Dunes stand as austere names in the history of casino gambling. However, a transformative shift occurred with the emergence of Caesars Palace, the Mirage, and the Bellagio, marking the advent of a new era in the industry. A more significant evolution unfolded when entertainment impresario Steve Wynn unveiled his eponymous resort, following conference mogul Sheldon Adelson's entry into the casino business with the Venetian. Each of these establishments became an icon of its time, though their endurance at the pinnacle varied. While some endured longer than others, it is uncommon for any to maintain their position at the peak for extended periods. Apple achieved such longevity in consumer electronics, but in the realm of resorts, it was the place itself, rather than individual establishments, that found enduring prominence. Las Vegas, as the birthplace of casino gambling, remains forever synonymous with the industry, having given rise to the largest companies in the business. The concept of integrated resorts represented the next phase in casino establishments, offering an audacious makeover where the casino facility, at least physically, receded in its conspicuousness. Although the casino remains the primary revenue generator within an integrated resort, its income is now complemented by a myriad of other revenue sources. Steve Wynn played a pivotal role in crafting the initial contours of this new business model during the days of the Mirage. The modern casino product underwent another major metamorphosis when the Singapore government subjected the new Las Vegas mold to the kiln in a more benign form. This "integrated resort" badge was quickly adopted in the Philippines and subsequently by Japan, albeit only skin deep in the former case in its anodyne interpretation. The integrated resort label connotes a brand association with quality, content-rich entertainment destinations symbolized in the industry by the two Singapore IRs.

Good branding contributes to success, yet it proves as elusive as squeezing water from a stone for many companies. The distinctiveness of certain brands evolves gradually over the course of their business, often taking years or even decades to fully develop. A robust brand becomes particularly advantageous in a competitive marketplace, although positive brand equity is beneficial regardless of the playing field. Similar to individuals, a company's brand undergoes evolution through nature, nurture, or a combination of both. The former, a naturally occurring characteristic, emerges as a result of the company's business operations over time. Nurturing a brand involves deliberately shaping the business to align with a specific identity, whether in terms of product quality, customer demographic segments, geography, or a combination thereof. Therefore, brand equity is either built or attributed, both being synonymous in the case of a company with a well-executed brand strategy.

Casino companies born in Las Vegas are imbued with the brand allure of their birthplace. This capital proved invaluable to MGM, Las Vegas Sands, and Wynn in securing their casino concessions in Macau, although Caesars (then Park Place) lost out. It reflected, to an extent, the shift in brand equity among the large Vegas casino marques, where the halcyon age of Caesars Palace dimmed after it changed hands repeatedly. In stepped the next breed of cognoscente in Steve Wynn and Sheldon Adelson, with big personas synonymous with their grandiose creations. Their names continue to loom large even after both were no longer involved in the businesses they created. The local casino operators in Macau inherited a different sort of brand association compared to their Las Vegas counterparts. The deregulation of the Macau casino industry in 2002 hasn't been entirely successful in shedding its old seedy history. The long-entrenched Chinese triad criminal elements, now corporatized, dug their claws deeper into the market, becoming even bigger than before. It was only when junket entities like SunCity became too prominent and extended beyond Macau shores that Chinese authorities decided enough was enough. Despite the criticism, Macau casino concessionaires profited handsomely for the better part of two decades from their association with their less respectable partners. Currency printing presses can churn up to 20,000 notes per hour, and the junket VIP room rivaled these minting machines with wagers in excess of tens of millions of dollars per day. But all that glitters is not necessarily gold and Macau casino companies found it challenging to shake off the tatterdemalion image when venturing overseas. SJM is so knee-deep in the morass that the Lisboa owner opted not to pursue new casino licenses in Singapore and Japan. Melco Entertainment went to the extent of vowing to disown its place of birth if the Japanese government were to accept it. Galaxy Entertainment struggled with its "Made in China" tag and has yet to expand to other shores.

One's origins are indelible, and a company's brand personality is similarly enduring and resistant to change. SJM is indelibly marked by the diverse associations of its founder. Malaysia's Genting Group, despite its financial prowess and business acumen, has struggled to enhance its brand equity. The rebranding of its casino business to Resorts World couldn't match the brand impact of its American counterparts, despite comparable revenue, profitability, superior cash flow, and lower debt. This conundrum illustrates the futility of a leopard changing its spots—an intrinsic transformation that goes beyond a mere name change. Genting remains primarily a mass-market brand, resonating more with the blue-collar demographic that associates it with 'casino' rather than 'resort,' despite elaborate makeovers in branding and product offerings. Considering its success in this space, the question arises: Is there a need for change? Herein lies the difference between Genting and SJM; the Macau company is comfortable in its own skin, while Genting aspires to evolve its brand image. The key lesson is that a company's true brand identity is perceived by its customers and reflected in its main consumer base. Operating and behaving beyond the comfort zone has limited tolerance unless a fully independent entity emerges by cutting the umbilical cord with the parent company. An example is the now-defunct Asian cruise operator, Star Cruises, which operated autonomously from its Genting owner, cultivating a distinct culture and brand. Creative Technology, arguably the most successful tech company from Singapore, attempted unsuccessfully to transcend its ubiquitous Sound Blaster audio product line and become the Asian equivalent of Microsoft and Apple. Despite having well-designed and competitively priced consumer electronics products with additional features, it failed to capture consumers' hearts.

As new Asian casino jurisdictions emerged following the deregulation of the industry in Macau, both regional incumbent operators and Western gaming companies eagerly competed for a share of the market. Homegrown players hold an advantage in market knowledge, while Las Vegas companies benefited from being at the industry's epicenter, a model Asia sought to emulate. The new jurisdictions sought a blend of both worlds—a Vegas-type entertainment resort customized to address the needs of the Asian demographic. In the absence of this ideal fusion, Western pop culture took precedence, given its influence on Asian consumerism, from Hollywood and Netflix to the iPhone and Tesla. Las Vegas companies had an inside track over their Western counterparts, having catered to Asian high rollers and being familiar with the premium customer segment. Consequently, Las Vegas Sands, Wynn Resorts, and MGM Resorts aligned with the Chinese government's long-term blueprint to revamp the Macau market. With demand surpassing supply, the Americans adapted effortlessly to the market. However, those who fine-tuned their businesses to the local vein thrived even more. Sands China struck a balance that propelled it to market leadership in Macau, repeating the feat with even greater success in Singapore, making Marina Bay Sands the world's most profitable casino. Wynn Resorts applied its finesse catering to the upper market echelons in Macau, solidifying its niche in the premium market space.

Outsiders perceiving Asia as one homogenous market were seriously mistaken; Singapore offered a distinct value proposition from Macau. The more than a dozen suitors for its two integrated resort licenses neatly fell into two camps. One group approached the opportunity unimaginatively, giving little thought to whether their brand and product aligned with the market requirements. The others industriously attempted to conform to the prescribed needs, but the reality of a square peg in a round hole applied to some. Among the over a dozen interested parties in Singapore, a large majority failed to come close to fitting the mold specified by the government. They tried to put their best foot forward, even vainly attempting to be something they weren't, but their track record would inevitably catch up with them—almost always, except in cases where inefficacious functionaries held the keys or when less than noble decision-makers were at play. New contenders have the advantage of no history, good or bad, to speak of, but lacking any history at all also meant zero experience, something governments were loath to entrust with such a critical socioeconomic pillar as a casino operating license. The Singapore government would strategically hedge its bets between an established big Vegas brand and another familiar to Asian consumers.

Like Singapore, Japan attracted a diverse range of suitors when considering the legalization of casinos. However, unlike Singapore, Japan lacked a filtering process, a surprising deviation from its typically ruthlessly efficient approach. The presence of a disparate bunch further complicated an already convoluted selection process, contributing to delays that transformed the wait for Japanese casinos from years into decades. Chinese junket companies, hesitant to operate openly in Singapore, confidently explored opportunities in Japan and were almost selected by one prefectural government. Additionally, a European operator with no experience managing facilities on the scale of large integrated resorts was chosen by another prefecture. Singapore, as a top-tier market with only a pair of casino licenses, had the luxury to accommodate the best-in-class casino resort operators. Consequently, all others were excluded from consideration at the outset of the process. Japan is a superior market to Singapore by every metric. There had been no reason for the country to encumber itself with any company less than the industry's *crème de la crème*.

A good operator possesses a keen awareness of its brand perception among consumers and its standing in the marketplace. Wynn Resorts effectively tailored its branding and products for the luxury segment. Las Vegas Sands dominated the large convention market, secured a prime portion of the premium mass segment, and matched Wynn in the top tier with its bespoke Paiza Club. MGM Resorts, yet to fully showcase the breadth of its entertainment prowess in Macau, may reveal its true colors with the upcoming MGM Osaka integrated resort set to open in 2030. During the nascent Asian casino market's early years, the Caesars brand was buffeted by a wave of mergers and acquisitions. Brand positioning obfuscation, combined with severe debt woes, left Caesars as the only one among the Vegas big players empty-handed in Asia. Despite Genting's branding conundrum, the grind market specialist secured one of the valuable Singapore IR licenses, leveraging its long-standing brand familiarity with Asian gamblers. The inclusion of a Universal Studios theme park sealed the deal. However, Resorts World Sentosa fell short in its attempt at a par excellence makeover to distinguish itself from its Malaysian cousin at Genting Highlands. Reluctance to let go of lucrative grind gamblers, coupled with its parent's rebranding of medium and large casino properties under the Resorts World name, hindered RWS' quest to position itself in the premium space.

Galaxy and Melco joined the elite group with properties surpassing the billion-dollar mark in revenue. Galaxy, akin to Genting in many ways, secured the lion's share of Chinese customers through its nationalistic positioning in Macau. It leads the market in turnover, trailing only behind Sands China in profitability. Melco, building up as a new contemporary brand, reinvents itself a little too frequently. The company faced mixed fortunes with short flings in Las Vegas and Vladivostok. While pulling out of Las Vegas might have seemed like a setback, it ultimately proved to be a strategic masterstroke for Melco. The move to exit Nevada preempted potential regulatory hurdles, paving the way for a smoother entry into the Philippines. In Japan, Melco, alongside Genting, persisted as other operators folded and cut losses in Yokohama, only to face setbacks when the port city withdrew its casino development plans after a mayoral change. The success of another Melco bet in Cyprus is still too early to tell and remains uncertain.

In Japan, Sands, MGM, Wynn, and Genting adhered to their size billing by exclusively showing interest in metropolitan casino licenses, while the relatively immature brands of Galaxy and Melco also explored more modest regional prospects. On the other side of the fence, the work of Japanese authorities was plagued by political meddling, besotting the IR process with nescience. Bad actors and unknown quantities fell through large cracks, partaking in the process and turning it into a circus. On one hand, national lawmakers focused on securing the biggest and best casino operators for Japanese integrated resorts. However, an extemporaneous approach in qualifying investors and a laissez-faire attitude at the prefectural level created a wide-open sieve, admitting anyone and everyone. This carapace of indifference to proper due process fueled speculation of a non-transparent framework, with also suggestions that government decision-makers may have already predetermined which prefectures would be given integrated resort licenses.

The problems faced in launching Japan's integrated resort industry highlight the importance of clearly defined entry requirements. The mixed signals about the market's true potential (glass slippers or comfortable moccasins or otherwise) attracted a diverse range of both desirable and undesired suitors, ultimately hindering progress. Conversely, companies with a good understanding of their brand equities will select and engage the right markets that suit their strengths—the shoe has to fit. Smaller European casino companies faced this dilemma when trying to present themselves as suitable large-scale integrated resort operators in new Asian jurisdictions. Attempting entry into regulated markets like Singapore and Japan for Nagacorp and the now-defunct SunCity was akin to walking a mile in shoes two sizes too small. The key lesson is that a company's success in a new market hinges on its ability to read the tea leaves. This means understanding the unique dynamics of the market, adapting its approach accordingly, and aligning itself with those dynamics while staying true to its brand and strengths. Tools like the IR Balanced Scorecard (Chapter 19) are useful for methodically assessing this in both quantitative and qualitative measures and determining if a company's brand and DNA fit the bandwidth of a new jurisdiction.

four

THE HERFINDAHL-HIRSCHMAN PRINCIPLE

Orris Herfindahl and Albert Hirschman were distinguished economists who shaped economic theory through their significant contributions to the field. The Herfindahl-Hirschman Index (HHI), developed by Herfindahl drawing on Hirschman's economic insights, is a measure of market concentration that indicates the level of competition. The HHI has been particularly valuable in antitrust cases, aiding in the evaluation of the competitive landscape and perceived market power of firms. A higher HHI signifies a less competitive market. This development of a quantitative measure offers valuable insights for policymakers and economists, enabling them to analyze market structure and competition more effectively.

Despite receiving high accolades for the successful implementation of its casino industry framework, the Singapore IR industry would be assessed with a high HHI. A favorable casino tax regime initially lured high-quality investments from the private sector. However, the regime, designed to attract high-quality investments, proved more successful than anticipated, contributing to the two Singapore integrated resorts becoming among the most profitable casino properties globally. To address this, the government implemented a clawback by raising the casino tax after the expiration of a moratorium on the quantum in 2022. Post this adjustment, the EBITDA figures of the two integrated resorts suggested that the businesses were still not materially deprived of their profits. While the favorable fiscal contract undoubtedly played a role in the resorts' success, the most crucial advantage contributing to their prominent positions was the duopoly market in Singapore. The fact that only two players engage in "house" games in a thriving marketplace bestowed upon them a tremendous advantage that every casino mogul would covet. As expressed by one of the fortunate two operators, it remains a highly profitable "cash cow" that continues to yield substantial returns.

The HHI score reaches its maximum of 10,000 in a monopoly, signifying a market with minimal competition. Duopolies and oligopolies also yield high HHI scores, though lower than monopolies, and generally, any form of market concentration can be detrimental. Insufficient competition can hamper innovation and stifle renewal. A market dominated by one or a few sellers tends to be inefficient, maintaining high prices without necessarily upholding quality. In Singapore, the government addresses this structural issue by imposing a ten-year limit on the duopoly market status. This strategy forces licensees to invest heavily in upgrades and expansions to keep their exclusive rights, creating an artificial sense of competition rather than a truly competitive market. Apart from this periodic interlude, the duopoly generally accepts the status quo, with Resorts World Sentosa somewhat resigned to its distant second position against Marina Bay Sands. Resorts World Sentosa, despite this, remains a top-ten global earner among casinos, leveraging its loyal clientele and the benefits of operating in a duopoly market. The contrasting customer demographics served by the two Singapore integrated resorts—Sentosa catering to working-class gamblers and Marina Bay Sands attracting white-collar and cosmopolitan crowds—accentuate the market circumstances. This divergence in focus further contributes to a subdued competitive landscape in Singapore. The phenomenal performance of Singapore's two IRs in their first decade of operation questions the initial policy of restricting the market to only two operators. Whether the government will introduce a third or fourth integrated resort upon the expiry of the current exclusivity period in 2033 will likely depend on two key factors: social considerations within Singapore's conservative society and the regional market dynamics at that time.

The small enclave of Macau has been a proven litmus test for the free-flowing tap characterizing the Asian casino market over the past twenty years. The deluge of new casino resorts that opened in 2002 served to whet the appetite of customers from the adjacent Guangdong Province in China, contributing to the development of an ever-growing customer base. The Cotai Strip, though smaller than the famed Las Vegas Strip, enjoyed a turnover multiple times greater than Vegas. In emulating the latter's cluster model, Macau created the same critical mass effect that helped it become the nexus of casino gambling in Asia. At its peak, up to 40 million people made the annual migration to Macau in search of fortune on the casino floor, akin to wildlife on their seasonal journeys for food, water, or spawning. Clustering also fosters intense competition among casino properties, all within a stone's throw of each other. This leaves gamblers spoiled for choice, with a dazzling array of brand-new, multi-billion-dollar resorts lining the man-made Cotai area. Despite near-perpetual halcyon days, the close proximity of different proprietors all basically touting the same wares conditioned each to fiercely and jealously protect their turf. First, there is the compulsion of keeping up with the Joneses, as each operator tries to maintain their lawn in parity with their neighbor across the fence. If one lured a huge crowd with a multi-day concert featuring a Hong Kong "Heavenly King," another trumped it with a sellout top K-pop girl act. One-upmanship is literally on display constantly as the resorts wrestle to claim the rights to the best show performance in town. Customers are bombarded with an ever-refreshing slate of attractions, entertainment, and amenities in the tussle to command the most footfall and highest spending under each store's roof. Every basis point of market share is keenly fought over, delighting casino punters who get showered with comps galore. High rollers enjoy the best of the situation, lapping it up with red carpet treatment and shopping door-to-door for handsome rolling chip rebates.

Despite intense competition, the Macau casino industry maintains an above-average HHI score due to consistently strong demand exceeding supply. All concessionaires remain profitable even with a lofty 40% casino tax rate. However, operating within China's centrally planned economy, the government exerts significant influence through policy and oversight to prevent excessive profitability. One control measure involves managing Chinese visitor visas to prevent market overheating, aligning with broader economic plans set by Beijing. The industry is also impacted by policies related to tourism, infrastructure development, and economic diversification. In recent years, a push for diversification has aimed to reduce reliance on gaming revenue and promote non-gaming offerings like entertainment, conventions, and family-oriented attractions. Additionally, the Chinese government emphasizes security and social responsibility, addressing issues like money laundering and problem gambling while promoting responsible gaming. This has helped regulate the growth of the market. Strict currency and financial controls, including regulations on fund transfers and currency exchange, along with the elimination of junket VIP rooms, have curbed money laundering. With the government's long-term goal of integrating Macau's casino market into broader regional economic plans, particularly within the Guangdong–Hong Kong–Macau Greater Bay Area, operators are encouraged through a combination of regulations and incentives to shift the industry closer to the Singapore model. However, the ultimate decision to maintain or alter the market equilibrium rests solely with Beijing.

Japan closely observed the rapid transformation of the Asian casino market in the new millennium, even as it contemplated legalizing casino gambling within the country. It studied various models, from the monopolistic regimes in Macau, Malaysia, and Phnom Penh to Singapore's new approach to integrated resorts. Notably, Singapore's success inspired the Philippines to revitalize its casino industry. After careful consideration, Japan envisioned legalizing casino gambling with up to ten Singapore-styled integrated resorts nationwide. The Diet (national legislature) enacted a bill allowing for three initial casino licenses, with the possibility of issuing more after seven years. This approach, however, limits Japan to a maximum of three casinos for nearly a decade. This stands in sharp contrast to Macau, which boasts over a dozen resorts despite being geographically smaller and less economically powerful than Singapore. With a geographical area over 500 times larger than

Singapore and a population exceeding 120 million, even ten casino resorts would essentially create regional monopolies in such a large country. The vast distances between these planned IRs suggest they are unlikely to pose direct competition to each other, raising concerns about a dearth of robust competition within the Japanese market.

Even before the first license was awarded, the structure of the Japanese casino industry revealed a glaring lack of competition. The Osaka Prefecture government's official IR tender process attracted only one bid, submitted by the ORIX-MGM consortium. Unopposed in the bidding process, the consortium submitted a proposal that met the minimum requirements by only a narrow margin. This lack of competition arguably gave the consortium excessive leverage, leading to concerns about the fairness of the process and whether the government would revise the rules and procedures for the two remaining concessions. Japanese media heavily criticized the Osaka government for granting the winning consortium a favorable deal at the expense of taxpayers, who bore the substantial cost of ¥79 billion for site rectification works. The consortium also holds an out clause until fall 2026, allowing them to abandon the project without consequence if market conditions become unfavorable.

Scheduled for a 2030 opening, the MGM Japan Resort appears set to enjoy a monopoly, not just in western Japan, but nationwide as it remains the only approved integrated resort in the country. This scenario threatens an unacceptably high HHI score for Japan's integrated resort industry. A three-license oligopoly, once considered concerning, now seems preferable compared to the current situation. Beyond the HHI score, it's crucial to consider the adverse effects of a monopoly on consumers and the industry. Restricted competition may stifle innovation and limit consumer options.

Without competition, a monopoly operator has weaker incentives to maintain high service standards, invest in quality, or prioritize renewal projects. Resorts World Genting, the once-iconic casino resort nestled in the Genting Highlands of Malaysia, has long enjoyed a dominant position in Asia. However, its historical lack of competition may have inadvertently hindered its evolution. While the resort maintains a certain vintage charm, it was only the emergence of modern integrated resorts in the region that finally necessitated a reevaluation of its modernization strategy. This situation bears some resemblance to SJM Holdings in Macau. Both Genting and SJM previously held monopoly positions within their respective markets. However, SJM's experience serves as a stark reminder of the dangers of complacency. Genting still has its domestic monopoly, but when Macau's market liberalized, welcoming five new operators, SJM struggled to adapt to the increased competition, ultimately succumbing the market leadership to the new entrants.

A resort cluster framework, like those in Macau's Cotai Strip and Manila, concentrates resorts in a designated area, fostering healthy competition. This framework also encourages collaboration on infrastructure and amenities, which could have created a more viable industry structure in Japan. However, implementing such a framework would require overcoming various obstacles, particularly navigating political and legislative complexities.

The expansion of integrated resorts across Asia continues, with the kingdom of Thailand emerging as the next new frontier. Parliamentary movements suggest the possibility of legalizing casinos within five mega-entertainment complexes, similar to the Singapore model. However, like Japan, questions exist regarding the impact of this approach on market competition and regional development. Thailand's economic landscape is characterized by a large disparity between urban centers, like Bangkok, and rural areas. Urban centers feature higher economic activity, higher income levels, excellent infrastructure, and better employment opportunities, translating to a generally higher standard of living for urban populations with easier access to education, healthcare, and amenities. In contrast, rural regions often face endemic problems like lower income levels, limited access to quality education and healthcare, and fewer job opportunities. Agriculture remains a fundamental pillar of rural economies, but its dependence on traditional practices often leaves these regions vulnerable to economic downturns and the escalating challenges of climate change, such as extreme weather events and water scarcity. This disparity extends to infrastructure development, with urban areas benefiting from better transportation, communication, and utility facilities. The Thai government reportedly views the proposed entertainment complexes as a tool for economic rejuvenation in rural areas, aligning with their goal of diversifying tourism beyond established destinations like Bangkok, Phuket, and Pattaya. While some of the complexes will most likely be located in these established tourist hubs, a focus on rural areas is evident. However, operating large-scale entertainment complexes in rural regions exposes shortcomings in existing infrastructure, such as transportation networks and utilities. One of the recommended criteria is that an entertainment complex must be situated within 100 km of an international airport. Additionally, questions remain regarding the availability of a readily available workforce with the required skills to operate and maintain these facilities and the impact of these projects on the social fabric and environment of rural communities. Thailand's foray into the integrated resort industry requires a strategic approach to cultivate a thriving competitive ecosystem. A "clusters and zones" model could achieve this, extending on the initial proposal of standalone entertainment complexes in five regions. Mirroring the success of the Las Vegas Strip, a cluster development model concentrates multiple resorts in a designated area. This critical mass of tourism offerings attracts a larger visitor base, stimulating economic activity across the surrounding rural region. These resort clusters act as a magnet, drawing visitors to the region. Once there, they're more likely to venture out and explore nearby attractions, generating additional revenue for the surrounding area. Densely populated areas like the Bangkok Metropolitan Region and the Eastern Economic Corridor are prime candidates for a zonal development strategy. This approach features integrated resorts with distinct styles, similar to Singapore's model, but physically distributed to balance visitor concentration across the zone. Imagine one resort in Bangkok, another in Pattaya, and a third in Rayong, all part of a greater zone. Developing adequate infrastructure (transportation, utilities) across wider zones necessitates a feasibility assessment to determine investment requirements. Additionally, exploring economic zone incentives could further sweeten the attractiveness of these zones for investors and businesses.

In the competitive realm of integrated resorts, distinct offerings are essential for fostering healthy market competition. This is perfectly illustrated by the contrasting approaches of Singapore's two prominent integrated resorts. The government strategically carved out unique niches for each resort: one focusing on business tourism by prioritizing conventions, meetings, and exhibitions (MICE), while the other caters to families, offering a plethora of leisure and entertainment options. This intentional divergence ensures the resorts complement each other, rather than overlapping in offerings. This enriches Singapore's tourism landscape with a diverse range of experiences that cater to various visitor segments.

Macau is actively pursuing a similar strategy to Singapore. Recognizing the homogeneity of their Cotai Strip resorts, Macau's renewal of concessions in 2023 for its six IR operators has focused on greater diversification with non-gaming offerings. This aims to avoid the pitfall captured in the adage, "If you've seen one, you've seen them all," and ensure each resort offers a unique value proposition. Their uniform approach to Japan's IR vision, regardless of location, fails to consider the distinct needs and scale of different markets. For instance, focusing solely on the MICE model in a rural setting with limited transportation connectivity and a small population base makes it unrealistic to expect a high volume of business travelers. This highlights the importance of tailoring IR offerings to the specific context and target audience. The onus, though, does not solely lie in the hands of government planners but also in the hands of the IR operators to manifest these plans into reality, not just on paper but also with the credentials to deliver on their promises.

The unchecked growth of the Asian casino industry over the past two decades has been propelled by rapid economic expansion in the region, particularly in China. The introduction of integrated resorts has dramatically transformed the competitive landscape, rendering satellite casino hotels in Macau nearly obsolete and demoting the previous monopoly operator to a minor player in the market. Similarly, regional and state-owned casinos in the Philippines have struggled to compete with the new integrated resorts in Manila. Meanwhile, resorts in Vietnam and Cambodia cater predominantly to niche grey markets due to the lack of a sufficiently robust regulatory framework to attract major gaming companies. Marina Bay Sands and Resorts World Sentosa have emerged as pivotal players, leveraging and stimulating the growing market demand. This intricate dynamic between scale and quality, bolstered by effective regulatory oversight and standards, is a fundamental factor in defining, rejuvenating, and shaping competition within the market.

The Asian casino industry demands constant evolution to stay relevant and competitive. A prime example is Malaysia's once-dominant Genting Highlands Casino. Faced with changing market conditions, it underwent a series of major transformations and rebranded itself as Resorts World Genting, with substantial investments that significantly reshaped the resort experience. This move reflects the necessity for continual upgrades and diversification to compete in the increasingly more competitive regional industry. Thailand is exploring the possibility of entering the industry by introducing "entertainment complexes" with integrated resort features, which would necessitate revising the nation's constitution to legalize casino gambling. While considering various investment levels for projects across the country, the government must ensure a minimum threshold for quality and scale for these complexes to compete effectively in the regional market. Striking a balance between financial feasibility and achieving desired visitor experiences is paramount in the dynamic Asian landscape.

five

LET THE NUMBERS DO THE TALKING

In the competitive casino industry, hard data is crucial for making informed decisions. It provides a neutral and objective perspective, free from personal biases and assumptions. By utilizing appropriate statistical models, casino operators can:

Identify and address cognitive biases: Heuristics (mental shortcuts) and ego-driven judgments can lead to poor decision-making. Data analysis helps mitigate these risks.

Optimize resource allocation: Data can reveal the optimal level of quality needed to attract target demographics, ensuring resources are used efficiently and effectively.

Creating a world-class resort requires a delicate balance between extravagant luxury and sound financial decisions. Steve Wynn's signature style, exemplifies the excessive opulence of some modern resorts. Wynn Resorts boasts an impressive art collection such as Pierre-Auguste Renoir's 'In The Roses,' a $23.5 million stunner that once resided at Wynn Las Vegas. Jeff Koons' 'Tulips' welcomes visitors at the rotunda connecting Wynn and Encore Las Vegas. Specific ownership of the artwork though can be a bit murky. The ill-fated lavish 'The 13' casino in Macau, envisioned by an owner driven by ego and unrealistic aspirations, never opened its doors and ultimately became a symbol of a failed investment. Fueled by a desire to create the next iconic landmark, some integrated resort owners have embarked on lavish spending sprees. Their ambitions are nothing short of monumental, aiming to rival the likes of the Louvre or the Guggenheim and surpass architectural marvels like Marina Bay Sands' SkyPark. However, this quest for instant iconicity is a risky and expensive gamble. IRs are, at their core, businesses with a responsibility to their shareholders. Casino executives, especially those with vast ownership and unchecked authority, can prioritize personal vanity and besting the competition over sound financial choices. These executives often overlook crucial factors: the subjective nature of beauty and the fact that iconic status is earned through time, not bought with extravagant displays. Furthermore, unrealistic expectations plague the pursuit of celebrity architects. Their brilliance is mistakenly seen as a guarantee for success across all projects, regardless of context. This aggressive chase for fleeting fame often leads to questionable investments and financial strain, jeopardizing the long-term viability of these businesses. Responsible management and data-driven decision-making must be prioritized over ego-driven pursuits to achieve sustainable success.

From the very beginning of an integrated resort project, two key elements should be developed simultaneously: the design vision and the financial model. This collaborative approach requires a strong partnership between business, design, and finance stakeholders. Market analysis guides the form and scale of the IR, and costs are carefully aligned with projected revenue and targeted financial returns. These costs include construction and development, ongoing operational expenses, and the cost of borrowing capital. Working capital and cash flow are crucial metrics for assessing a project's financial viability. Seamless collaboration across all disciplines forms the bedrock of a sound integrated resort design and business plan. Unfortunately, a common pitfall arises when the business development team and operations team function in silos. This isolation hinders informed decision-making, as both sides rely heavily on each other's input. To bridge this gap, fostering open communication channels is paramount. Regularly scheduled meetings involving both teams create a space for a holistic view of projects, allowing for the exchange of insights and concerns. Furthermore, developing shared metrics and visual dashboards ensures everyone is on the same page from the outset. By monitoring key performance indicators (KPIs) together, both business development and operations can prioritize design vision, financial feasibility, and operational efficiency throughout the entire process.

The first rendering of an integrated resort is often entrusted to architects, who develop the design concept based on given specifications and incorporate broad parameters set by their client. Many casino companies, lacking internal design expertise, rely on third-party architectural firms. While some firms excel in this arena, others may struggle due to a limited understanding of the casino industry's specific needs. This can lead to a problematic imbalance: either a lack of intelligent client input or an over-reliance on it. It's a misconception that early-stage design details are not as critical; in fact, they can profoundly impact a project's success. Clients who grant architects excessive autonomy, believing that details can be finalized later, risk creating hollow spectacles. This approach reduces the design process to a superficial competition, prioritizing aesthetics over functionality and practicality. This is evident in the submissions made in response to the integrated resorts Request for Concepts exercise conducted by the Singapore government in 2005, where many flashy submissions are lacking in substance and fail to meet the project's true requirements.

A well-structured conceptual plan for an IR, regardless of its length, should be anchored by two key elements:

1. *Robust Framework*: A strong "wireframe" outlining the core principles and functionalities of the resort. This detailed framework ensures the design aligns with the project's overall vision.

2. *Balanced Financial Structure*: A comprehensive financial plan that encompasses more than just securing development funding. This plan should be supported by data, a clear business model, and preferably backed by a proven track record.

Superficial plans may seem to get by in limited competition or favorable conditions, creating a false sense of security. However, they under-deliver on the full market potential, leaving companies vulnerable if the environment changes to a competitive market. The oil and gas industry offers a prime example of under-delivering. The term 'giveaways' arose from situations where subpar design and operation resulted in substantial revenue losses. Inefficiencies can often stem from flaws in the physical design, which will be compounded in daily operations. To break free from the recurring pattern of underperforming resorts, ensuring financial viability must be a core principle from the planning stages. Prioritizing financial modeling allows the form and function of the integrated resort to organically adapt to an optimal scale and configuration and eliminate unnecessary "giveaways." This data-driven approach acts as the foundation upon which the entire project is built, ensuring all components harmonize and contribute to a cohesive and financially viable entity. By prioritizing realistic financial projections, we can leave costly, underperforming "white elephant" resort components in the past. Integrated resorts aimed to transcend the limitations of the glorified casinos of old. They envisioned a complete transformation and a paradigm shift rather than just a cosmetic makeover.

However, despite bearing the "integrated" label, many of the more mature integrated resorts, particularly those outside Las Vegas, struggle to move beyond their core focus on casinos. Legacy industry giants like SJM and Genting are some stalwarts saddled with this issue. Their deeply entrenched practices, habituated over decades, are practically synonymous with their brands. Shedding this deep-rooted identity requires a visionary leader to take the reins such as Steve Wynn, who boldly reinvented his stable of properties to cater to the modern consumer and steer the industry in a new direction. On the other hand, newer players in the IR market, while lacking experience, have a unique advantage: they are unburdened by historical baggage. Picking up the torch from Howard Hughes' legacy of transformation in Las Vegas, Sheldon Adelson introduced a groundbreaking concept with The Venetian in 1999. This resort successfully balanced the appeal to both mass and premium demographics, while also integrating large conventions into its offerings. Building on MGM's entertainment legacy, Kirk Kerkorian introduced a new era of spectacle with shows like the iconic 'O' by Cirque du Soleil. This focus on grand productions has become a defining characteristic of MGM Resorts, transforming it into an entertainment powerhouse. Successful IR leaders like James Allen stay ahead of the curve by constantly adapting their strategies to evolving consumer preferences. The Hard Rock empire, under Allen and the

Seminole Tribe, epitomizes this. Over two decades, they've transcended their music-themed roots by introducing a diverse range of non-gaming experiences. For them, the focus has shifted from just gambling to a broader, all-encompassing experiential journey.

The casino industry today is witnessing a generational shift in leadership, marked by the retirement of old-school leaders and the rise of tech-savvy successors. Lawrence Ho, at the helm of Melco Entertainment, is carving a path distinct from his father, the legendary Stanley Ho who once "owned" the Macau casino industry. Across the South China Sea in Malaysia, Lim Keong Hui is expected to inherit the reins of Genting Group from his father, KT Lim, in the coming years. To navigate this increasingly competitive arena with discerning consumers, these new leaders will need intelligent, market data-driven strategies. The traditional revenue equation is being disrupted. The focus has shifted beyond the casino floor, led by the industry revolution in Las Vegas. Here, successful resorts have adopted a balanced model, with non-gaming revenue challenging the dominance of casino income. Traditionally, the casino reigned supreme as the sole profit engine. Everything else, from restaurants to shows, existed as mere cost centers, solely there to support the casino and not expected to generate much independent income. While casinos remain and will always contribute a significant revenue stream, this perspective is outdated and represents tunnel vision. The winning strategy is about empowering the whole. Modern consumers seek more than just gambling. A successful integrated resort offers that diverse smorgasbord of experiences. Viewing non-gaming amenities as mere supporting cast ignores their growing importance. This outdated mindset also fosters an unfair management hierarchy, where the casino takes precedence over the teams that create the entire resort experience.

In an integrated resort, the casino undergoes a seismic shift. It relinquishes its sole, sun-like dominance and becomes more akin to Earth – the third rock, vital but dependent on a well-functioning ecosystem for its continued success. Just as Earth thrives within a solar system where all the other seven planets play critical roles, all aspects of an IR – hotels, theme parks, entertainment, food, and shopping – contribute to the overall experience and attract guests. Here's the crucial distinction: non-gaming elements are not mere decorations for the casino. They're not cosmetic trimmings; they're the essential components of the resort's ecosystem. Each amenity should be viewed as a vital contributor, a business unit in its own right. The hotel is vital to the success of an integrated resort, allowing guests to extend their stay and experience the entire "solar system." However, labeling it a "casino hotel" diminishes its importance. It shouldn't be an instrument solely for the casino's benefit, but a critical partner within the resort's ecosystem. Unfortunately, a prevalent issue exists. Often, the Casino Department controls room inventory, prioritizing space for high-rolling players. This restricts the hotel manager's autonomy, hindering their ability to develop a strategic perspective for hotel operations. Rooms may be held vacant until the last minute for casino patrons, creating an inaccurate picture of occupancy and revenue (RevPAR). This casino-centric dynamic ultimately harms the hotel's service and product quality, rendering it a "satellite moon" orbiting and serving the dominant casino.

When an integrated resort operates with only superficial integration, non-casino attractions and amenities function under limited control, subject to the caprices of the casino department. While the casino undeniably serves as the engine that drives initial traffic, it's only one part of a complex system. Imagine a high-performance car – the casino is the engine, but peak performance requires a seamless transmission, a powerful battery and alternator, an efficient cooling system, exceptional suspension, and precise steering. A truly integrated resort thrives when every department operates at its peak. Each element – hotels, restaurants, theme parks, and shopping – functions as a finely tuned gear, propelling the entire resort forward and leaving competitors in the dust. This holistic approach maximizes yield by capturing every possible revenue stream. When all departments work in harmonious alignment, the resort becomes more than just the sum of its parts. It becomes a well-oiled machine generating a symphony of profits. The key to unlocking this success lies in strategic planning from the very beginning. Every element of the IR, from the casino to the spa and restaurants, should be envisioned as a profit center in its own right. By empowering each department to focus on its own financial performance, while adhering to an overall resort strategy, individual departments can generate positive cash flow, ultimately contributing to a collective windfall for the entire business.

While getting all the parts of an integrated resort functioning optimally is crucial, it's equally important to first ensure there's a market for each component to thrive. Integrated resort success hinges on market fit. Simply transplanting a model from Manila to Singapore, or vice versa, wouldn't work. Before diving headfirst into design and construction, a thorough understanding of the target market is essential. Stop and consider, not to smell the flowers, but to conduct in-depth market research to identify who and where the customers will come from. A past Bloomberg News headline aptly captured the inherent uncertainty in economic forecasting: 'Fed Officials Put a Finger in the Air' on interest rates. This highlights the difficulty faced not just by central banks, but also by businesses across other industries in accurately gauging market potential. In the development of integrated resorts, a sector known for its large-scale investments, a purely intuitive approach can be particularly detrimental. Many senior casino executives, under pressure to make critical decisions, may resort to a form of market assessment based on gut feeling and preliminary estimations. While this approach, sometimes referred to as "guesstimating" or a "SWAG" (scientific wild-ass guess), may serve as a starting point, it falls short of the rigor required for a successful IR project.

The Osaka government's official development plan for Japan's first integrated resort projects a staggering annual revenue of 520 billion yen, with 80% attributed to the casino. These figures are based on an annual target of 20 million resort customers, consisting primarily of domestic visitors alongside international tourists. However, the question remains: how precise are these projections? The answer (and devil) lies in the details and the methodology used to arrive at these figures. There are two general approaches to such forecasting: top-down and bottom-up.

Top-Down Approach: This method may break down the projected casino revenue, detailing the income distribution between table games and electronic games. It could also segment the customer base into mass market and premium players. For non-gaming, revenue could be delineated across its various sources like hotels, conventions, retail, and other amenities.

Bottom-Up Approach: This method builds the revenue projection from the ground up. For example, it could involve estimating the average spending per visitor across all areas of the resort, including accommodation, food and beverage, entertainment, and gambling. It might also consider the expected visitor mix and their spending habits.

While all projections are inherently forecasts, a closer look at the methods employed in Osaka's plan can reveal its level of accuracy. Here's how we might assess its plausibility:

Market Research: Were established market research techniques employed to project visitor demographics and spending patterns?

Benchmarking: Did the plan consider the performance of similar IRs regionally or globally to create realistic expectations?

Economic Factors: Did the projections account for macro-economic factors that could influence tourism spending?

By analyzing the methodologies used, we can move beyond a casual assessment and gain a more informed understanding of the likelihood of achieving the projected figures. We can subject the Osaka projections to a quick examination by scrutinizing their projection of 6 million foreign resort visitors per year. This can be done by testing its robustness using historical data. Prior to the COVID-19 pandemic, Osaka hosted 12 million foreign tourists in 2019. Assuming that international arrivals rebound to pre-COVID levels by 2024, and projecting a healthy compounded annual growth rate of 10% thereafter, the prefecture would welcome 23 million international visitors in 2030, coinciding with the planned opening period of the resort. Based on this estimate, one permutation is that roughly 10% of visitors, or approximately 2.3 million, would need to stay at the integrated resort for at least two nights to achieve the government's target of six million visitors. This scenario may be difficult to realistically achieve, given the abundance of tourist attractions in the Kansai region. This makes it unlikely for 10% of all visitors to patronize the integrated resort. Simply applying top-down projections from other IR destinations in the region to Japan might be misleading, as there are unique factors in every market's dynamic. For instance, while it may be plausible for 1 out of 10 visitors to visit an integrated resort in the small island nation of Singapore, expecting the same outcome in Osaka would be unrealistic. Further validation of the projections can be pursued by reconciling the projected 520-billion-yen revenue with visitor figures. Alternatively, validation can be performed to derive revenue by estimating daily casino patrons and the average win per customer, and comparing it to revenue projections. The more validations made by testing a broader mix of parameters and perspectives, the more rigorous the projections will be.

For the investors in integrated resorts, financial projections are more than just numbers on a spreadsheet - they're the lifeblood of the project. With hundreds of millions, or even billions, of dollars on the line, any overestimation or miscalculation can be catastrophic. Deep industry experience is essential for crafting reliable projections. In Japan's fledgling IR market, many proposals suffer from flawed forecasts due to a lack of expertise, reliance on dubious advice, or resorting to mere "SWAGging" (guesswork). This often stems from a misconception that the casino industry is immune to failure. The belief that casinos are guaranteed moneymakers is a dangerous myth. While this might have been true in less competitive markets, today's landscape demands critical analysis that delves beyond market trends to consider political shifts, regulatory changes, and other external factors. In highly competitive jurisdictions, overspending and inflated projections spell certain disaster. The past two decades saw a boom in the Asian casino industry, fueled by China's economic surge. During this period of economic prosperity, even poorly-run establishments enjoyed some degree of success. This is far from a sustainable or foolproof business model. Industry leaders like Las Vegas Sands, with their experience managing multiple successful properties, understand the vital role of financial planning. They understand the importance of judicious financial analysis for success in any market, regardless of location or competition. Ultimately, the buck stops with the leader who greenlights the project.

The initial responsibility for financial projections falls on the investor's business development team. Their job is to impartially and objectively analyze the data and ensure the accuracy of the projections. These projections need to be robust and withstand rigorous testing and sensitivity analysis. The true strength of the projections lies in their ability to hold up to scrutiny from both top-down and bottom-up approaches. Bottom-up estimations are crucial as they provide reality checks based on more specific data. By thoroughly analyzing the market size, and addressable customer base reconciling with the business strategy, the bottom-up approach creates realistic business scenarios. This serves as a vital test for the validity of the top-down projections.

Let's delve into some bottom-up analysis for integrated resort financial projections. Bottom-up analysis involves precise bean counting, starting with the fundamentals—determining the size of the market. This market comprises both domestic and international customers, with the domestic market being a subset of the local population. In larger jurisdictions, the domestic market is divided into two segments: the base market and the greater local market. The base market typically consists of individuals residing within up to a three-hour commute time from the resort by land transportation. Due to its small geography, Singapore's unique case is that the base market encompasses the entire domestic market, with no greater local market. When distinguishing between casino and non-gaming segments in the analysis, each has different and sometimes overlapping addressable markets. Regulations often impose minimum age entry requirements and other restrictions for the casino, while non-gaming amenities have no such limitations. Demographic data for the analysis can be sourced from published government census data and demographic ring study reports. From these data sources, an aggregate available market for the integrated resort can be derived. For instance, Osaka Prefecture boasts a greater metropolitan population of over 5 million people, resulting in a base market comparable in size to Singapore. However, the prefecture has a critical edge over Singapore with access to a vast domestic market of 123 million people, all within a 90-minute flight. Another key advantage for Japanese integrated resorts lies in their proximity to a colossal outbound Chinese tourism market, with most of these travelers within a convenient 3-hour flight. This positions Japan to capture a substantial portion of the 100 million Chinese tourists who travel abroad annually.

Refining the available market data sets the stage for more accurate projections, aligning top-down estimates with gaming revenue forecasts. Accurate distribution of gross gaming revenue estimates hinges on a thorough evaluation of expected per-day slot wins, table wins, and average win-per-player. This not only ensures accuracy but also allows for optimizing gaming positions on the casino floor, maximizing yield and occupancy across seasonal fluctuations. A moderately busy casino, even if slightly overcrowded during peak periods, is preferable to a large, empty one that creates an uninviting atmosphere. This not only avoids the drawbacks of wasted space but also allows for more efficient management of capital expenditures. Gaming equipment carries operational and maintenance burdens and occupies valuable space. While the initial budget may seem negligible compared to overall resort costs, these recurring factors can have a long-term impact on operations. The casino industry once relied on over-generous hotel capacities, with the casino subsidizing other amenities. This outdated model contrasts with the integrated resort paradigm. Integrated resorts justify large hotels with their diverse amenities. By maximizing room inventory yields, they ensure a seamless experience for all guests, whether they partake in gaming or not.

To determine the accessible market for a resort in a new market, analyzing traveler volume at key entry points like airports and railway stations is crucial. This data helps identify the specific demographics and volume of potential customers who can easily reach the resort. Take Nagasaki Prefecture's rejected IR plan in Japan, which projected 1.5 million annual international visitors. Assuming a 2.5-night stay, this translates to 600,000 unique visitors, which is far greater than the recorded foreign arrivals in Nagasaki in 2019. For resort projections to align with current visitor counts, the number of foreign tourists to Nagasaki prefecture would need to increase fivefold - assuming one in five of these tourists visit the resort. However, this assumption is unrealistic and casts serious doubt on the validity of the IR projections. This example highlights how bottom-up analysis can stress-test macro projections. Significant deviations from data trends, as seen here, raise concerns about the project's viability and increase the risk of failure.

While attention to detail is crucial, focusing solely on granular figures built upon shaky assumptions can also be misleading. Such excessive focus risks getting lost in minutiae details, which is not much different from relying solely on speculative top-down estimates. We must always ensure the analysis considers the broader context to avoid losing sight of the bigger picture.

six

URBAN MASTER PLAN

Urban master planning for new structures and amenities involves careful consideration of various factors, including zoning regulations, land use, infrastructure, environmental impact, accessibility, and community engagement. These factors are essential to ensure the harmonious integration of new developments with existing structures and the overall vision for a precinct. Integrated resorts, which are essentially large-scale mixed developments, occupy vast real estate—sometimes equivalent to a hundred or more football fields combined. It is evident that these billion-dollar landmarks, designed to serve tens of thousands daily, profoundly impact the physical and functional characteristics of their vicinity. Every day, hundreds of tour buses ply in and out of an integrated resort, and the resort's operational machinery relies on thousands of onsite employees, significantly burdening transportation infrastructure. Convoys of delivery vehicles are required to fulfill the resort's mammoth supply chain, representing a logistical undertaking of mega proportions for just one business. The scale of modern-day integrated resorts, acting as central hubs, demands diligent zoning scrutiny to assess their impact on traffic, infrastructure, and the surrounding community. Placing such a large-scale development in an existing built-up ecosystem without due consideration for existing constituents is a recipe for an unmitigated urban planning disaster. This not only disrupts the cohesive elements of the area's original master plan but also strains existing infrastructure, especially in densely built-up areas. The host jurisdiction and the integrated resort operator share a symbiotic responsibility to ensure the resort integrates seamlessly into the social fabric. The operative word here is "integrate." True *integrated* resorts demonstrate integration both physically and operationally within their walls. Besides this internal integration, which is covered in Chapter 17, the resort must integrate with the external elements that form the foundation of the urban master plan.

The first essential element for a successful integrated resort originates not from the business operator itself, but from its inception within a comprehensive master plan. In this plan, the resort acts as just one component of a grander mission. A successful master plan seamlessly integrates the resort with various aspects:

Civil: Zoning, infrastructure, connectivity, and accessibility.

Environmental considerations: Conservation, sustainability, resilience, and adaptation.

Social elements: Aesthetics, culture, and security.

Flexibility: Adapting to changing needs and future growth.

The plan for Singapore's two integrated resorts is the ultimate embodiment of this approach. The seeds for their development were sown in the country's long-term National Master Plans. The plan outlined a vision for Singapore's development over 40 to 50 years, emphasizing land use, infrastructure, and environmental considerations. A subsequent Master Plan provided specific details for the following 10 to 15 years, covering zoning, land use policies, and development guidelines.

A prime example is the 360-hectare bay area designated in the plan for a new downtown. This aimed to enhance Singapore's role as a global business and financial hub, creating a vibrant 24/7 environment for residents to live, work, and play. Leveraging its waterfront location and green surroundings, the district was expected to attract investments, visitors, and talent, while also serving as a public recreation space.

In the Master Plan, Sentosa and Singapore's southern islands were envisioned as "island playgrounds." Here, high-energy world-class attractions and theme parks would blend with the unique charm derived from the islands' rich natural and cultural heritage. This holistic approach to tourism development aims to create an immersive and engaging experience that celebrates both the contemporary excitement of modern attractions and the timeless allure of the islands' heritage. Such a combination has the potential to appeal to a diverse range of visitors seeking entertainment, cultural exploration, and a connection with nature.

The two integrated resorts were intricately incorporated within the broader and detailed master plans for the bay area and Southern Islands, fitting within these larger development schemes. At Marina Bay, the integrated resort was envisioned to embody a sophisticated, elegant, and contemporary concept, emphasizing upscale accommodations and extensive conference facilities tailored for business travelers and affluent clientele. Strategically situated in close proximity to the central business district, the resort was to offer a seamless experience for conference delegates, minimizing commute times between meeting venues and the bustling business district. As dusk settled over the quiet post-business hours, this tranquil scene would transform into a vibrant nightlife. Weary executives could shed their professional attire, venture to the resort, and immerse themselves in relaxation, fine dining, captivating performances, or a touch of excitement amid the lively atmosphere of dazzling entertainment options or find a little fun amid the din of coruscating one-armed bandits in the casino. The Southern Islands embody the vision of the ultimate tropical leisure gateway. The addition of an integrated resort within its lush setting stands as the boldest expression of its continual transformation. The resort, with its world-class facilities and attractions, would serve to reinforce the island's status as the premier leisure destination of choice for families and sun seekers.

An effective urban master plan does more than combine design maps and zoning regulations. Successfully incorporating an integrated resort demands careful groundwork well before resort construction begins. In the case of Marina Bay Sands, the government initiated the reclamation of 266 hectares of land to create a new downtown, envisioned in a grid-like design by the late architect I.M. Pei. This ambitious undertaking involved transforming an existing highway into a major arterial road and burying a new 3.5-kilometer stretch of highway underground, including a half-kilometer section beneath the seabed that traverses the mouth of the bay. These preparatory measures aimed to welcome tenants to the new Singapore downtown, comprising an integrated resort and a 101-hectare garden with climate-controlled conservatories, alongside other upscale commercial and residential real estate. These extensive infrastructural efforts were complemented by a strategically placed subway line with a station directly beneath the integrated resort, ensuring seamless connectivity for residents, workers, and the millions of visitors it attracts annually. In anticipation of increased visitor traffic to the new Resorts World integrated resort, a new S$80 million bridge was built parallel to an existing one, connecting

Sentosa Island to the mainland. Roads on the island were expanded to accommodate the increased volume of vehicles. A new third passenger terminal was constructed at Changi International Airport to manage the expected rise in air traffic due to the integrated resorts and other tourism initiatives.

The Cotai Strip, envisioned as a rival to Las Vegas, sought to consolidate leisure, entertainment, and gaming on a newly created landmass between Macau's two islands. This ambitious project involved reclaiming the channel between Coloane and Taipa, effectively combining them into a single larger island. The goal was to shift the focus away from the crowded Macau peninsula and establish a world-class integrated resort and entertainment destination. This strategy aimed to strengthen Macau's position as a major gaming center while broadening its appeal to a wider range of tourists. However, the Cotai master plan fell short in anticipating the strain on the existing infrastructure on Taipa and access to the Macau peninsula, leading to unforeseen bottlenecks and delays while also negatively impacting the quality of life for residents. Despite a new three-way dual carriageway bridge supplementing the existing two, the increased traffic volume quickly overwhelmed the island's access routes. Accessibility was further restricted by insufficient improvements to the road network around the reclaimed area. A fourth bridge, under construction, is a belated attempt to rectify the issue nearly twenty years after the first Cotai resort opened, highlighting the prolonged response to the infrastructure problems.

The Cotai Strip now suffers from unprecedented daily traffic congestion. Limited public transportation options further exacerbate the problem. The bus network is inefficient, with each resort operating its own separate fleet, leading to redundancy and a lack of cohesion. The limited-route light rail system risks becoming an underutilized resource. Taxis are also scarce compared to Hong Kong, making hailing a cab a constant grouse. Taxi rides can be frustrating for visitors, as drivers often only speak the local language, making it difficult to get to desired destinations. Without ride-hailing apps prevalent in other Asian travel hubs, alternative transportation options are scarce.

Connectivity to Macau, especially for international tourists, remains limited. Land, sea, and air borders become strained during peak holidays. While additional land crossings ease access for mainland visitors, international tourists primarily fly through Hong Kong due to Macau International Airport's limited routes and operating hours. The success of Macau's integrated resorts, fueled by high demand from Chinese gamblers, underscores the potential of the city as a tourism hub. However, unaddressed external integration deficiencies act as a roadblock to fully realizing this potential.

Similar planning issues arose in the Philippines with the development of Entertainment City, built on a reclaimed section of Manila Bay. Like Cotai, Entertainment City featured a meticulous design with wide streets, spacious sidewalks, and designated development zones for casino resorts, retail, commercial, and residential use. However, its proximity to the densely populated districts of Pasay and Parañaque severely constrained its ability to manage the influx of visitors to the new area. Entertainment City's infrastructural limitations mirrored those on the Cotai Strip. Both developments, acting as magnets, drew tens of thousands of people daily. This substantial influx inevitably strained surrounding areas, overwhelming infrastructure and causing severe traffic congestion. While traffic congestion is a daily reality for many Filipinos, the drastic change in traffic patterns disrupted these affected zones, making the area less appealing to foreign visitors to Entertainment City.

However, the Philippine government seems to prioritize immediate revenue generation, unlike Macau. Entertainment City flourishes due to the influx of Chinese junket operators displaced from Macau, who contribute significantly to the government's tax coffers. The extensive land reclamation works also raised environmental concerns, particularly regarding the impact on fishermen's livelihoods. Local case studies demonstrate how reclamation altered coastal ecosystems, disrupting marine biodiversity and natural habitats. These changes in water circulation and sedimentation patterns likely influenced the bay's overall ecological balance. Fishing communities, heavily reliant on the bay's resources, experienced reduced fishing grounds, directly impacting their catch and income.

Many localities in Japan favoring integrated resorts have also unwittingly chosen sites with a myriad of urban planning obstacles. The first approved integrated resort in Osaka, for example, has encountered multiple issues due to zoning and land-use planning. Inadequate assessments by local authorities regarding soil quality compromised the site's suitability. This oversight led to tens of billions of yen in unexpected public costs to address soil contamination and liquefaction issues, resulting in long delays to the resort's construction schedule.

On the other hand, rural prefectures grapple with serious accessibility issues that hinder them from attracting large numbers of international visitors. A prime example is

Nagasaki Prefecture, which designated the city of Sasebo for its integrated resort location. Sasebo is roughly an hour away from Nagasaki Airport, with public transportation extending the travel time further. Nagasaki Airport primarily serves domestic routes, forcing international visitors to connect through major hubs like Tokyo, Osaka, and Fukuoka. This significantly reduces the appeal of Sasebo as a major international destination for the integrated resort. The poor connectivity raises serious doubts about the prefecture's target of attracting 1.5 million international tourists annually to a Sasebo integrated resort, given that the entire prefecture recorded only 600,000 foreign visitors in a given year.

Hokkaido and Wakayama are two other regional prefectures that initially expressed interest in developing integrated resorts but have since withdrawn. Unlike Sasebo, both of their designated sites, Tomakomai and Marina City, were at least relatively close to international airports. Hokkaido eventually retracted its IR plans, officially citing concerns about the environmental impact on its fauna. In contrast, Wakayama belatedly conceded to growing community opposition to the development. Similar to Wakayama, the metropolis of Yokohama also yielded to the will of the people, albeit involuntarily, when disgruntled residents voted out the mayor in elections. These observations point to a common pitfall in integrated resort planning: the inadequate consideration of social factors. While comprehensive feasibility studies (including economic analysis, infrastructure, and environmental impact) are crucial, a truly successful master plan requires meaningful engagement from all stakeholders. These include not only residents but also local businesses and community groups. Prioritizing financial gains alone overshadows critical social concerns, potentially leading to future issues and conflicts. Superficial attempts at community engagement through uninspired PR exercises are inadequate. Integrated resorts, as major corporate members within a community, must strive for genuine integration with their surroundings. This requires both government and operator to actively address the needs and anxieties of local residents. Japan serves as a prime example of this shortcoming. The national IR legislation focused heavily on financial aspects, and many local governments offered only minimal efforts to address public concerns, with similar disregard for public anxieties shown by many operators.

Community engagement and feedback are integral to urban planning, especially in the context of the gambling element. The public opposition faced in the initiation of the Japanese integrated resort industry is largely attributed to this failing. In hindsight, the national government and local officials should have heeded the people's call for a referendum to obtain tacit approval. Demurring against a referendum due to fears that consistently high disapproval polls against casino gambling might lead to rejection in a plebiscite only served to delay the inevitable, as experienced by Yokohama and Wakayama officials. Even Osaka is not entirely free from challenges, despite receiving the green light from the national government for its integrated resort. Dissenting voices persist in the prefecture, with numerous lawsuits filed by various citizen groups challenging the local government's approach. Local leaders seem to have overlooked the essence enshrined in the term "urban master plan." The term "urban" originates from the Latin *urbanus*, meaning "belonging to city dwellers." It is for, and ultimately belongs to, the people, making it only right to seek their approval. This serves as a valuable learning lesson for mayors of other Japanese municipalities contemplating integrated resort developments when the national government resumes tendering the remaining IR licenses.

Japan is representative of most Asian collectivistic societies where a prevailing stigma against gambling exists, rooted in cultural values that prioritize community well-being over individual pursuits. The prevailing social ethos prioritizes social order and financial security, placing gambling at odds with these core collectivistic principles. Within these societies, the stigma serves as a deterrent, reflecting a broader concern for the impact of individual actions on the interconnected fabric of the community. This perspective influences attitudes toward gambling, shaping a narrative that discourages such activities due to their perceived risks to both social cohesion and economic stability. An exception may be the Philippines, once dubbed the 'Pearl of the Orient,' a designation rooted in its breathtaking landscapes and rich cultural heritage. This epithet emerged during Spanish colonization and later American occupation and indelibly shaped the country's cultural and political landscape. The exposure to Western ideals, governance, and education during these periods laid the foundation for a more pronounced Western liberalism in the Philippines compared to many other Asian nations. This fusion of influences is evident in the Philippine democratic institutions, legal system, and educational practices, reflecting a balance between its Asian roots and Western legacies. Gambling was already widespread and normalized in the country due to the prevalence of casinos, lotteries, and cockfighting.

This likely contributed to the minimal objection faced by the development of Manila Entertainment City and other integrated resorts.

The kingdom of Thailand presents a starkly different scenario. In the intricate tapestry of Thai society, conservatism is deeply interwoven with the threads of Buddhism, the predominant religion. Buddhism serves not only as a spiritual compass but also plays a central role in shaping Thai societal norms and values. Traditional Buddhist teachings in Thailand emphasize harmony, humility, and adherence to societal hierarchies. Concepts such as filial piety, respect for authority and royalty, and preservation of cultural customs are intrinsic to Thailand's conservative ethos. These values extend beyond religious practices and permeate various aspects of daily life, from family structures to interpersonal relationships. As the Thai government considers the deregulation of casino gambling through integrated entertainment complexes, it's crucial to acknowledge this cultural context. Learning from mistakes witnessed in Japan, where prioritizing financial gains overshadowed social concerns in some integrated resort projects, is vital. For instance, neglecting public anxieties surrounding potential disruptions to traditional ways of life in certain communities led to resentment and litigations. Understanding how Thais perceive gambling's potential impact on these core values will be instrumental in crafting a successful and socially responsible approach to integrated resorts. Dissent against these plans has already surfaced among certain segments of the Thai population. To ensure a socially responsible approach, the government needs to actively listen to public concerns during its planning process. The wisest approach is to conduct a local referendum in each *amphoe* (district) provisionally designated for entertainment complex development. This referendum should clearly determine whether residents approve of developing an integrated resort within their district. The plan should also include alternative locations in each province or region in case the primary choices face rejection.

Receiving explicit approval from the people can be a big step toward realizing a vision of Thai entertainment complexes to rival the success of integrated resorts in Singapore. With a greater abundance of flora and fauna, along with a richer culture, traditions, and history compared to Singapore, Thailand's entertainment complexes can offer a distinctly unique value proposition. As already the top tourist destination in Asia, the kingdom possesses all the essential elements for a thriving integrated resort industry. By prioritizing public engagement and adopting a comprehensive approach similar to Singapore's successful strategy – with its emphasis on social safeguards – Thailand's entertainment complexes are well-positioned to become regional leaders in the industry.

Crafting a master plan for Thailand's entertainment resort industry requires careful consideration of several factors. Chief among these is infrastructure, particularly accessibility and connectivity, to determine the optimal scale and structure for both metropolitan and regional complexes. A crucial element is to avoid replicating Japan's uniform integrated resort model regardless of location. Integrated resorts can serve as powerful catalysts, driving regional economic revitalization and transformation by stimulating targeted infrastructure upgrades, such as improved high-speed rail connections to enhance accessibility for tourists from major cities. In urban settings, they can create vibrant hubs. However, their proximity to religious institutions, schools, and densely populated residential areas might necessitate careful planning to avoid potential social conflicts. Dense urban areas with limited space may face constraints for further infrastructure upgrades, such as expanding roads or parking facilities. Thus, plans for entertainment complexes in the Bangkok Metropolitan Region should prioritize less-congested city limits over central districts.

Thailand's rich cultural heritage presents a unique opportunity to craft a truly distinctive integrated resort experience. The IR master plan should leverage this by seamlessly integrating local traditions, architectural styles, and practices into the design. Imagine vibrant handicraft workshops alongside contemporary art galleries, or traditional dance performances captivating audiences within the resort. This not only strengthens the resort's authenticity but also promotes Thailand's soft power on a global stage. Beyond cultural immersion, a successful IR plan requires a holistic approach. Ensuring new developments align with existing infrastructure is critical to minimize disruptions and optimize resource use. This includes considerations for transportation, utilities, and public services, fostering a human-scale design that prioritizes accessibility for all. Additionally, incorporating the preservation of natural landscapes into the blueprint for regional entertainment complexes can contribute to environmental conservation and create economic benefits for local communities through ecotourism opportunities.

Investors and operators venturing into a new gaming market often lack the ideal conditions present in Singapore, where a comprehensive urban master plan guides IR development and fosters a responsible tourism environment. In contrast, some landscapes can be daunting. South Korea, for instance, faces challenges with its casinos having no access to the local market, severely limiting potential revenue. It leaves IR operators with virtually no other option than to rely heavily on junkets to keep their businesses running. This approach, while potentially lucrative in the short term, poses many long-term issues such as vulnerability to money laundering concerns and dependence on a single customer segment. Similarly, at the Hoiana Resort in Vietnam, the restriction on locals gambling creates an overreliance on open borders to attract Chinese high-rollers, making it susceptible to fluctuations in geopolitical relations.

Experienced operators in less-than-ideal regulatory environments often seek to negotiate changes. Renowned for his focus on well-established frameworks, Sheldon Adelson demonstrated Las Vegas Sands' willingness to withdraw from markets like Vietnam, South Korea, and Japan when conditions proved unfavorable. To secure a more favorable agreement, MGM Resorts engaged in extensive negotiations with the Osaka prefectural government in Japan before proceeding with their integrated resort project.

Thailand's emerging gaming market garners both supporters and critics. While the regulatory framework would likely not match Singapore's level of rigor, investors have options. They can either proactively advocate for adjustments as legislation is developed or wait until regulations are finalized to assess the market's appeal. Investors recognizing opportunities in new markets should share the responsibility of shaping its development. Robust long-term plans that incorporate well-defined gaming legislation and policies, framed within a comprehensive urban master plan, ultimately benefit both investors and the jurisdiction.

seven

X MARKS THE SPOT

At their core, integrated resorts are large-scale, mixed-use prime real estate developments. Unsurprisingly, integrated resort operators share the near-fixation on location with real estate developers. This principle demonstrates the powerful impact of strategic location choices on an IR project's market viability. This location-centric principle holds true even in the realm of industrial and logistics developments, which prioritize proximity to transportation hubs, supply chain efficiency, and access to highways and distribution networks over traditional considerations for "prime" areas in residential and commercial real estate. Integrated resorts fall into the latter category, serving as mass tourist destinations that demand excellent accessibility and connectivity—crucial components of an urban master plan where an integrated resort stands as a central element, as detailed in the previous chapter. Singapore's two integrated resorts were purposefully incorporated into the island nation's long-term urban master plan. One serves as the centerpiece of its new downtown, while the other anchors a popular island getaway, functioning as a jewel in its tourism industry strategy. These locations fulfilled all the essential criteria for investors as they were designed to stimulate economic growth, particularly by establishing Singapore as a leading regional tourism destination. The Philippine government, aiming for similar success, established an entertainment zone for casino resorts on a reclaimed area along Manila Bay. The Manila Entertainment City plan, though conceived before Singapore's vision, only gained higher momentum afterward. It was described by the then-chairman of PAGCOR (the country's gaming regulator) as the country's largest tourism development project by investment and a major job-creation initiative, representing a landmark commitment to economic growth. While Manila Entertainment City may not have achieved the same global recognition as the Singapore resorts, it has demonstrably contributed to the Philippines' tourism industry, nearly doubling tourist arrivals since its opening. Manila Bay's selection maximized economic potential due to its proximity to the country's main airport. It also boasts a readily available customer base of 13 million Filipino residents in Metro Manila, including a high concentration of both the middle class and the country's elite. These factors have translated into substantial profits for the Manila casino operators.

Within a broader master plan, the location for an integrated resort development is set, as was the case in Singapore. However, alternative approaches also exist. In many American state jurisdictions, the onus is left to investors and casino operators applying for a casino license to identify and secure suitable sites for their development, as well as obtaining, all necessary zoning consent from municipal or county authorities. American tribal casinos generally operate on reservation land belonging to Native American tribes, except for landless tribes, which can seek federal approval to place non-reservation land in trust for casino construction. Unlike other Asian countries with centralized oversight by national governments, Japan takes a more collaborative approach. Prefectural governments compete for the three available integrated resort licenses by submitting detailed bids to the national government, including chosen operators and investors. If left solely to the investor's discretion, the location of an integrated resort would likely be chosen for purely economic gain, targeting the most densely populated and wealthiest area with the best infrastructure. However, for governments, other factors often come into play. While capital cities invariably attract the most business interest, focusing excessive investments primarily into these areas risks exacerbating existing economic and social imbalances. Governments have a responsibility to balance investments and developments between urban centers and other areas, aiming to foster inclusive growth and reduce regional disparities. The nature of large-scale casino resorts makes them excellent instruments for rejuvenating less developed regions, thereby spurring development, creating job opportunities, and enhancing infrastructure.

The Philippine government has set its sights on revitalizing the Clark Freeport Zone, a former US Air Base, as the next frontier for its booming casino industry. Despite facing prolonged economic hardship, the region has witnessed a gradual resurgence with the development of industrial parks and a growing presence of technology firms. Modern casino resorts are envisioned as the final cornerstone, transforming Clark into a strategic business and tourism hub. This ambitious plan is bolstered by the expansion of Clark International Airport, aiming to establish it as the country's second major international gateway. Understandably, investor expectations and interest for areas like Clark, a former military base undergoing revitalization, are lower compared to densely populated regions. This is because integrated resorts require certain basic infrastructure and accessibility for commercial viability. This major drawback was what deterred major casino companies from pursuing an integrated resort in Nagasaki. Similarly, a pilot initiative by the Russian government to create a casino tourism hub in remote Vladivostok struggled due to its inaccessible location and harsh climate. Unlike Sasebo in Nagasaki, Tomakomai City offered a more promising proposition – an exurban location near New Chitose International Airport, boasting superior connectivity. However, this advantage was tempered by limited winter accessibility.

Location aside, a development site's topography, land composition, and soil conditions heavily influence its suitability for an IR project. Constructing a resort on reclaimed land, like Marina Bay Sands in Singapore and the upcoming MGM Resort Osaka project on Yumeshima Island, presents unique problems. The land for Marina Bay was reclaimed using soft marine clay, known for its instability. This necessitated extensive soil improvement measures, specialized foundation designs, and deep piles to ensure a stable base for the massive structures. While these techniques mitigated settlement risks, they caused a one-year delay in the project, prompting the hiring of additional workers to meet the three-year deadline.

Developing an integrated resort on Yumeshima Island proved unexpectedly complex and costly for the Osaka city government. The discovery of unsafe levels of arsenic and fluorine, compounded by the soil's liquefaction potential, necessitated extensive safety countermeasures. These measures resulted in an unforeseen 79-billion-yen expenditure, leading to a delay in the resort construction start date to 2025. A 4.4-kilometer access road necessitated soil decontamination, resulting in another 75.6 billion yen of additional expenses. Similarly, extending the subway line proved more expensive than estimated due to the need to stabilize soft ground and remove underground obstacles. Exacerbating the underlying site issues, strict guidelines are expected to dictate the construction pace to ensure no disruption to the Osaka Expo running from April to October 2025, which will be staged directly adjacent to the IR site.

Unlike the artificial land chosen for MGM Resort Osaka and Marina Bay Sands, Hokkaido Prefecture designated a verdant natural area for its planned IR site. This area boasts captivating landscapes, including forests which are a major tourist draw due to their diverse flora and fauna. Slender white birch trees with their distinctive peeling bark stand out against the greenery, offering a striking scene throughout the seasons. However, the mayor's plan for a large integrated resort amidst the towering birch trees has sparked opposition due to its potential environmental impact. Clearing fifty hectares of pristine forest, threatening both flora and fauna, highlights the role these trees play in mitigating climate change by absorbing carbon dioxide. Opponents argue that building a large resort contradicts Japan's national climate goals, including achieving carbon neutrality by 2050. The lack of comprehensive environmental studies also raised concerns about the potential destabilization of the soil structure, which could lead to increased erosion and altered water cycles. Habitat disruption from the project was another major concern, potentially leading to extinction and a loss of biodiversity, particularly for protected goshawks whose nesting areas and overall ecosystem would be disrupted by the project. All these concerns prompted the prefectural governor to eventually reconsider the project after learning about the extent of the disruption.

In some cases, a seemingly unsuitable location can surprisingly be the most suitable site for an integrated resort. This unusual approach stems from the belief that placing casinos away from urban centers, where accessibility is limited, may discourage individuals from frequent gambling. The idea is to create a physical barrier, making impulsive visits less likely and potentially deterring the development of addictive behavior. Proponents argue that remoteness not only limits exposure to gambling opportunities but also encourages responsible gambling practices by making it a less convenient and habitual activity. However, this approach necessitates careful consideration of other possible drawbacks and thorough evaluation to ensure its effectiveness in reducing gambling addiction. While a similar strategy seemed successful in South Korea, where the only citizen-accessible casino is located in the remote Jeongseon County, the Kangwon Land casino still thrived due to its monopoly status in the South Korean market.

The same strategy was also considered by the Taiwanese government, who considered establishing casinos off the main island in Penghu County and the islands of Kinmen and Matsu. While only accessible by air and sea from the Taiwanese mainland, these locations held a strategic business advantage for investors due to their proximity to mainland China where the locations were closer to China's Fujian Province than Taiwan's main island. It was precisely this proximity that attracted former top gaming executive William Weidner, who pledged over $1 billion to develop a resort on Matsu. However, his efforts were ultimately in vain, as Taiwan's casino legislation plans were rejected in local referendums. Matsu's failure marked just another setback for Weidner after his phenomenal successes with Las Vegas Sands in Macau and Singapore, adding to similar struggles in the

Bahamas, Danang in Vietnam, Wakayama in Japan, and the Philippines.

Manila Entertainment City's success on several fronts can be attributed to its prime location and planning. A large metropolitan population provides a steady stream of revenue for the integrated resorts. The city boasts excellent connectivity, particularly with key markets in North and Southeast Asia. The proximity of multiple resorts fosters a synergistic cluster effect, creating a critical mass of consumers and enhancing the overall appeal and economic impact. Unlike its Asian neighbors, casino gambling enjoys broad social acceptance in the Philippines. The local population and government view it as a new form of entertainment and a source of revenue for the country. Government policies have actively supported the gaming sector, with a particular focus on expanding the online casino sector. This support includes adapting regulations to stimulate economic growth, establishing a free port zone for online operators, creating a broader framework for Philippine Offshore Gaming Operators (POGOs), and offering a separate online license (PIGO) for land-based casinos. However, despite all the positive developments, the Philippine gaming industry faces a higher risk compared to Macau and Singapore over the long term. This is because the focus on loosely regulated policies could create instability down the road. The recent boom in the Philippine gaming industry is heavily driven by Chinese investors. These backers operate VIP gaming rooms and proxy gambling within integrated resorts and dominate the online casino landscape. The former gained traction after similar practices were banned in Macau and restrictions were imposed on junkets in Cambodia. Crackdowns on grey gambling activities in other countries created a safe haven in the Philippines for hemmed-in Chinese investors. This influx fueled the industry's recent boom, leading to heady forecasts predicting tens of billions of dollars in annual gross gaming revenue by 2027.

Despite the current euphoria in the Philippines, a broader perspective is crucial for a balanced assessment. The country enacted the Anti-Money Laundering Act (AMLA) in 2001 to combat money laundering linked to terrorism and illegal weapons sales. A decade later, a report card by the Financial Action Task Force exposed continued weaknesses in its regulatory framework and implementation. Ten years on, concerns persist, with the FATF specifically highlighting the casino sector as a key area of vulnerability. By 2022, when "Bongbong" Marcos became president, the Philippines found itself on the FATF's grey list, signifying it would be subject to increased monitoring due to deficiencies in its anti-money laundering and counter-terrorism financing controls. This designation spurred President Marcos to issue a directive demanding action from all government entities to address these issues. The target: removal from the grey list by 2024. The gaming authority, PAGCOR, had come under particular scrutiny. The prevalence of Chinese junkets within integrated resorts, coupled with rising POGO-related crimes like human trafficking, swindling, and kidnapping, underscores the need for urgent action. This alarming trend has even prompted the Chinese government to demand firmer action from Philippine authorities. In response, an e-visa system for Chinese nationals was abruptly suspended. These developments in the Philippines unfolded alongside China's ongoing anti-corruption campaign to cut off the snake's head to eliminate the problem at its root. These broader developments pose the risk of negating all the gains made in the Philippine gaming sector. The proliferation of these operators could prompt Chinese authorities to take sterner action to limit their activities, similar to the crackdowns in Macau and Cambodia.

In Vietnam, a similarly lax regulatory regime has allowed Alvin Chau, the former owner of SunCity, to establish his first major integrated resort outside Macau. This came after he was banned from Australia and withdrew from a project in Japan. However, with Chau's imprisonment and the dismantling of SunCity's vast junket network, the future of the now-divested multibillion-dollar Hoiana Resort becomes uncertain. With Vietnamese citizens prohibited from gambling in casinos and the junket channel gone, Hoiana's success now largely depends on attracting Chinese and South Korean tourists, who currently represent a third and a quarter of Vietnam's international visitors, respectively. However, relying solely on tourism revenue, especially without the substantial contributions from junkets, makes recouping the massive investment a significant uphill battle.

The circumstances surrounding Cambodia, the Philippines, and Vietnam serve as a stark warning about the importance of considering its regulatory framework when choosing gaming investment locations.

—

A thorough analysis of factors relevant to integrated resort locations reveals several key parameters crucial for selecting a site that optimizes commercial success alongside social well-being:

1. *Accessibility and Connectivity*: A well-functioning transportation network is a key backbone.

2. *Urban Integration*: Seamless alignment with existing and future urban development plans.

3. *Community Consensus*: Local community support is vital for long-term success.

4. *Market-Driven Scale*: The resort size should correspond to the available market and minimum investment requirements.

5. *Regulatory Framework*: A well-defined and robust regulatory framework is necessary.

6. *Environmental Impact*: Minimal disruption to the surrounding environment should be prioritized.

Thailand's established tourism industry and cultural richness make it a potential contender as Asia's next premier casino destination. We can apply the above location parameters to evaluate the suitability of site considerations for its entertainment complexes outlined in a Thai parliamentary report.

Thailand, with a population of 66 million and 10% residing in Bangkok, presents a similar demographic to that of Singapore and Osaka. The capital's Suvarnabhumi and Don Mueang airports handle most of the 40 million tourists that visit the country annually. The parliamentary report had proposed the development of five or more entertainment complexes across the kingdom. To broaden reach and support regional tourism, the report recommends locating these resorts in provinces with existing tourism economies or those that share a common border with neighboring countries. Each site should ideally be situated within 100 kilometers of a major international airport, including the two in the capital and the U-Tapao airport, which is being developed into Thailand's third major international gateway. The development plan outlined a tiered model with three investment scales to cater to different markets. The premium tier is for sites in densely-populated areas, focusing on a high-end clientele with an estimated investment of at least $3 billion. The remaining two tiers emphasize exurban revitalization, with more modest investments ranging from $30 million to $600 million. The Thai government, newly elected in 2023, prioritizes economic growth through its pro-business election manifesto. Recognizing that tourism is one of Thailand's main economic sectors, the administration, within its first three months in office, has implemented a visa exemption scheme for visitors from 64 countries. Building upon the previous administration's efforts, a fresh parliamentary committee has revived the entertainment complex plan, a key element in the national tourism strategy. Furthermore, the Prime Minister has approved a series of public infrastructure projects. Suvarnabhumi International Airport's capacity will increase from 45 million to 60 million passengers with a new terminal. Phuket, a leading global destination, will be bolstered by a second airport and new highways. Similarly, the adjacent provinces of Krabi and Phangnga will see airport expansions and a new international airport, respectively. Key airports in other provinces will also undergo upgrades to handle increased capacity and serve regional routes. Improvements are also planned for overland transportation infrastructure. The first phase of a 600km high-speed rail connecting the northeast to the capital is targeted for completion in 2026. Another line linking the two main international airports to Bangkok is scheduled to open in 2029, with an additional 700km of track planned to reach Chiang Mai in the north. These major investments in transportation infrastructure will considerably improve accessibility throughout the country, making Thailand's plan to open entertainment resorts in various regions more achievable.

1. Accessibility and connectivity

Urban Proximity: Resorts located near major urban centers like the Bangkok Metropolitan Region (BMR) offer greater accessibility due to a higher concentration of domestic customers. Other densely populated regions like the eastern provinces (Nakhon Ratchasima, Udon Thani, Khon Kaen) and Chiang Mai also hold considerable potential. These areas, collectively representing over 20% of Thailand's population, constitute a significant domestic market.

Connectivity Infrastructure: Efficient transportation infrastructure plays a crucial role in attracting tourists. A resort situated within the BMR is likely to attract a higher proportion of international visitors due to its proximity to major airports. However, less-connected locations might require a greater focus on domestic clientele.

Income Disparity: It's important to recognize that median income (and spending power) tends to be lower in suburban and exurban areas compared to the capital region. Businesses must adapt their models and marketing strategies accordingly to align with the chosen location's demographics.

High-Speed Rail Integration: Thailand's national high-speed rail roadmap presents a strategic opportunity for entertainment complexes. Proximity to major railway stations facilitates easier access for tourists arriving by rail from neighboring countries, effectively expanding the tourist customer base by providing a convenient and potentially more affordable alternative to air travel.

Last-mile connectivity: Although proximity to an airport is a major factor, last-mile connectivity is equally important. This necessitates a robust infrastructure network with efficient transportation options like highways, railways, and public transport.

2. Urban planning and site suitability

Tier 1 Developments: High-investment resorts in densely populated areas require a comprehensive urban design impact assessment. This goes beyond traffic concerns and evaluates the overall impact on the urban environment. For example, in Bangkok, a city with high population density (5,700 people/km^2) and traffic congestion, a large-scale entertainment complex would severely disrupt its urban equilibrium. Large employee numbers (over 10,000) and daily visitors (up to 100,000) create substantial strain on existing resources. A thorough urban impact assessment empowers planners to anticipate and manage the diverse effects of a development on the city. Factors like density limits, accessibility, and impact on transportation systems, public transit, road capacity, and pedestrian pathways need careful consideration.

Environmental Responsibility: Sustainable practices must be prioritized. This includes responsible water management to avoid pollution and over-usage, controlling dust, emissions, and noise pollution during construction and operation. Additionally, the development should blend seamlessly with the natural landscape, minimizing visual intrusion. Respecting cultural traditions and heritage associated with the environment is equally important.

Exurban Development: Building entertainment complexes in natural environments requires strict environmental considerations to ensure sustainability. Large resorts can occupy vast areas, leading to habitat loss. Optimizing the development footprint and prioritizing areas with minimal ecological value is crucial. Similar to the Hokkaido case, assessing the presence of endangered species and ecosystems is essential, along with implementing necessary protective measures. Investing in exurban locations hinges on the presence of essential infrastructure. Choosing overly remote sites with poor accessibility and a lack of essential utilities like power, water, and waste management jeopardizes a project's viability.

3. Community consensus

Public polls: While a public survey conducted as part of the Thai parliamentary study indicated significant support for legalizing casinos through entertainment complexes, its limited sample size of 3,000 necessitates a cautious interpretation of the results. This caution is further emphasized by the case of Japan, where neglecting public concerns during casino deregulation led to a turbulent process. Numerous studies by Thai academics over the past two decades highlight widespread societal anxieties and resistance to introducing casinos within the kingdom. Thailand's Theravada Buddhist values heavily influence its social fabric, emphasizing moral conduct and discouraging vices. This is reflected in the strict gambling regulations enforced by the government, which have inadvertently forced gambling underground and fueled a thriving illegal market. Thai society's Buddhist teachings promote ethical behavior and avoid activities deemed harmful, including gambling. Similar to many Asian cultures, a social stigma surrounds gambling in Thailand, viewing it as a deviation from societal norms and potentially bringing shame to individuals and families. Despite the conservative cultural and legal landscape that disapproves of such activities, the prevalence of illegal gambling establishments and the allure of these activities for some reveal a complex social reality. This highlights the need for a more comprehensive approach to gauge public opinion. Therefore, seeking a broader consensus, if not explicit approval, from the general population is crucial before formally establishing casino legislation. Local referendums conducted within specific districts (*amphoe*) or sub-districts (*tambon*) can provide a clearer picture of community sentiment and allow local leaders to advocate for or against development in their respective areas.

Feedback: Public feedback channels play a crucial role in ensuring accountability, transparency, and inclusivity in the planning process. However, it's important to remember that achieving complete public consensus may not be possible. Open communication allows all stakeholders to understand the rationale behind the plan and ask questions. This early community input can reveal potential social, economic, environmental, and infrastructural impacts that might be overlooked. Public feedback channels enable residents to voice their concerns and propose solutions, ensuring their perspectives are heard and considered throughout the planning stages.

Dialogue: Open dialogue can lead to a more informed and comprehensive development plan, even if it cannot address every individual's specific needs or desires. This doesn't diminish the importance of public input; it simply acknowledges the inherent complexity of balancing diverse viewpoints within the planning process. Offering various feedback mechanisms is crucial. These can include online platforms, open forums, written submissions, and one-on-one meetings.

Citizen advisory committees, community surveys, and public hearings are also valuable tools. Additionally, dedicated social media channels can facilitate real-time communication, information sharing, and discussion among community members.

Transparency: Potentially divisive legislation like casino gambling warrants setting aside time for substantive discussions within the legislature, even if the proponents hold a majority vote. An extended deliberation fosters a well-informed and thorough debate among MPs. Examining the proposed legislation from various perspectives allows them to consider both its economic and social consequences. Such discussions provide an opportunity for opposing viewpoints to analyze the merits and drawbacks of casino-related policies. Incorporating expert opinions and considering the experiences of other jurisdictions allows for a more comprehensive analysis. Furthermore, this process ensures that diverse voices within the House of Representatives have the opportunity to express their concerns, share insights, and propose amendments. This contributes to a well-informed and balanced legislative outcome. Overall, this deliberative process strengthens transparency, accountability, and the quality of decision-making surrounding casino legislation.

4. Market-Driven Scale

The tiered investment structure proposed by Thai lawmakers signifies a prioritization of broader societal benefit distribution, moving beyond solely maximizing economic value in specific regions. While an entertainment complex in Bangkok might attract the highest investment, exurban developments can act as catalysts for economic revitalization. These developments offer opportunities for local businesses, entrepreneurs, and residents to increase economic activity, improve quality of life, and promote social equity.

Expert vetting: Effective vetting of investment proposals requires a firm grasp of the integrated resort industry's business fundamentals. Engaging professional industry consultants is highly advisable. These consultants can assist a government in the planning and evaluation processes, contribute to building a robust regulatory framework, and advise on qualitative assessments of bids while considering factors like management expertise, market size, and market risks. Subject matter expertise is crucial for several aspects:

- Drawing comparisons with similar developments in other gaming jurisdictions (size, industry, risk profile) to understand relative attractiveness.

- Conducting thorough due diligence to verify bidder suitability and the accuracy and completeness of information provided in proposals.

- Enhancing transparency and accountability through the involvement of independent experts.

Investment quantum: Integrated resorts, by definition, are high-quality, multifaceted entertainment complexes distinct from other leisure and entertainment businesses. The substantial investment observed in Macau, the Philippines, Singapore, and Japan underscores the high financial commitment required to establish a world-class integrated resort destination. Exurban integrated resorts may require less expenditure compared to their urban counterparts. However, the idea of integrated resorts typically involves a minimum scale and quality that warrants a considerably higher investment than the $30 million designated for Tier 3 entertainment complexes in the Thai parliamentary report. This necessitates a general reevaluation of the tier system. Tier 1 could be set at a minimum of $3 billion, with Tier 2 investments between $1 billion and $3 billion, and Tier 3 investments pegged up to $1 billion. Subsequently, the market can refine these figures based on the attractiveness of each location.

5. Regulatory structure

For all the qualities and rich potential of a Thai casino industry, the kingdom will have to address certain hurdles to attract the major casino companies. Established casino brands prioritize well-defined regulations and strong governance. Transparency International reports have pinpointed weaknesses in Thailand's regulatory environment that necessitate further strengthening. Instances of past corruption and police involvement with illegal gambling could deter investors seeking a stable and transparent operating environment. Calls for stricter regulations, comprehensive reforms, and a more robust anti-corruption framework have yet to yield meaningful progress. This raises a crucial question: does the Thai government possess the will and capability to establish a strong casino regulatory framework?

A robust regulatory framework offers several advantages. Firstly, it will attract big and reputable casino operators who value well-defined regulations. Secondly, it fosters a business environment that prioritizes responsible gaming practices. Finally, a strong framework enhances the overall image of the industry and garners public trust. By establishing a solid regulatory foundation, Thailand can position itself as a legitimate and highly competitive destination for the entertainment complex industry, ultimately shaping its reputation within not just the regional but global market.

eight

DESTINATION RESORT?

Turn the glossy pages of any issue of Condé Nast Traveler, and you'll sense the allure of a single word: *Destination*. Evocative and resonant, it promises an arrival with a capital A, a mythical place of unparalleled luxury where you could linger indefinitely. Here, every need is anticipated and fulfilled with effortless grace, offering a glimpse of nirvana...almost. By definition, a destination resort is a self-contained establishment offering a wide range of amenities, activities, and entertainment options, often situated in a remote, scenic location. Designed as the primary attraction for visitors, it provides everything needed for a complete vacation experience – accommodation, dining, recreation – all within the resort's boundaries. The term though is liberally used in the industry regardless of whether a property fulfills the description. While some genuinely earn it, others merely drape themselves in the alluring cloak of the term. Club Med stands as a pioneer in the truest sense of a destination resort. It revolutionized the all-inclusive concept that includes a comprehensive package of services and amenities in the overall cost. This typically covers meals, drinks, accommodations, and leisure activities. These self-sufficient "villages" are mini-universes where guests need never step outside their luxurious bubble.

Casino resorts are increasingly striving to become all-encompassing "destinations." This strategic shift aims to fulfill a wider range of guest needs within the resort itself. By offering diverse amenities and experiences, casino resorts encourage guests to linger longer, maximizing their potential engagement with gaming options and ultimately driving revenue. Similar to how Club Med eliminates clocks and internet access for full immersion, casino resorts inundate guests with a whirlwind of activities and attractions, intentionally blurring the distinction between day and night. That in essence is what modern-day Las Vegas is all about. Gone are the days when the main attraction was the ubiquitous all-you-can-eat breakfast $2.99 buffet. The opulent resorts along the famed Strip have been transformed into captivating playgrounds, offering a non-stop entertainment smorgasbord from sunrise to sunset. Traditional cabaret revues and magic acts have given way to more extravagant features like rooftop rollercoasters, indoor zoos, lava-spewing volcanoes, pirate ships, and iconic replicas such as the Pyramids, Eiffel Tower, and the Statue of Liberty. A notable new attraction on the Strip is the MSG Sphere, a 366 feet tall and 516 feet wide spherical theater, adorned with over a million LEDs covering 580,000 square feet, which showcases 16K-by-16K wraparound visual illumination—an out-of-this-world spectacle bright enough to be visible from space.

Becoming a destination resort requires substantial costs, including both substantial capital investments for expansive facilities and considerable ongoing operating expenses. In Las Vegas, maintaining competitiveness within the concentrated 4-mile stretch of Las Vegas Boulevard, often referred to as the Strip, demands a continuous effort to outshine rivals. The intensely competitive Nevada market has witnessed numerous mergers and acquisitions over the past three decades, the most recent being the 2020 acquisition of Caesars

Entertainment by Eldorado Resorts. In this near-saturated market, ambitious projects during the height of the industry consolidation like Boyd Gaming's Echelon Place and a planned casino resort by Melco Entertainment faced such harsh economic realities that they never materialized. CityCenter once envisioned as the epitome of Las Vegas's future, experienced a tumultuous journey marked by financial struggles, construction delays, and ownership disputes. Whereas the big LV Strip properties vie for the ultimate destination rights in the face of cutthroat competition, that necessity was driven by different circumstances in the early days of Las Vegas. The El Rancho in the 1940s, often considered the first true Las Vegas destination resort, emerged as an oasis in a barren desert, providing refuge from the surrounding nothingness in pioneer Las Vegas. Similarly, Club Med destinations and casino resorts like Atlantis in the Bahamas adopted a self-sufficient ecosystem model due to their remote locations. Drawing a parallel, the Hard Rock Punta Cana in the Dominican Republic stands as a secluded sanctuary, exchanging urban landscapes for endless stretches of pearl-white sand along the Caribbean Sea. Guests can either indulge in its tranquil remoteness or immerse themselves in a myriad of amenities and activities. The resort boasts a plethora of experiences, from a dozen sparkling pools, a lazy river, all-encompassing dining options, a championship golf course, open-air concerts at dusk, nightclubs, and a Hard Rock Casino.

Comparable Asian destination resorts set amid untamed tropical landscapes include Resorts World Genting and Laguna Lang Co in Vietnam. The preamble raises the question: is an integrated resort a destination resort, or, more pointedly, must its design adhere to the destination resort model? This inquiry leads us back to the fundamental reasons why a resort seeks destination status. In remote, rural settings, it becomes a necessity driven by isolation and the need for self-sufficiency. Elsewhere, the motivation is fueled by competition – the relentless pursuit of becoming the ultimate 'go-to' destination. These rationales, however, were largely abandoned during the boomtime of the early 2000s, when Asia witnessed a surge of new integrated resorts. Sparked by the dismantling of Macau's gaming monopoly and further fueled by Singapore's integrated resort duopoly, casino developers embarked on a spending spree. Those halcyon days of Chinese nouveau riche, affluent Southeast Asians, and easy credit that intoxicated the region were a time of staggering opulence. Ten-figure capital investments became commonplace, with each resort vying to outdo its rivals in a no-holds-barred battle for supremacy, offering every conceivable amenity under one roof. This unsustainable model was brutally exposed when the heady market succumbed to a slowdown triggered by the COVID-19 pandemic and the demise of Macau's junket operators. Macau experienced mass job losses as operations contracted.

The pursuit of destination status by every Cotai resort has led to a uniform landscape marked by an unoriginal fusion of commonplace, undistinguished offerings that weighed on their bottom lines as the market recalibrated. Even without the advantage of hindsight, the destination model appears unsuitable for Macau. It does not align with the established criteria of either remoteness or a fiercely competitive market. The Macanese government could have outlined the Cotai blueprint to foster better differentiation among the six concessionaires; in its absence, each operator should have boldly differentiated their resort designs for a more distinctive identity. Macau's compact charm has always favored quick escapes. Its size lends itself to immediate experiences, making it a perfect day-trip destination for China's mainland residents. The vibrant urban landscape, while lacking in polished sophistication, holds a distinct appeal. However, this transient nature and the absence of a truly urbane scene currently limit its potential for destination resorts. That might change in the future. The government's Beijing-backed master plan hints at a transformation. Envisioning a bigger Macau, incorporating Hengqin Island, and shaping new casino concessions, this plan could be the first step towards reinventing the territory as a regional tourism hub - a wholesome Las Vegas, reimagined for a new era.

The specific parameters of competition in the casino industry can be subjective, depending on the players involved and the broader market dynamics. In the unique case of Singapore, with its existing status as a highly urbanized and metropolitan Asian city and a duopoly casino market, becoming a destination resort wasn't crucial for the resorts. The bustling metropolis itself served as the primary draw for visitors. However, when the Singaporean government entered the industry with its sights set on dominating the regional tourism market, the integrated resorts were designed to compete head-to-head with established players in the Asian gaming and hospitality sector. The substantial investments made by Las Vegas Sands and Genting in Singapore were ultimately justified and handsomely rewarded. This success can be attributed to several factors: the significant embellishment provided by Singapore's broader tourism strategy, the high regard and trust in the government's impeccable track record, and the sheer scale and grandeur of the resorts themselves. Japan, as the second-largest economic powerhouse in Asia after China, saw similar optimism and investor interest following its initial casino deregulation. Measured by the same merits as Singapore, the scale of a Japanese integrated resort industry was considered to be markedly larger. Additionally, its close geographical proximity to China offered a clear strategic advantage. Based on these factors, Japan attracted even stronger investor interest than Singapore had at the outset. The spectacular failure of the nascent Japanese IR industry has thus come as a big shock. The blame has largely been directed towards a negative culture of political expediency, which resulted in unwieldy legislation and flawed policies. One of the most glaring shortcomings was the misconception that integrated resorts should function solely as destination resorts. This led to the creation of a single, overly broad set of mandatory criteria for Japanese IRs, vaguely similar to those established for Singapore's resorts. This one-size-fits-all approach proved to be ill-suited to the unique circumstances of the Japanese market and was one factor that contributed to the industry's state of disarray. The government had mooted two categories for Japanese integrated resorts:

Metropolitan resorts: Located in major population centers, designed to maximize economic value and guarantee the greatest success.

Regional resorts: Intended to drive rural revitalization and gentrification.

Despite the distinction, both categories were governed by a single template. This oversight was compounded by a wave of investors blinded by the runaway successes of the Singapore and Philippine integrated resort industries, despite the differing reasons for their success. Notably, the Philippines had been fueled by opaque funds from Chinese junket conduits. The bullish climate led to inflated investment pledges in Japan, exceeding $10 billion for Yokohama and Osaka IR developments, with even rural locations in Hokkaido and Nagasaki prefectures inexplicably attracting low ten-figure bids. The entire situation had resembled pouring gasoline on a fire. Integrated resorts in metropolitan areas justify higher investment due to their proximity to large customer bases and superior accessibility. However, this comes at a cost of high investment and fierce competition for customer attention. Conversely, exurban resorts require strategic investment in a wider range of offerings to function as destination resorts. Despite limited investment capital, they benefit from less competition and the captive audience of a remote setting, which translates to longer customer stays and a niche market presence.

The key takeaway is that while an integrated resort can adopt a destination resort model, it doesn't mean all integrated resorts inherently need to be destination resorts. In urban settings, they don't necessarily need to function as independent destinations themselves. As discussed earlier, the Singapore integrated resorts' destination design model stands as an exception, driven by the government's wider regional tourism strategy. In most cases, the city itself should be considered the primary destination, with the integrated resort serving as a valuable component within it.

What, then, are the nuanced considerations in designing an urban integrated resort? Prime among them is seamless integration within the area's urban master plan, both in form and in function. The resort should not only exist as a self-contained entity but actively complement and collaborate with the surrounding business and social fabric. When overlap with existing businesses occurs, competition should be harnessed as a catalyst for progress. It should spark innovation, fresh ideas, and new perspectives, shaking up established routines and pushing incumbents to adapt. While healthy competition can lead to improved offerings and customer service, a fine line separates this from detrimental head-on conflict. Cannibalization of market share and local resentment must be avoided. Price wars, triggered by direct competition, ultimately benefit no one.

Instead, differentiation is key to fostering a vibrant and diverse business landscape. Wherever possible, the resort should seek synergies through partnerships or cross-promotions, enriching the customer experience and contributing to the destination's overall success. When the resort site isn't pre-determined, the operator faces a balancing act. The business imperative to maximize revenue through a prime location must be weighed against the social responsibility to avoid disrupting the existing fabric. Establishing a buffer zone around sensitive areas, like schools, places of worship, and residential communities, is crucial to mitigate concerns about noise, light pollution, and security issues. Existing entertainment hubs, with their established infrastructure and security, offer the opportunity for an IR to integrate seamlessly into a pre-existing ecosystem. Alternatively, the urban periphery or areas undergoing redevelopment offer suitable site options. These minimize disruption to established communities while presenting opportunities for revitalization.

The characteristics of the reclaimed land parcels of Odaiba and Aomi in Tokyo's Koto Ward mirror the ideal site for an urban integrated resort, as outlined earlier. Nestled on Tokyo Bay, these areas offer both convenient proximity to the city's heart and physical separation from the mainland, further buffered from residential districts by the largely commercial wards of Minato, Chuo, and Shinagawa. A Tokyo integrated resort need not adopt the Singapore template. Unlike Singapore, Tokyo already possesses the captivating blend of ancient and contemporary, deep-rooted traditions, and a vibrant cultural fabric that forms the bedrock of any successful destination. The city itself possesses an allure that renders a destination resort model superfluous. Therefore, the ultimate Tokyo integrated resort should be a bespoke endeavor, not an all-inclusive behemoth. It should offer elevated and finely selected experiences that seamlessly blend exclusivity with broad appeal. This would add to the quintessentially Tokyo experience, offering guests an authentic immersion in the city's vibrant culture. Imagine bespoke collaborations with local artisans and chefs, private tastings with Michelin-starred talents in hidden kitchens, and the transformation of mere structures into a vibrant embodiment of the city's soul. Architectural heritage, artistic pulse, and cultural rhythm would be woven into the very fabric of the resort, delivering hyper-personalized experiences.

In essence, a Tokyo integrated resort wouldn't simply offer a break from the city; it would actively transform the visitor's relationship with it. The resort would provide a gateway to a deeper understanding of the city, unveiling its authentic heart and allowing for an unforgettable, fully immersive journey.

Thai entertainment complexes demand an examination beyond a simple yes/no decision regarding the destination resort model. This context-specific approach is critical due to the varied urban contexts and population dynamics across the country. Consider Bangkok, a vibrant metropolis with a resident population of approximately 6 million. However, during peak daytime hours, the city transforms, bustling with an influx of commuters and visitors, pushing the daily population beyond 10 million. When we expand our lens to encompass the whole Bangkok Metropolitan Region, which incorporates the surrounding urban sprawl, the picture becomes even more striking, revealing a formidable urban agglomeration of 14 million inhabitants. An entertainment complex in the inner suburbs of Bangkok might, therefore, thrive on the city's existing dynamism, potentially mirroring the model of a Tokyo integrated resort. The one-size-fits-all approach, the bane of the Japan IR industry, must be scrupulously avoided to prevent similar pitfalls in Thailand. Locations on the urban fringes, such as the ancient capital of Ayutthaya or the edge cities within the Eastern Economic Corridor's transitional zones, might be better served by a subtler, partial destination resort model. This approach would cater to niche interests and seamlessly complement existing urban dynamics. Similarly, Phuket, despite its modest resident population of approximately 500,000, boasts a gentrified landscape shaped by its status as Thailand's premier tourism destination. Such contexts necessitate a strategically tailored approach to entertainment complex design. Finally, for mooted exurban locations in Krabi, Phangnga,

the north, and the northeast, a full-fledged destination resort design could be optimal. These areas possess the necessary space, resources, and unique qualities to warrant a comprehensive development model.
Integrated resort...destination or not? The answer to the question can be found in the existential query of the need be a destination.

nine

ICONICITY

Iconicity, as defined by the Cambridge Dictionary, is the captivating ability of a subject to reach beyond its physical form and resonate with something far greater. In the realm of architecture, this power to transcend bricks and mortar and become a symbol of an era, a culture, or even a universal sentiment, imbues structures with enduring magic. Think of the Taj Mahal, its white marble a tear of love frozen in time, whispering tales of imperial grandeur and eternal devotion. Or the Pyramids of Giza, their stoic silhouettes piercing the desert sands, testaments to a civilization's ambition and its quest for immortality. These titans of the past stand as beacons of human achievement, their very presence inspiring awe and igniting the imagination. In modern times, the torch of iconicity has been passed to such marvels as the Sydney Opera House, its shell-like exterior echoing the sea's embrace, and the Louvre, its grand galleries housing not just art, but the shared journey of humankind's creativity. And among these contemporary giants, the Marina Bay Sands in Singapore emerges as a bold newcomer, staking its claim to the pantheon of icons. Conceived by the visionary architect Moshe Safdie, the Marina Bay Sands is a symphony of steel and glass, its three towering hotel structures gracefully intertwined by the sinuous ribbon of the SkyPark. This aerial oasis, longer than the Eiffel Tower and capable of housing four Airbus A380s, transcends its engineering feat to become a modern allegory of Noah's Ark, offering refuge amidst the urban tropical landscape. The construction itself was a testament to human ingenuity, with each prefabricated segment of the SkyPark delicately lifted and slotted into place, overcoming the multitude of challenges of the reclaimed land site and defying gravity with seemingly impossible grace. It is this very struggle against engineering odds, this audacious leap of imagination, that imbues the Marina Bay Sands with its iconic spark. However, like the elusive essence of perfume, iconicity cannot be bottled and replicated. The "mini-me" sky decks scattered across the globe pale in comparison to the original; mere echoes failing to capture the magic of the first spark. This, perhaps, is the true allure of an icon – its uniqueness, its organic genesis from a confluence of vision, daring, and a touch of serendipity. Like the late Whitney Houston, who transformed classic songs into masterpieces, architects may occasionally find themselves breathing new life into established forms. But in the realm of pure iconicity, true magic lies in the creation of something entirely original, something that transcends its bricks and mortar to become a symbol of its time, whispering its story to the ages.

Marina Bay Sands in Singapore remains a captivating testament to the transformative power of architecture and sparked a pursuit among new integrated resort developers to emulate its success. In Macau, a tapestry of new resorts has unfurled across the Pearl River Delta, each vying for attention with increasingly outlandish concepts. The Parisian Macau, with its scaled-down Eiffel Tower, offers a familiar European veneer, yet lacks the originality and sheer scale that imbues MBS with its iconic aura. Similarly, the boxy MGM Cotai, reminiscent of a misplaced shipping container, and the lotus-shaped

Grand Lisboa, while visually striking, fail to resonate beyond architectural circles. Even the technically-marvelous, exoskeleton-clad Morpheus Hotel remains confined to the glossy pages of industry publications. Southward, in Manila, the Okada Manila's pale imitation of the Bellagio's iconic water fountains and the City of Dreams Manila's "fortune egg" monument struggle to capture the soul and narrative power that define true architectural icons. Their fleeting mentions in architectural journals stand in stark contrast to the coveted must-see status their creators envisioned. The Japanese port city of Yokohama has harbored dreams of joining the pantheon of iconic integrated resorts, witnessing a flurry of conceptual designs that never saw the light of day. One sought to conquer the vertical frontier with audacious contours, while another envisioned a monolithic structure echoing ancient sentinels. A third, catering to the Wild West enthusiast, even proposed a Conestoga wagon-inspired design. Sadly, these extravagant dreams, like unlit bonfires, remained unrealized as Yokohama's IR plans ultimately dissipated.

The insatiable pursuit of iconicity often throws practicality out the window. In their desperate quest for the "wow" factor, architects and developers sometimes lose sight of the fundamental purpose of integrated resorts: to serve large numbers of guests effectively. Designs become over-flamboyant and impractical, sacrificing functionality for fleeting fame. This is particularly detrimental in the context of resorts, where comfort, accessibility, and a seamless guest experience should reign supreme. The allure of architectural iconicity is undeniable. However, true iconicity cannot be manufactured or replicated. Chasing after an unattainable replica often leads to architectural folly, leaving behind a trail of impractical structures and disappointed patrons. The true path to architectural iconicity in integrated resorts lies not in mindless imitation, but in embracing originality and purpose. By understanding the needs of their users and creating spaces that are both functional and evocative, architects can design structures that not only resonate with the present but also stand the test of time, earning their place among the true architectural icons of the world.

While architectural iconicity undoubtedly holds immense power, the concept of iconicity extends far beyond the realm of brick and mortar. The very notion of iconicity thrives not just in imposing structures but also in the captivating performances, artistic expressions, and experiences that breathe life into an integrated resort. Consider legends like Elvis Presley and Beyoncé, whose iconic voices transcended music charts and resonated with generations. Similar magic can be woven into the fabric of an integrated resort, attracting and captivating guests through artistic and experiential offerings. Las Vegas, a city synonymous with dazzling entertainment, embodies this concept. By securing residency contracts with renowned performers, resorts transform their stages into platforms for iconic moments. From the flamboyant flair of Liberace and the timeless crooning of Sinatra to the contemporary energy of Bruno Mars and the soaring vocals of Celine Dion, these residencies draw crowds and generate substantial revenue, often reaching tens to hundreds of millions. Take, for instance, the legendary duo Siegfried and Roy, whose thirty-year reign at the Mirage intertwined their white tigers and magical feats with the very identity of Las Vegas. However, as times shift and sensitivities evolve, certain elements may lose their iconic luster. With animal rights concerns gaining traction, the majestic white tigers and menageries of lions, leopards, and dolphins at the Mirage are destined to become a memory. In their place, Hard Rock International, the new owner, envisions a different kind of iconicity – a tribute to music's greatest legends through the largest collection of memorabilia in history. Similarly, the kitschy volcano at the Mirage, once a novelty in the 80s and 90s, will make way for experiences that resonate with contemporary sensibilities. This shift underscores a crucial truth: iconicity is not static. It is a dynamic force, evolving with changing tastes and societal values. A true understanding of this fluidity is vital for integrated resorts as they strive to cultivate lasting appeal. Rather than clinging to outdated notions of spectacle, the path to enduring iconic status lies in embracing fresh expressions, incorporating artistic and experiential elements that resonate with the current cultural landscape and possess the capacity to become legends in their own age.

The world of professional sports has long intertwined with the seductive aura of integrated resorts. I'm not alluding to sports betting, which became a permanent fixture in casinos when the mafia introduced it to Vegas in 1976, immortalized in the movie 'Casino' with Robert De Niro as Chicago Outfit mob boss Frank 'Lefty' Rosenthal. Hollywood's éclat, however, didn't translate into real-life success, with sportsbook revenue representing less than 3% of gambling turnover in Nevada. Sports betting on the internet tells a different story, but I digress. Consider Don King, the boxing promoter, as the human equivalent to the Janusian characteristic of Las Vegas, and you're on the right track. There's a feral fascination with the spectacle of two adult men legally inflicting bodily harm on each other, where prize boxers pummeling each other above the belt becomes as entertaining as music superstars belting out their hits. Caesars Palace reached iconic entertainment venue status because it views Adele and Rod Stewart no differently from Marvin Hagler and Thomas Hearns—they all draw the masses under its roof. In 2015, MGM Grand hosted the highest-grossing boxing match in history, the 'Fight of the Century' between Floyd Mayweather and Manny Pacquiao. Tickets for the event sold out in sixty seconds, and the priciest ringside seat cost a staggering $10,000. Such demand is unmatched, perhaps only rivaled by Taylor Swift concerts, thanks to the millions of ardent Swifties worldwide; and she didn't need to get a scratch on her face for that.

Mixed martial arts, another contact sport, is heavily featured in integrated resorts. While this modern combat sport lacks the long history of boxing, UFC enthusiasts might consider former UFC champion Conor McGregor a polarizing icon, known as much for his controversies outside the cage as his skills within it. This is, after all, a generation that loves its antiheroes. Nevertheless, the Fertitta brothers profited handsomely from their acquisition of the UFC franchise, making UFC fights a staple at their Station Casino (now Red Rock Resorts) properties and subsequently a mainstay event at casino resorts worldwide. While not achieving mainstream icon status, UFC fights drew fiercely loyal crowds to venues. The Fertittas weren't complaining; their $2 million purchase of UFC in 2001 multiplied two thousandfold when they sold it fifteen years later for $4 billion.

The famed five-mile stretch of Las Vegas Boulevard, aptly named "The Strip", is an iconic collective that cemented the desert city's reputation as an entertainment mecca. Its dazzling lights, world-class casinos, and electrifying performances have captivated millions for decades. While smaller-scale imitators like Macau's Cotai Strip have emerged, none have quite matched the cultural and historical significance of the original. Despite boasting larger casinos and generating even higher gambling revenue at its peak, Cotai Strip never achieved the same level of iconic status as Las Vegas. This wasn't solely due to its shorter history; Cotai Strip lacked the captivating energy and cultural cachet that made Vegas a global phenomenon. With its vast landmass and lack of geographical constraints, Thailand could be the next contender in the arena of iconic entertainment clusters. As it contemplates legalizing casino gambling, the country has the capacity to develop a genre of resort complexes unlike any other, one that surpasses the limitations of its predecessors. However, as explored in the previous chapter, judicious urban planning and a clear vision are instrumental in creating a truly iconic destination that transcends the sum of its parts.

Brands, too, can reach iconic heights, although it's not simply a matter of popularity. Iconicity is subjective and often associated with qualities like paradigm-shifting innovation, enduring legacy, or groundbreaking achievements. Think IBM, Nike, Apple, Disney – these brands didn't become iconic overnight; it was a gradual process, built over years and sometimes even generations. Marina Bay Sands epitomizes an iconic resort property. Its breathtaking architecture is only part of the equation; the property's success hinges on a combination of shrewd business decisions, effective marketing, and a deep understanding of its target audience. This holistic approach to development is what truly elevates Marina Bay Sands to the realm of the iconic. In the world of gaming, owning an iconic property isn't always enough. Las Vegas Sands, the owner of Marina Bay Sands, is a prime example. While its flagship resort is instantly recognizable, the company name itself doesn't carry the same level of prestige. Conversely, older Vegas brands like The Sands, Stardust, and Horseshoe were steeped in history, both glorious and infamous, achieving iconic status in their own right. Some, like Horseshoe, are even making a comeback on the Strip. Caesars Palace stands as a classic example of an iconic brand struggling to maintain its edge. Despite its enduring legacy and regal reputation, it hasn't kept pace with competitors like Wynn Resorts, the Venetian, and Bellagio. Frequent changes in ownership haven't helped, and Caesars notably missed out on new casino licenses in Asia. However, the recent acquisition of Caesars Entertainment by Eldorado Resorts presents a new opportunity. With careful rehabilitation and strategic planning, the Caesars brand could yet make a play for the burgeoning Thai market, capitalizing on its iconic status and adapting to the unique demands of Southeast Asia's second-largest economy.

There's an old adage that claims the way to a man's heart is through his stomach. In the realm of integrated resorts, this translates to the undeniable allure of celebrity chefs. Award-winning culinary maestros like Gordon Ramsay, Alain Ducasse, and Anthony Bourdain possess an almost mythical power to draw droves of gourmands to their restaurants. Take nahm, nestled within Bangkok's Como Metropolitan Hotel. Chef David Thompson's unique take on Thai cuisine has transformed the hotel into a culinary pilgrimage point for discerning palates. But like a delicate spice, scarcity can be the key ingredient in the recipe of iconicity. nahm's exclusivity starkly contrasts the over-expansion that plagued celebrity chefs like Jamie Oliver and Gordon Ramsay, ultimately leading to the closure of many of their restaurants. This is the heart of being an icon – exclusivity breeds allure, while ubiquity dilutes the magic.

As the sun dips below the horizon, another facet of resort life ignites: the pulsating world of nightclubs. These dimly lit sanctuaries trade culinary artistry for liquid libations, pulsating beats, and uninhibited revelry. Live music fills the air, bodies contort on dance floors, and inhibitions melt away beneath the dazzling strobe lights. Among the countless contenders vying for legendary status, some venues stand out. Las Vegas, the undisputed playground of adult escapism, once boasted the Copa Room at the storied Sands Hotel. For four glorious decades, the Copa hosted a veritable who's who of the entertainment industry, transforming itself into an icon of glitz and glamour. Now, its legacy lingers in the Venetian, whispering tales of legendary performances and electrifying nights. Today, Vegas pulsates with a multitude of nightclubs – Tao, XS, Omni, Hakkasan, Marquee – each striving to reach the same stratospheric heights as the Copa. In Singapore, third-generation scion Lim Keong Hui, heir to the Genting empire, has boldly acquired Zouk, the city's iconic club operator, and integrated it seamlessly into the essence of the Resorts World entertainment portfolio. The anticipation lingers for the emergence of the next true icon, destined to ignite the imagination of a generation and carve its name into the annals of nightlife history. The alchemy of iconicity lies within a potent blend of uniqueness, exclusivity, and a hint of scarcity, complemented by audacious innovation. Only a select few venues can masterfully distill these elements into an intoxicating elixir, with the potential only limited by our own vision. Iconicity in the world of integrated resorts isn't a trophy claimed, but a crown bestowed by time and the collective awe of visitors. It's an exclusive club whose members share a lineage of audacious vision, groundbreaking innovation, and stories woven into the very fabric of their being. In this arena, perhaps no force has evolved with more dramatic strides than technology. Computer-aided design and simulation have pushed the boundaries of civil engineering, birthing marvels like the sky-grazing MBS SkyPark. Today, the pursuit of the next revolutionary frontier in this field burns brighter than ever. We stand on the precipice of a new dawn, waiting for the unveiling of MGM Resorts Osaka, poised to be the most extravagant integrated resort the world has ever seen. Yet, mere extravagance doesn't guarantee a seat at the iconic table. Renderings that ignite the imagination are but a pretty teaser trailer. The true showstopper lurks beneath the surface. Will MGM Osaka's magic lie in autonomous air taxis flitting between airport and resort? Or perhaps, in an AI-powered symphony of seamlessly personalized guest experiences that would make the producers of Black Mirror blush? Reaching such Netflix blockbuster proportions might be the key to unlocking iconic status. However, even without achieving such apotheosis, leadership can be earned. Adopting cutting-edge technology early, even if for a fleeting decade, can grant a resort a temporary hold on that elusive *je ne sais quoi*. Think of it as holding the torch of innovation before it passes on, leaving its mark on the industry's DNA.

So, while we wait for the next resort to truly capture the zeitgeist, we can take solace in the ongoing dance between technology and imagination. For it is from this fertile ground that the icons of tomorrow will spring, forever pushing the boundaries of what's possible and rewriting the very definition of an unforgettable experience.

ten
"KYC"

KYC, an acronym for "Know Your Customer," refers to the standards and processes financial institutions implement to safeguard against fraud, corruption, money laundering, and the funding of illicit activities. These measures involve a comprehensive verification of client identities and the ongoing scrutiny of financial transactions. Beyond its regulatory implications, KYC holds profound significance for businesses of all stripes. A deep understanding of your customer base is an essential cornerstone of success. A company that intimately knows its customers is one that truly knows itself—not merely as its annual report might suggest, but as perceived by those it serves. While KYC is undeniably crucial for risk management, statutory compliance, and due diligence, this chapter ventures deeper, exploring its fundamental meaning. You may be surprised to learn that many companies lack a genuine understanding of who their customers truly are.

While companies often articulate their market positioning and loyal demographics in their mission statements, expressing their aspirations, it's crucial to distinguish these goals from their actual customer base. The latter may not always align with the initial vision, particularly for nascent businesses still refining their identities. It takes time for any company to develop and nurture its operations and offerings to attain its corporate mission and win over the target market it aspires to serve. In some cases, businesses wisely adapt their vision to better reflect market realities and focus on customer segments that naturally gravitate toward their products or services. A shifting market from evolving consumer preferences, technological advancements, or economic changes can create unforeseen opportunities or challenges that necessitate a pivot in the target audience. For some, a company's ability to cater to its desired customer base might be hindered by limitations in funding, expertise, or infrastructure, leading to a reevaluation of its target market. In a competitive environment, aggressive strategies or innovations by rivals can force a company to rethink its customer focus and reposition itself to remain competitive.

Macau ascended to the pinnacle of global gaming in the early 2000s, following the dissolution of its long-held industry monopoly. The emergence of opulent, multi-billion-dollar resorts unleashed a wave of Chinese nouveau riche eager to indulge in these expansive pleasure palaces. Grandiose casino halls, resplendent with riches, luxury boutiques, and a symphony of fine dining options awaited their arrival. Macau embodied the "if you build it, they will come" philosophy, a veritable "field of dreams." This insatiable demand eased the industry inception of local upstarts Galaxy Entertainment and Melco Resorts and gave them little incentive to discover their true mettle amidst abundant profits. However, a stark reality emerged in 2022 with the renewal of casino concessions after two decades of windfall. Stricter regulations, heightened government expectations, and the elimination of junket companies marked the end of a lucrative era. Faced with a diminished market, concessionaires were forced to innovate and develop strategies to maintain their share. For the first time, Galaxy and Melco faced an introspective journey to uncover their inner strengths—a struggle that was evident in their endeavors beyond Macau, particularly in their unsuccessful attempts to secure Japanese integrated resort licenses. Relying on their home market performance against the pedigree of their American peers, fell short as a strategy. A decade has not been sufficient for them to forge a distinct identity in the broader industry outside Macau. Brand identity hinges on a cognitive understanding of one's prime customers— a fundamental element for effective market entry. A casino license tender resembles a beauty pageant, where each participant must strategically showcase their most compelling attributes. A contestant maximizes their competitive edge when the company's strengths are woven into both the individual components and the collective impact of its integrated resort vision. Ambiguities in this concept can expose weaknesses in customer strategy and market comprehension. In Japan, the evolving brand identities of these two Chinese companies served to work against them.

Market leaders leverage the strength of their deep-rooted DNAs. Las Vegas Sands applied its renown as a conventions powerhouse in anchoring a massive one-million-square-foot MICE space as the central theme of its integrated resort blueprint in Singapore. Genting harnessed its family-friendly legacy to conceptualize Resorts World Sentosa, a multifaceted entertainment haven, featuring a Universal Studios theme park, an oceanarium, and a water park. Each Seminole Hard Rock resort property pays homage to its musical roots through distinctive guitar-shaped hotels, an acclaimed collection of music memorabilia, and vibrant Hard Rock Live concert arenas. MGM Resorts excels in the realm of sports entertainment, boasting an impressive array of partnerships with prominent professional sports leagues and events, an asset it can bring to each new MGM venue. The Caesars Rewards program serves as a cornerstone of its competitive advantage in the U.S. domestic market. Boasting a database of over 65 million members, the program's hyper-personalized CRM technology facilitates the tailoring of rewards and offers to individual preferences and behaviors, culminating in a highly engaged customer base that the company can tap into wherever it opens a new property. These established brands infuse their unique strengths into every aspect of their resort design that resonates with each of their specific target audiences.

When the epicenter of the gaming industry shifted from the West to the East, major U.S. casino operators had to adapt their business practices to new demographic landscapes and had to be mindful of different cultural nuances to avoid imposing their domestic demographic assumptions in the highly heterogeneous Asian ethnic and cultural melting pot. In many cases, the customer universe in Asian gaming jurisdictions is structured to balance between attracting international clientele and managing domestic participation responsibly. Some countries, like Cambodia and Vietnam, cater exclusively to international gamblers through regulations prohibiting local entry. In others, like Malaysia, only certain local demographics, such as non-Muslims, are permitted to enter the casino. Singapore's regulations aim to manage domestic participation by imposing a casino entry fee for residents. In Macau, the government offers tax incentives to encourage operators to attract more international customers. Singapore and the Philippines employ tiered tax regimes that particularly benefit premium gaming, while Japan prioritizes the MICE segment as a fundamental principle for its integrated resort industry. These regulatory layers create different serviceable addressable markets for each jurisdiction. In assessing the viability of a new jurisdiction, a company should not solely gauge the attractiveness based on its serviceable addressable market but rather on the market subset that aligns with its brand strengths. Strong brand equity is an asset for jurisdictions focused on international tourists and that is what the big Las Vegas companies bring to the table. The superior brand values of Las Vegas Sands, MGM Resorts, and Wynn Resorts are integral to the Beijing government's vision to transform Macau into a genuine global destination. This, coupled with their expertise in the MICE segment, secured Sands the Singapore Marina Bay IR license. Despite lacking international experience, Galaxy and Melco's deep understanding of the Macau market allowed them to effectively compete with American operators in the Chinese enclave. Similarly, Bloomberry Resort's distinctive native edge has firmly established its position as the market leader in the Philippines. Genting's unmatched understanding of Southeast Asian cultural demographics sets them apart as a regional powerhouse, enabling them to thrive even against competition from American companies. On account that China represents the largest nationality group patronizing almost all Asian casinos furnishes a strategic benefit to Galaxy, Melco, and Genting which all have ethnic Chinese owners. That shared ethnicity fosters a sense of familiarity and trust with a better understanding of the customers' values, preferences, and cultural nuances which are all critical to developing stronger customer loyalty and advocacy.

The arrival of American casino operators in the early 2000s wasn't just an influx of fierce competition; it was a transformative wave that reshaped the entire Asian gaming landscape. Armed with sophisticated strategies, cutting-edge marketing, and tech-driven innovations, these newcomers disrupted the antiquated industry in a region where consumers were already captivated by American popular culture. Before their arrival, the Genting Highlands Casino stood alone as the only automated casino operation. Linked progressive jackpots, now commonplace even in the smallest casinos and dingy Cambodian border establishments, were then exotic rarities. This American invasion sparked a virtuous cycle of improvement, that ultimately benefited the entire market. Before their arrival, Asian casino operators (except Genting) employed a simplistic binary model: categorizing players as either 'grinders' or VIPs. This limited approach offered little in the way of personalized experiences or targeted marketing. The Americans brought with them their enterprise management systems that automate not only the electronic gaming machines but also real-time management for table games. These systems, now ubiquitous across integrated resorts and standalone casinos, with brands like Acres and Bally (now Light & Wonder) dominating the market, unlocked the power of big data. With fully automated casino floors, operators could now leverage detailed player data to develop a multitude of demographic segments, enabling the creation of tailored product offerings and marketing campaigns for each distinct group. For millennials, esports tournaments, live music, tech-infused slots, and electronic table games became commonplace draws. Baby Boomers, the loyal core of high-volume bus programs, find comfort and nostalgia in familiar offerings like electronic slots mimicking classic reel games and traditional poker and blackjack card tables. High Rollers are pampered with VIP programs and exclusive lounges offering personalized services. Resorts World Sentosa was the first Asian property to recognize gender inclusivity, offering women-only gaming areas and amenities. Female-friendly slot themes and ladies' nights designed for this group further enhance inclusivity. Through loyalty programs, frequent players earn tiered benefits like free rooms, dining credits, and invites to exclusive events. These membership benefits extend beyond the casino to the non-gaming attractions and amenities in an integrated resort. For the first time, Asian casino operators began to pay attention to their non-gambling customers. At Singapore IRs, they can contribute as much as 30% of total revenue. Moving beyond demographics, big data empowers operators to analyze game preferences, risk tolerance, and spending habits to personalize recommendations and promotions. Understanding players' psychographics, including their motivations for visiting the resort, allowed for even more finely tuned experiences. Behavioral patterns, tracked within responsible gaming protocols, help identify VIPs, predict future spending behavior, and optimize marketing efforts, showcasing the dynamic evolution of casino segmentation strategies.

This new finesse could not have arrived at a better time. The colossal scale of integrated resorts necessitates automation to streamline the countless repetitive tasks and improve efficiency. Technology allows for personalized services, quicker responses to guest requests, and improved communication, contributing to an overall positive guest experience. Companies like Las Vegas Sands wield technology as a competitive edge, dynamically mapping their casino floors to keep pace with ever-evolving customer mix and preferences. A stark illustration of this adaptation is the declining presence of junket players. The widening ban on these middlemen, who once fueled Chinese premium gaming through high-volume rolling chip play, is rippling across the industry, causing significant disruption. It set off far-reaching tremors that shook even the Singapore IR market, and its full effects are yet to be felt across the region. The disruption may have triggered "false positives" in some jurisdictions, such as the Philippines and the Indochina grey market, where the exiled junkets from Macau are finding temporary sanctuary. Operators, especially those in highly regulated jurisdictions, must adjust their business strategies and customer targeting to offset the loss of the junket segment. This high bar necessitates rigorous clientele oversight, mirroring financial institutions' KYC audits. These audits verify customer identities, monitor their transactions for suspicious activity, and identify risks associated with financial crimes. Advanced technology solutions not only empower casinos to streamline customer relationship management through efficient data analysis and demographic segmentation, but can also ensure compliance with KYC and AML regulations, minimizing risk and fostering responsible gaming practices.

Market-specific customer segmentation is a fundamental principle for market leaders. Las Vegas Sands' Bethlehem Resort (now Wind Creek) had deviated from its parent's core business leisure and premium gaming strategy as it didn't align with the demographics of the Allentown suburbs. Caesars Entertainment showcases the power of strategic brand alignment through its diverse brand portfolio, ranging from the luxurious Caesars to the mid-market appeal of Harrah's, Horseshoe, and Silver Legacy to precisely match the varying demographics of each property's market. When a company's strategic niche perfectly aligns with the profile of a specific market, the results can be extraordinary. Marina Bay Sands, for example, found its sweet spot in Singapore by catering to high-rolling international VIPs and the MICE market, propelling it to the top of the global casino profitability rankings. Genting's brand resonated with Malaysia's ethnic-Chinese working class, proving a winning formula. Similarly, Galaxy Entertainment's deep Chinese heritage appealed to Macau's mainland Chinese clientele. Integrated resorts thrive by designing every element, from attractions to amenities, to resonate with their target demographics. Take Hard Rock Hollywood, for example: live music at Hard Rock Live magnetizes young adults and millennials seeking high-energy entertainment, while trendy restaurants and tech-savvy amenities cater to their digital-native preferences. In keeping with the brand's all-age appeal from 8 to 80 years old, there's always something for families and multigenerational groups—from the ubiquitous Hard Rock Cafe to the Roxtars kids' program and facilities. Accommodations are designed with a range of room sizes and configurations, catering to families and large groups traveling together. For premium customers, there are exclusive luxurious suites and private access amenities, upscale dining, and VIP gaming lounges. Every element in the resort speaks to a distinct audience.

The decision to enter a new jurisdiction hinges on the level of synergy between the addressable market and a company's established customer demographics. When little or none exists, the company must make a clear-eyed assessment to determine whether it should consider foregoing the new market. The same consideration should be made by jurisdictional authorities vetting prospective licensees. Companies without strong international experience, particularly in the Asian market, will always be at a disadvantage when competing to penetrate prime Asian jurisdictions against already established regional operators. Focusing on smaller, secondary markets can offer a stepping stone for such companies to gain international experience and build a foundation before tackling larger territories. This is clearly exposed in the travails of American tribal operators like Foxwoods and Mohegan Sun, European outfits such as Casino Austria, Groupe Partouche, and Barriere Group, when they chose Japan for their first venture into the Asian market. In hindsight, Japanese regulators should have prequalified companies before allowing them to bid for integrated resort licenses. Many bidders were evidently unqualified to achieve the broad goals set by the government, which requires a robust experience in high-impact tourism.

Integrated resorts are poised to encounter escalating pressure to comply with KYC regulations in the future, driven by various factors. Governments worldwide are tightening regulations to combat money laundering and terrorist financing, with heightened scrutiny on high-risk industries such as casinos. Advanced technologies like facial recognition and digital identity verification enhance the efficiency and robustness of KYC and anti-fraud systems, prompting regulatory bodies to advocate for mandatory implementation. The growing public awareness of financial crime and its societal impact is mounting, increasing the pressure on authorities to hold industries like casinos accountable. The first domino has already fallen in the online gaming sector, and as offline and online gaming converge, similar KYC practices are likely to be applied across the entire casino landscape. KYC aims to exclude undesirable segments and the actors associated with them. Singapore, for instance, has stringent probity requirements that discourage Chinese junket companies, often linked with money laundering, from participating in its integrated resort market. This stands in stark contrast to Japan, which lacks such suitability checks: despite regulations restricting junket activities, this gap allowed a major Chinese junket company to nearly secure an integrated resort bid in a Japanese prefecture.

Most major integrated resort operators adhere to rigorous ethical and governance standards, which prevent engagement in jurisdictions that fall short of those benchmarks. Further complicating matters, they must navigate complex sanctions compliance regimes, ensuring adherence to restrictions on trade and financial transactions with sanctioned countries or individuals. This stringent regulatory landscape explains why many American operators circumvented the Philippines market although President Marcos Jr.'s efforts to delist the Philippines from the Financial Action Task Force's anti-money laundering watchlist could possibly alter this dynamic in the future. Similarly, the future of Thailand's entertainment complex industry hinges critically on how it regulates its gaming market. The design of these regulations will ultimately determine the type of industry actors Thailand attracts, shaping its trajectory to resemble either the highly-regulated Singapore model or a more permissive environment like the Philippines. Thailand's entry into the industry is poised to reshape the integrated resort landscape in the region, with its gaming regulations acting as a key driver to the kind of market it will become. A U.S. gaming-compliant framework in Thailand could erode Singapore's market dominance and attract major American gaming brands.

Companies seeking to enter the lucrative Asian market have to be mindful of the social and cultural sensitivities surrounding gambling. The large Las Vegas operators like Sands, MGM, and Wynn have traditionally catered to middle-class and higher-end demographics, a niche that sits well with the concerns of Asian governments about social cohesion and responsible gambling. In contrast, operators who generally cater to a broader mass market may find themselves less welcome in this cautious environment. The high risk of addiction and social harm among the vulnerable working-class demographic is simply too high for some Asian governments to gamble with. This presents a clear advantage for Vegas operators, whose brands are synonymous with luxury, exclusivity, and responsible gaming practices. Furthermore, this strategy aligns with mature tourism destinations like Singapore and Thailand, which are prioritizing higher-yielding visitors. Long-stay budget travelers strain infrastructure and manpower resources while offering comparatively less economic value. Their low average daily spend makes large-scale tourism infrastructure investment unjustified. Additionally, large volumes of these visitors can diminish a destination's appeal for high-value segments.

The landscape of consumer preferences is not merely shifting; it's undergoing a vibrant evolution, offering opportunities for resort operators to embrace the diverse segments emerging within it. The active aging phenomenon and multi-generational travel fuel a thriving, age-agnostic market that aligns well with integrated resorts, given their plethora of attractions and amenities, particularly for brands like Hard Rock. This evolving generation has given rise to distinct demographics with unique preferences and considerable buying power, demanding attention. One noteworthy phenomenon is the surge in solo travelers, reflecting a growing trend of individuals seeking personal growth and independence. Norwegian Cruise Lines successfully tapped into this segment, introducing accommodations tailored for single travelers, predominantly single women. A cut above the conventional casino bus program retirees are the silver surfers, an active and tech-savvy demographic with higher disposable income and travel desires. They prioritize health and wellness, cultural experiences, and multi-generational travel over just a day out at the slot machines. Sustainability is no longer a niche market but a core value for a diverse cross-section of consumers. This segment prioritizes ethical practices, social impact, and transparency in their choices. Major casino companies, for example, are adapting by offering sustainable options and ethical practices, aligning with the values of environmentalists and eco-conscious consumers driving this movement. From Gen Z's commitment to social and environmental causes to Gen Alpha's focus on authenticity and purpose, younger generations demand businesses resonate with their values. New integrated resorts are increasingly responding by weaving social impact initiatives and eco-friendly practices into their core offerings, cultivating authentic experiences. The COVID-19 pandemic intensified interest in the health and wellness sector, leading to increased demand for healthier food options, fitness activities, and personalized wellness solutions. Caesars

Entertainment had emphasized a wellness-centric theme, focusing on the medical tourism sector in their proposal for an integrated resort in Osaka. As traditional gender roles become more fluid, businesses are adjusting marketing, product design, and consumer engagement strategies across various industries. Active efforts in inclusive marketing extend to specific segments within the LGBTQ+ community, aiming to authentically address their needs and represent their diversity. Inclusivity further extends to businesses ensuring accessibility for individuals with disabilities, going beyond wheelchair-friendly approaches to cater to neurodiverse consumers, including those with autism, ADHD, or other neurodivergent conditions, by providing accessible products, services, and communication channels.

In the realm of business model development, both Clay Christensen and Alexander Osterwalder share a fundamental truth: the customer reigns supreme. Harvard Business School's Christensen positions customer value proposition, profit formula, and key resources/processes as pillars of a successful model. Osterwalder's "business model canvas" echoes this sentiment, prominently featuring customer segments and value propositions alongside product offerings, infrastructure, and financial viability. Both frameworks emphasize that understanding and defining your target customer is the cornerstone of any effective business model. This customer-centric perspective extends beyond theoretical frameworks. It's at the heart of every successful business venture. Just as Osterwalder's canvas lays bare the nine vital blocks underlying a model, the "customer comes first" credo holds true from the very inception of a business model. Before spreadsheets overflow with revenue and profit projections, the critical question of "who are we serving?" first has to be answered. This is particularly relevant for integrated resort development. Discerning the target demographics is the first step in assessing feasibility and shaping a resort design. The resort takes form not in a vacuum, but in direct response to the needs and aspirations of the customer segments you aim to attract. Ultimately, the success of your integrated resort hinges on this fundamental truth: it all starts with the customer.

eleven

RISE OF THE DIGITAL-NATIVES

A traditionally staple segment in casino gambling is retirees and the older generation. The significance of this demographic is apparent in the widespread incorporation of bus programs into every casino's marketing strategy. These programs offer transportation services, typically through chartered buses, directly ferrying passengers from their local communities to nearby casinos. Often bundled with additional perks in package deals, such as free slot play, dining vouchers, or discounted hotel stays, casino bus programs primarily target day trippers. In developed economies, this group, comprising mainly senior citizens, represents an important customer demographic with disposable income and leisure time. They are enticed by discounted fares and the convenience of dedicated schedules that offer a morning journey to the casino and a timely return home for dinner. For certain U.S. regional casinos, particularly those in close proximity to urban centers, these bus programs emerge as substantial contributors to their overall success. The cruise business is another sector renowned for its predominantly elder-generation clientele. This demographic is drawn to the all-inclusive nature of cruises, with the onboard casino adding an element of entertainment and excitement to their journey. Integrated resorts reduce dependence on this demographic by offering a variety of activities and attractions that appeal to a broader range of demographics. This shift also marks the first time that casino companies make a deliberate effort to focus on generating non-gaming revenue. The wider appeal of this new genre, with multifaceted offerings, shatters the negative perception of casino-centric resorts and overturns long-held opposition towards casino legislation in Singapore, Japan, and Thailand.

The late 1990s witnessed the concurrent convergence of two major trends: the explosive growth of the internet and the emergence of large-scale integrated resorts like the Mirage, Bellagio, and Venetian in Las Vegas, and Marina Bay Sands and Resorts World Sentosa in Asia. This period also saw the birth and accelerated maturation of the "digital native" generation, individuals raised amidst omnipresent digital technology and wired from a young age for seamless online interaction and immersive experiences. Often classified as individuals born in the mid to late 1990s and beyond, the first wave of this tribe has reached their 30s, a prime age demographic for integrated resort businesses. With the Baby Boomer generation reaching their twilight years, digital natives are poised to become the dominant consumer segment within the integrated resort market. Raised on smartphones and social media, this generation craves unique experiences, seamless connectivity, and personalized digital interactions – features not yet fully embraced by the casino industry, although they represent an opportunity for adaptation and innovation in catering to this emerging market segment.

The dawn of the internet at the turn of the millennium triggered a seismic shift in the casino industry. Companies like Cryptologic, the brainchild of the Rivkin brothers and Microgaming, emerged with a vast portfolio of online software platforms and games like slots, table games, and even live dealer experiences. This paved the way for mega-operators like PartyGaming, Pokerstars, 888 Holdings, and Pinnacle Sports, mainly based in Europe, to tap into the lucrative US market. Unburdened by physical borders, these operators found great success, drawing the bulk of their profits from American players. This unregulated surge in online gambling prompted the US authorities to re-examine the Wire Act, a 1961 law targeting illegal sports betting by organized crime. The Act restricted the transmission of gambling information across state lines, and the Department of Justice (DOJ) used it to crack down on online operators, arguing that transmitting bets over the internet violated federal law. Most operators complied, retreating from the US market. However, the passage of the Unlawful Internet Gambling Enforcement Act (UIGEA) in 2006 aimed to tighten the screws further. This act targeted the financial aspect, prohibiting financial transactions related to online gambling. UIGEA dealt a harsh blow to these publicly listed companies in Europe, causing a significant drop in their market values. The infamous "Black Friday" on April 15, 2011, marked a turning point. PokerStars, Full Tilt Poker, and Absolute Poker, the three largest online poker operators serving U.S. players at the time were shut down and executives were charged with bank fraud, money laundering, and violations of gambling laws. Black Friday prompted a reevaluation of the legal status of online poker in the U.S. It also led to a shift in the landscape, with the states of Nevada, New Jersey, Delaware, Pennsylvania, Michigan, West Virginia, and Connecticut later legalizing and regulating online poker independently.

Asia boasts the world's largest and fastest-growing digital consumer base, with digital natives making up over 80% of the population aged 15 and above. The

ASEAN bloc leads the way, adding 125,000 new internet users daily and projecting a $1 trillion digital economy within a decade. It's no surprise then that Asia has become the epicenter of online gambling, attracting operators to a market conservatively estimated at $10-20 billion but likely multiple times higher closer to $100 billion. While many countries officially prohibit online gambling for their citizens, a thriving, albeit complex, ecosystem operates beneath the surface. Hundreds of online operators offer a diverse array of offerings, from live dealer games and virtual poker to sports betting and offshore lotteries, flourishing in this unregulated to pseudo-regulated space. While some operators target Asian markets from licensed bases like the Philippines, others operate entirely unconstrained. The legal conundrum is no country in the region explicitly allows online gambling for its citizens, placing all operators in a grey area. Governments constantly attempt to block unauthorized sites through internet filtering, payment restrictions, and even legal action. However, these efforts are met with technological countermeasures in a perpetual cat-and-mouse game.

Historically, the online and land-based casino industries operated in distinct spheres. However, 2013 marked a turning point when Atlantic City casinos were allowed online operations, opening the door for convergence. Seven years later, the Philippines followed suit, permitting Manila integrated resorts to operate online under the Philippine Inland Gaming Operator (PIGO) framework. Atlantic City's online gambling success is undeniable. From $39 million in 2013 to $1.7 billion in 2022, internet gaming revenue saw a staggering 43-fold increase. Its share of total gaming revenue also skyrocketed, leaping from a mere 2% to 38% in just nine years. Notably, the peak summer of 2023 even saw online revenue briefly surpass land-based casinos for the first time. However, online gaming revenue for the Manila IR operators fell short of expectations, likely due to competition from other licensed Philippine online casinos and the prevalence of illegal operators targeting the Asian market. City of Dreams Manila eventually suspended its internet casino operations indefinitely within a year of coming online. The other Manila resorts persevere, possibly leveraging the online platforms for wider customer reach and brand recognition, despite the financial drawbacks.

Elsewhere in Asia, legislative rumblings are stirring. A 2022 Thai parliamentary committee report recommended legalizing both casino entertainment complexes and online casinos, but the latter was subsequently dropped due to concerns about the difficulty of regulatory oversight. Navigating the existing online regulatory landscape remains a complex equation. Offshore online licensing models like the Philippines POGO raise concerns about antagonizing neighboring countries for targeting their citizens and replicating PIGO within Thailand might yield similar underwhelming results as Manila, given the fierce competition from unregulated operators. Undeniably, online casinos have impacted the brick-and-mortar casino industry. While some argue they cannibalize business, others see them as complementary. The impact varies depending on location, regulations, and demographics. A 2018 study by the University of Nevada, Las Vegas, cited up to 15% decrease in annual casino revenue in states that legalized online gambling compared to those that didn't. This dip is attributed to competition and convenience offered by online platforms. Another report by the American Gaming Association in

2020 revealed a drop of almost 10% in average daily attendance at casinos nationwide between 2014 and 2019 as a result of some shift in consumer preference towards online gambling. The future of online gambling in Asia remains uncertain. As technology advances and public attitudes evolve, governments will likely need to adapt their approaches and strike a balance between preventing harm and safely addressing the demand for online gambling.

Brick-and-mortar casino operations have largely stayed disconnected from the World Wide Web, with a notable exception in Asia. Proxy betting, the act of placing bets on behalf of someone else in a casino, was once common in Macau's high-stakes baccarat VIP rooms. Initially facilitated through humble telephones and later mobile devices, the internet's emergence allowed the live streaming of physical baccarat games in a casino to bettors remotely. However, in 2016, the Macau government banned this practice due to its rampant use for laundering illicit funds, given the anonymity of the actual bettor, making the money's source hard to trace. In the case of the junket kingpin, Alvin Chau, sentenced to 18 years in jail, he was alleged to have made illicit gains of $1 billion through online proxy betting. VIP proxy betting, nevertheless, remains legal in the Philippines. Genting employs similar technology, albeit in an intranet environment, providing a convenient way for customers to remotely wager via mobile devices on selected gaming tables in some of its casinos. These tables are simultaneously live-streamed within the permitted perimeter of the casino floor.

The clanging reels and flashing lights of classic slot machines, once a casino staple for over a century, have undergone a dramatic metamorphosis in the age of technology. Today's slots have transcended their one-dimensional image, morphing into compelling game worlds that blur the lines between traditional casino games and immersive computer experiences. Gone are the days of generic fruit symbols and spinning bars. Modern slots boast lavish themes, often inspired by popular culture and captivating video games. These themes are interwoven into the gameplay, complete with stunning graphics, animations, and immersive soundtracks that transport players to fantastical worlds or beloved narratives. These experiences aren't merely passive. Some slots incorporate interactive elements, allowing players to make choices, complete quests, and even progress through storylines, adding a layer of engagement and agency. This shift towards skill-based mechanics caters to a wider audience, attracting not just traditional gamblers but also players who enjoy the strategic depth of video games. In today's connected world, even slot machines are embracing social features. Multiplayer options allow players to compete or collaborate in real-time, fostering a sense of community and adding a new dimension to the gameplay experience. The trend toward gamification isn't limited to slots. Electronic table games (ETGs) offer arcade-style representations of classic casino games like blackjack and roulette, eliminating the need for physical equipment. These games, available in pods or consoles, offer key advantages. They remove the physical limitations of traditional tables, allowing for higher game turnover, faster gameplay, and more convenient electronic payments. Since their introduction in the early 2000s, ETGs have taken the Asian casino world by storm, proving highly profitable for both operators and suppliers. They've attracted new demographics and even converted some traditional baccarat and roulette players through hybrid ETGs that combine the physical table with electronic wagering.

In a bold departure from traditional casino offerings, Caesars Entertainment is betting on transforming its LINQ hotel property in Las Vegas to establish itself as a pioneering hub for tech-driven entertainment. It is another example of the gaming industry's strategic shift, redefined by a new generation, to cater to evolving preferences. This prioritizes interactive experiences and cutting-edge technology over the typical casino atmosphere for guests. Step into the LINQ's interactive world and engage in holographic game battles, immersive VR adventures, and mesmerizing dances by life-sized holographic performers. An innovative zone reinvents table games with electronic versions featuring virtual dealers on expansive screens. The sportsbook experience evolves into a tech-savvy haven with plush couches, expansive TVs, and even VR Fan Caves. The casino itself becomes an interactive art installation, a mesmerizing playground where LED sculptures and screens react dynamically to visitor interaction. One of the newest attractions at the LINQ is a collaboration between Jimmy Kimmel's Comedy Club and Proto, an advanced projection technology that beams real-time, interactive holograms across distances. This installation features a hologram of comedian Kimmel and his guests, beamed live from Los Angeles, who crack jokes and interact with the audience as if they were physically present. All of these represent a deliberate strategy to resonate with a target audience increasingly drawn to dynamic and engaging digital experiences. For Caesars, The LINQ serves as a crucial testing ground for future innovations, with successful elements to be rolled out across their broader portfolio.

Lawrence Ho, Melco Entertainment's CEO, had commissioned an exhibition in Japan in 2017 that would not be out of place among The LINQ's installations. The 'Kimono Roboto' 10-day showcase, nestled in Tokyo's trendy Omotesando Hills, embodied Ho's digital-native spirit and resonated with his youth among industry leaders. This multi-million-dollar spectacle had served as a cornerstone of Melco's bid for an integrated resort license in Japan. Blending cutting-edge technology with Japanese cultural heritage, the installation used sound, motion, and VFX to weave a mesmerizing narrative of the kimono's evolution. Four-meter-high, 24-meter-wide walls became projection canvases for bespoke robot models adorned in flowing kimonos, accompanied by a specially composed score that enveloped the senses. Thirteen exquisite kimonos adorned a circular space, while a central animatronic robot took center stage in a "hero" kimono. The visual feast culminated in a music video by Swedish artist Björk, weaving together diverse media to create an immersive journey through time and textiles. From burlesque to animatronics, the evolution shows how far the industry and its demographics have altered in one generation. Lawrence Ho has always believed in pushing boundaries through technology. His early success with Mocha Slots, the first all-electronic gaming lounges in Macau, challenged the dominance of traditional table games. Now, Melco Resorts continues its legacy as a tech pioneer by utilizing blockchain for secure transaction audits and responsible gaming tools that monitor player activity, breaking new ground for innovative responsible gaming practices.

Integrated resorts are increasingly creating digital touchpoints, not just for reaching and marketing to customers, but also to act as real-time guest concierges, offering convenience and enhanced experiences. MGM Resorts has enhanced its MGM Rewards app across desktop, Apple, and Android platforms, turning it into a resort-wide digital companion for their customers. This app transcends its initial purpose as a customer loyalty program, transforming into a digital passport for a holistic MGM experience. Similar to integrated resorts themselves, the MGM Rewards app blurs the lines between gaming and non-gaming, engaging customers across the entire MGM universe. Users can seamlessly check-in, access their rooms via mobile key cards, and leverage the app's digital concierge to book dining reservations, shows, and concerts. The loyalty program, too, has evolved. Points are now awarded for both casino play and non-gaming transactions, fostering a more inclusive experience. Members can track points and tier status in real-time, receive personalized recommendations for maximizing benefits, and even earn rewards across both online and offline gaming with the app's integration with the company's BetMGM online casino platform. The company leverages the power of digital engagement with immersive virtual Las Vegas experiences through its mySTRIP and myVEGAS online social games. Accessible on mobile devices and Facebook, these interactive platforms transport players to the heart of the Strip, offering access to iconic landmarks within MGM resort properties. Beyond sightseeing, players embark on captivating missions and challenging quests, immersing themselves in the vibrant energy of Las Vegas. They can participate in exciting virtual competitions, test their skills on free-to-play versions of popular MGM casino games, and even stand a chance to win real-world prizes like hotel stays, meals, and show tickets. The newest resort on the Strip, Resorts World Las Vegas boasts a GamingPlay digital wallet technology that disrupts traditional cash management systems, offering a seamless and data-driven approach to customer engagement. Direct integration with bank accounts, credit cards, and PayPal allows for frictionless deposits and withdrawals, eliminating the need for cumbersome chip purchases and cage visits. On the customer loyalty front, members can earn points at slot machines simply by entering their phone number and dispensing with a physical plastic card, using a digital rewards card. These digitalization tools serve to streamline gameplay and personalized experiences to enhance customer satisfaction and encourage longer playing sessions. However, all these unification of gaming and non-gaming experiences faces hurdles in the Asian context. While casinos are generally normalized in Western culture, perceptions in Asia still often stigmatize casino gambling. A similar unified app launched by an operator in Singapore ran afoul of regulations for potentially violating responsible gaming guidelines. In Asia, the golden rule remains "nary the Twain shall meet" between gaming and non-gaming.

The rise of non-gaming revenue in integrated resorts has prompted a shift in investment priorities, leading operators to allocate resources beyond the casino floor. Technology plays a crucial role in this evolution, streamlining operations and enhancing guest experiences, particularly at large-scale facilities like Marina Bay Sands. The integrated resort has introduced a Smart Hotel app, a mobile companion that goes beyond a digital key card. Like the MGM Rewards app, Smart Hotel supports in-room amenity requests, dining orders, and reservations for restaurants and shows. But it goes a step further, offering features like facial recognition check-in and contactless check-out that eliminate the need for queues at the front desk for both incoming and outgoing guests. Artificial Intelligence is ushering in a transformative era for the gaming and hospitality industry. Major resort operators are now investing in AI-powered chatbots and virtual assistants that not only adeptly address guest queries but also offer insightful recommendations, efficiently handling a myriad of service requests. This technological innovation not only elevates guest experiences but also liberates staff to focus on more intricate tasks, contributing to an enhanced operational landscape. Beyond immediate customer interactions, AI assumes a pivotal role in data analytics, empowering hotels to delve into valuable insights regarding customer preferences, behavior patterns, and emerging trends.

To cater to digital natives, we are witnessing a growing trend where theme parks, shows, and performances are shedding their passive past and embracing the digital wave. Gone are the days of predictable narratives and static experiences; the future lies in interactivity and immersion, blurring the lines between reality and imagination. Universal Studios is leading this charge, crafting a metaverse where virtual reality (VR) and augmented reality (AR) seamlessly blend with physical park elements. Theme park rides are being reinvented – no longer mere rollercoasters, but interactive journeys where emotions and choices shape your personal adventure. While Cirque du Soleil's legacy endures, the showmanship genre is evolving. Passive audiences are giving way to hyper-personalized experiences where you're no longer just a spectator but also a co-creator.

Productions like the House of Nod's experimental VR project demonstrate this shift, utilizing brain-computer interfaces to tailor the narrative based on your emotional responses. Each viewer embarks on a unique journey, a choose-your-own-adventure theater meets a live-action video game within the confines of the VR headset. Sensory-immersive spectacles are another evolving genre. Attractions like Madame Tussaud's are transforming into multi-sensory playgrounds. The 'Forest of Mirrors' is an example of this trend, utilizing VR headsets and haptic feedback suits to create a hyper-realistic trek through a mystical forest. Environmental sensors dance to your movements and emotions, altering the soundscape and even the virtual textures within your grasp. Even musicals and operas are getting a gamified makeover. Imagine stepping into the next integrated resort in Osaka or Bangkok, only to find 'Jersey Boys' and 'Lion King' infused with a touch of interactivity. Reward points, plot challenges, and collaborative tasks could weave their way into the performances, turning theater into a giant, shared experiment. VR Opera's collaboration with the Opéra National de Paris serves as a prime example, letting the audience choose their own perspective in the story, actively engaging with the opera from different character viewpoints.

For integrated resort operators, the future is now and the digital natives are already in the house.

twelve

THAT'S ENTERTAINMENT

Beneath the casino's glitz, integrated resorts pulsate with a medley of experiences. Thrill seekers swap cards for the electric atmosphere of a live sports event or the dazzling energy of a world-class musical extravaganza. Families forge cherished moments as they shop, dine, and shriek with laughter under the rollercoasters' roar. For some, solace lies in hushed museum halls or tranquil gardens blooming with serenity. And behind the calming spa walls, weary souls find sanctuary, their anxieties dissolving in the warmth of healing balms and pools. But what combination of these makes an integrated resort tick? The answer lies in an intricate balance between vision and reality. Licensing authorities shape the landscape with urban masterplans, while operators orchestrate the symphony of attractions, tailoring them to their target demographics. Space, capital, and market forces become the stage directors, dictating the form and scale of each offering. This chapter delves into the diverse compendium of integrated resort attractions, exploring not only their present manifestations but also peering into the horizon to imagine their future forms.

Thrills and spills

Integrated resorts with theme parks act as powerful magnets for family tourism, attracting a diverse demographic seeking shared experiences and lasting memories. Witness the success of Resorts World Sentosa in Singapore, where a Universal Studios theme park sits as a jewel within the 49-hectare resort. Theme parks are more than just entertainment anchors; they're economic catalysts. Their impact extends beyond the resort walls, stimulating ancillary businesses, fostering job creation, and driving regional development. This wasn't the Genting Group's first theme park rodeo. For decades, they operated both outdoor and indoor parks at their Malaysian resort. But Sentosa offered a strategic shift. Malaysia's park catered primarily to the domestic market with generic attractions, while Singapore's Universal Studios leveraged a globally recognized brand to attract a wider international audience. The investment was substantial, but justified by the immense potential of the Singapore IR market. The power of a strong brand is undeniable. Look at theme park-crazy Japan with its 200 amusement and theme parks. The industry generates over $5 billion annually, with Tokyo Disney Resorts alone capturing over 50% of that market. It's a stark illustration of the muscle of an established international franchise. The next highest-grossing Japanese theme park pales in comparison, clocking in at just one-fifth of Disney's revenue. Genting had looked to replicate its Singapore success with Universal Studios by partnering with 21st Century Fox to upgrade the theme park at their Malaysian resort. Unfortunately, that plan hit a snag when Disney acquired most of Fox's television and film media assets. The Mickey Mouse company was known for its long-held stance against gambling. Popular Star Wars-themed slot machines were removed from casino floors after Disney acquired Lucasfilm in 2012. It was thus somewhat ironic when Disney formed a tag team with the Florida casino monopoly holder, the Seminole Tribe, to advocate for a gambling amendment referendum to prevent the expansion of gambling in the state. As recently as 2019, Disney CEO Bob Igor categorically proclaimed that the company would not be getting involved in the business of gambling in any way in the near term. Five years later, the Disney-owned ESPN sports network struck a $2 billion deal with Penn Entertainment to launch the ESPN Bet sportsbook. Genting will rue that the "near term" ended a tad too late for them. So, perhaps there is renewed hope for a Fox theme park in future integrated resorts, maybe in Thailand? However, there are other world-class options for integrated resort developers. A Paramount theme park is expected to materialize in a later phase of the newly-opened Inspire Entertainment Resort in South Korea. Warner Bros. is expanding its amusement universe indoors, introducing a Harry Potter World in Tokyo in 2023. Depending on each developer's demographic strategy and capital resources, other alternatives in the $100 billion amusement and theme park sector include Blackstone-owned Merlin Entertainment, which operates Legoland and other theme park brands, Six Flags, and SeaWorld, among other choices.

While big franchise theme parks dominate the scene, an appetite exists for unconventional and unique experiences. Puy du Fou in France boasts bespoke themes deeply rooted in the local culture, offering immersive journeys into the soul of a destination. Forget rollercoasters, there is not a single ride here; this historical park transports guests to bygone eras with authentically recreated villages, themed hotels, and spectacular productions re-enacting rich French history. Full-scale sets and captivating theatricality draw over two million visitors a year, proving immersion trumps thrills. Puy du Fou's theatrical magic is already crossing the Pacific to Shanghai, weaving Chinese legends and history into spellbinding shows with iconic characters and periods. Imagine stepping into ancient China, witnessing dynasties rise and fall through captivating performances. In the same vein, picture the next Japanese integrated resort with an immersive theme park bringing to life 1,000 years of history. From the rise of the samurai to the shogunate's reign, and from peasant uprisings to the Meiji Restoration era, each age unfolds in vibrant detail, transporting visitors to the heart of Japan's past. Thailand's rich cultural landscape is also well-suited for a Puy du Fou touch. Imagine a historical theme park nestled within a Thai entertainment complex, where the Sukhothai and Ayutthaya Kingdoms rise again, and the Chakri Dynasty's legacy comes alive.

Yet, some push the boundaries of immersion even further. Utah's Evermore theme park isn't just a backdrop; it's a living, breathing world. Here, medieval and Renaissance influences blend seamlessly into a real-life 'Westworld.' Guests can chat with potion-peddling shopkeepers and interact with costumed actors deeply committed to their roles. The lines between observer and participant blur, and they become characters in the unfolding narrative. Visitors can join guilds to offer backstories and get role-playing opportunities, allowing them to craft their own adventures through quests and tasks.

Moving beyond established themes of castles and thrill rides, innovative attractions are reshaping the landscape of leisure by embracing the unique historical and natural contexts of their locations. One such case emerges from the unlikely location of Transylvania. Forget vampires; the true wonder lies beneath the earth's surface, where an ancient salt mine has been transformed into a remarkable subterranean destination. Descending 120 meters below sea level, visitors embark on a multi-faceted adventure at Salina Turda - from an awe-inspiring Ferris wheel to a museum delving into the mine's rich history. A serene salt lake offers boat rides and the therapeutic benefits of its mineral-rich waters, reputed to alleviate joint pain and inflammation. For those seeking a more heart-pumping experience, the Arabian Gulf prepares to unveil a revolutionary feat of engineering in 2025. A colossal 1.6 million-square-foot resort and "extreme" theme park will rise from the waves, perched atop an oil rig interconnected by a network of platform bridges. This ambitious project, backed by the Saudi Arabian sovereign wealth fund, promises to redefine the boundaries of leisure with exhilarating roller coasters and aquatic adventures, all within the unprecedented setting of an offshore paradise. Oscar Wilde's quip, "Imitation is the sincerest form of flattery that mediocrity can pay to greatness," holds a potent warning for IR developers tempted to blindly replicate successful concepts. A case in point is the failed attempt by an Asian integrated resort to mimic the magic of Xcaret's natural water theme parks in Mexico. The folly of this approach lies not only in the absence of the original's deep expertise but also in the fundamental misunderstanding of what makes Xcaret tick. Its unparalleled success hinges on the unique natural environment of each site, an inseparable and irreplaceable element of the product. The true greatness of successful theme parks lies in originality and authenticity. Learning from existing concepts is valuable, but only as a springboard to craft something distinct and immersive, rooted in the specific context and character of each location. For IR operators seeking to venture into this realm, a wiser path often lies in collaboration rather than imitation by partnering with theme park experts. While sprawling exurban landscapes have traditionally been the playground of theme parks, innovative minds are challenging this paradigm. Enter Thinkwell Group, a Los Angeles-based design firm specializing in theme park experiences and production. In 2016, they unveiled iPort, a revolutionary concept developed in collaboration with Hollywood producer and director James Cameron. This groundbreaking idea reimagined theme parks as vertical wonders for Harrah's (now Caesars) IR bid in Singapore. iPort, a five-level, one million-square-foot indoor odyssey brimming with cutting-edge technology, soared beyond convention. Imagine two 140-foot "video cyclones" cloaked in high-resolution LED, immersing guests in a world never seen before. Unfortunately, iPort remained a breathtaking blueprint as Caesars lost the bid to Las Vegas Sands. However, the seed of vertical theme park brilliance was sown. Fast forward to 2019, and Thinkwell's vision materialized in China with the Lionsgate Entertainment World in Zhuhai—a 10-story haven that brings Lionsgate franchises like 'Hunger Games' and 'Twilight' to life through thrilling rides and captivating attractions. It stands as a testament to the idea that theme parks can defy gravity and deliver pulse-pounding experiences within cityscapes. So, perhaps a theme park for a Bangkok entertainment complex may not be out of the question.

It's Showtime

From Sinatra's crooning to Dion's powerhouse vocals, from Siegfried & Roy's white tigers to Cirque du Soleil's gravity-defying acrobatics, and from Liberace's sequined spectacle to the Blue Man Group's rhythmic paint splatters, the stage has always been a canvas for evolution in entertainment. And unlike the static monuments of museums or theme parks, live performances offer a dynamic pulse within integrated resorts – a heartbeat that keeps the experience fresh and relevant for diverse audiences.

With stage shows, resorts can curate experiences tailored to specific demographics, whether it's a nostalgic blast from the vaudeville and revue era for older generations or a contemporary dose of Lin-Manuel Miranda's hip-hop-infused storytelling for millennial visitors. This fluidity, this constant reinvention, is the very lifeblood of repeat visitation - an especially crucial factor for attracting the domestic, non-gaming market. Genting's resorts in Singapore and Malaysia tap into the Baby Boomer nostalgia by regularly scheduling concerts featuring iconic artists like Engelbert Humperdinck and legendary 60s and 70s Asian songbirds, resonating with their desire for familiar tunes and a trip down memory lane. In contrast, Marina Bay Sands caters specifically to its affluent theatergoers with dazzling productions of international Broadway hits like 'Wicked' and 'Hamilton,' captivating and retaining their loyalty through high-caliber cultural experiences.

Shows are not just entertainment; they're strategic tools to sculpt the guest experience, diversify revenue streams, and optimize seasonal peaks and troughs. Family-friendly musicals like 'Charlie and the Chocolate Factory' can be strategically scheduled during school break periods. High-energy dance shows and popular artist residencies in the summer can entice millennials and drive foot traffic during shoulder seasons. Local cultural performances can be organized during major regional holiday periods to cater to tourists. Strategic partnerships with renowned artists and exclusive productions can boost customer acquisition by enhancing a resort's appeal. Securing residencies with legendary artists or exclusive debuts of prestigious productions allows for highly focused marketing, maximizing appeal to a resort's desired customer base. Loyal fans and curious newcomers alike are drawn to the charm of witnessing performances unavailable elsewhere, transforming a resort into a pilgrimage destination. The seamless exclusive integration of 'O' into the Bellagio's identity creates a powerful brand synergy. Guests associate the resort's iconic fountains with the show's mesmerizing underwater world, leading to a heightened perception of luxury and exclusivity. Treasure Island exclusively houses another Cirque du Soleil production, the captivating, gravity-defying acrobatics of 'Mystère' which serves as a powerful magnet, attracting thrill-seekers and reinforcing the resort's image as a premier destination.

The dilemma for every integrated resort operator is whether they should gamble on the familiarity and prestige of award-winning international show productions or take a daring leap with new, original creations. Both options present distinct advantages and drawbacks. Shows with industry recognition have proven track records, along with built-in hype and critical acclaim, attracting established fan bases and guaranteeing a certain level of quality. They instantly elevate a resort's cultural cachet, signaling a commitment to high-caliber entertainment. The shows' global renown does much of the marketing work, potentially lowering promotional costs. However, these come at high costs in licensing and talent fees, squeezing profit margins. This direction offers little opportunity for creative differentiation, making the resort experience less unique in the absence of any form of contractual exclusivity. Additionally, the genre typically caters to a specific demographic, potentially neglecting diverse audience segments.

On the other hand, original productions stand out from the crowd with a fresh, never-before-seen experience that can be choreographed specifically to resonate with a resort's desired demographics. Unlike run-of-the-mill entertainment options, original productions have the power to stand out from the crowd. They offer guests a fresh, never-before-seen experience that can become a cornerstone of the resort's identity. However, there's no guarantee of success, and they can either be an unmitigated success or potentially lead to financial losses and negative publicity. A meticulously crafted production may not resonate with the target audience as anticipated. Just like the thrill of discovery, there's also the possibility of disappointment. Margins can be high since the resort owns the intellectual property, allowing greater control over costs and profits, although this may be moderated by a higher marketing burden to build awareness and excitement for an unknown entity. Ultimately, the best choice depends on a resort's specific goals, budget, and target audience. Award-winning shows guarantee immediate prestige by association, but original productions can cultivate truly unique brand equity. Choosing the right path demands careful consideration, strategic planning, and a healthy dose of creative ambition, the last of which isn't really the forte of an integrated resort operator. The contrasting approaches adopted by two integrated resort operators in Singapore highlight this dilemma. One operator opted for the security of internationally-acclaimed stage productions, while the other embarked on the ambitious path of creating original productions. Unfortunately, the latter's ventures faced criticism for underwhelming storylines and repetition, leading to shorter runs and ultimately being replaced by less elaborate offerings.

Culture and the arts

The Japanese government's IR policy document repeatedly emphasizes "Japanese tradition, culture, and art." Late Prime Minister Shinzo Abe further underscored this point in a 2018 meeting, stating, "Incorporating content that utilizes Japan's traditions, culture, and art will foster stay-type tourism, attracting visitors from across the globe." This mandate leaves little doubt that bidders must integrate rich Japanese content into their integrated resort designs. This trend of governments demanding "culturally resonant" offerings in multi-billion-dollar resorts requires careful consideration. While promoting national culture and arts has its merit, successful implementation necessitates a delicate balance between commercial viability and authentic cultural representation. The key lies in unique experiences, realistic expectations, and operator autonomy over content decisions. Some of the challenges this poses to operators are:

Commercial Viability: Cultural offerings, if poorly conceived or executed, can alienate target demographics and lead to financial losses.

Authenticity vs. Appropriation: Striking the right balance between authenticity and mass appeal while avoiding cultural appropriation is critical.

Operator Agency: Government interference in content decisions can stifle business decisions and planning.

The Sentosa resort's admirable concept of a museum tracing the ancient maritime Silk Road, featuring life-sized replicas of junks and dhows and marketplaces from its various ports of call, underscores the dilemma. Despite renovations and upgrades, the museum's niche appeal and mixed reviews ultimately contributed to its closure, as it struggled to compete with the broader appeal of Universal Studios and the oceanarium within the resort. Countries like France, Italy, Japan, India, and Spain, boasting rich historical sites, diverse traditions, acclaimed art scenes, and distinct cuisines, possess a natural advantage in cultural tourism. South Korea, on the other hand, has captivated the world with its modern pop culture phenomenon, the Hallyu Wave. Mohegan's Inspire Resort in Incheon attempts to capitalize on this asset by infusing its 15,000-seat arena with K-pop performances and showcasing an integrated cultural space that combines shopping, dining, and entertainment.

A testament to Japan's rich theatrical heritage, Kabuki, a vibrant theatrical tradition dating back to the 16th century, faces declining relevance in connecting with new generations and international audiences in today's world. This multi-faceted treasure trove of music, dance, and drama, considered one of the world's oldest surviving performing arts, found its day-long performances of yore increasingly out of sync with the modern, fast-paced world. To adapt, productions have been shortened to cater to modern attention spans and fit tight tourist schedules. To enhance accessibility for non-Japanese audiences, the performances are accompanied by in-ear simultaneous interpretation available in a variety of languages. Fresh interpretations of classic plays further attempt to bridge the gap with contemporary sensibilities, while genre-bending experimentation – from musicals to elements of Western theater – broadens the appeal and attracts new fans. Super Kabuki, for instance, masterfully blends tradition with action-packed elements like special effects and modern music to increase its appeal to younger audiences. The use of multimedia elements like projection mapping and digital sceneries further enhances the immersive experience and visual spectacle. The upcoming MGM Resorts Osaka, opening in 2030, might be the perfect international stage to showcase this evolving Kabuki experience. This could even be an opportunity to push boundaries further by breaking the glass ceiling for female performers in this historic art form.

In Macau, the authorities are strongly encouraging casino concessionaires to introduce more non-gaming entertainment options. This mandate was a key requirement for concession renewal in 2022. Chairperson and executive director of MGM China, Pansy Ho, believes art and culture embody the next iteration of Macau's integrated resort industry. To support this vision, MGM China has dedicated over 150,000 square feet of space in its two properties to facilitating cultural events, fashion showcases, and art exhibitions. Pansy Ho saw the 'rich storytelling' potential of Macau's 442-year colonial legacy, with its fascinating blend of trade and cultural exchange. However, these historical realities also encompass stark realities like unequal power dynamics, the lingering scars of the Opium War, and restricted mobility for Macau's people. These elements could be contrary to the Chinese government's preferred narrative of a unified and ever-strong China throughout history.

Not all cultural programs will become blockbusters. A mix of mainstream and niche offerings catering to diverse demographics is key. Ultimately, cultural experiences must be high-quality, engaging, and held to the same standards as other resort amenities. Culturally resonant elements can extend beyond dedicated attractions, with traditional practices and nuances woven into the fabric of the entire resort design and operation. Here, the design philosophy of *feng shui* is subtly woven into the very fabric of the resort. This focus on balance, harmony, and positive energy creates a unique and aesthetically pleasing atmosphere that resonates not only with Chinese guests but also with visitors from around the world seeking a tranquil and luxurious experience.

Museums are institutions dedicated to showcasing and safeguarding objects of historical, cultural, artistic, or scientific significance. They educate audiences, fostering understanding and appreciation of these treasures for present and future generations. Often serving as pillars of culture, museums preserve and showcase the unique stories and expressions of their respective nations. Some museums, like the Louvre, the Acropolis Museum, the Smithsonian Institution, and the National Museum of China, achieve such high cultural and historical significance that they are often considered on par with national monuments. The Louvre in Paris and the Guggenheim Museum in Spain stand out not only for their groundbreaking designs and historical significance but also for their enduring influence on the architectural landscape, making them major tourist landmarks in their own right. Demographic trends of museum-goers vary. While adults over 50 represent the largest group in many countries, families with children and young adults are increasingly drawn to museums with engaging experiences, innovative installations, and social media appeal. Museum visitors are more likely to have higher education and reside in urban areas. These demographics align with key target groups for integrated resorts. For resorts targeting a broad clientele, a museum can provide a premium offering that caters to the high-end segment of their diverse audience.

The image of traditional museum halls, characterized by hushed reverence and guarded displays, seems like fitting a square peg in a round hole amidst casinos, clubs, and entertainment. However, this distinguished institution is undergoing a dynamic metamorphosis driven by the need to engage diverse audiences and embrace the evolving cultural landscape. Many museums are shedding their restrictive cloaks and transforming into vibrant ecosystems of cultural dialogue. This shift transcends mere trend-chasing; it represents a strategic response to the changing demographics and artistic sensibilities of an increasingly interactive and tech-savvy generation. Modern museums are redefining the visitor experience. Interactive exhibits now replace passive observation, immersing visitors in narratives that transcend static displays. These encounters foster deeper engagement, transforming viewers into active participants in the artistic conversation. Amidst the digital dynamism, sanctuaries of quiet contemplation still remain. Bare walls and natural light provide havens for those seeking the hushed communion with art that once defined the museum experience. This modern museum, thriving in a carefully presented duality, is a perfect complement among the elements of an integrated resort.

A prime example is the ArtScience Museum at Marina Bay Sands in Singapore. Rather than fitting into a single genre, it exists at the intersection of art, science, and technology. The museum showcases visually stunning art in diverse forms, from traditional to contemporary installations and multimedia pieces. The realm of science is woven into the museum's fabric through interactive displays that explore concepts in physics, biology, and technology, offering both educational and entertaining experiences. Innovative technology seamlessly integrates into the exhibits, blurring the lines between art and science. Virtual and augmented reality, holographs, and interactive platforms transport visitors to other worlds and challenge their perceptions while celebrating various cultures and perspectives. The museum's seasonally rotating installations act as a magnet for repeat visits among the resort's target white-collar demographic, perfectly complementing its prime downtown location. Curating dynamic exhibits plays a key role in the resort's marketing strategy, targeting different market segments through specific campaigns. For instance, the 'Sensory Odyssey' exhibition provided an educational escape during summer break, attracting families with its immersive exploration of natural environments. Similarly, the 'Marvel Studios: Ten Years of Heroes' exhibition capitalized on the franchise's peak popularity in 2018, drawing legions of fans from across demographics. By strategically aligning exhibition themes with broader marketing campaigns, the ArtScience Museum effectively contributes to the resort's overall target audience engagement.

Certainly, Asian integrated resorts could do with more cultural attractions. To enhance Japan's integrated resorts as national tourism gateways, MGM Resorts will support the government in the development of a museum showcasing traditional Japanese art and culture in Osaka. Picture yourself strolling through a fourth Guggenheim Museum nestled amidst a modern entertainment complex in Bangkok, a possibility if Thailand legalizes casinos. Alternatively, imagine exploring a South Asian art museum collaborating with the renowned MoMA (Museum of Modern Art) within a third Singapore integrated resort.

Game on

The traditional dominance of entertainment in Las Vegas, bathed in the glow of stage lights and neon allure, has undergone a transformative evolution over the past 30 years. The likes of Bruno Mars and Cirque du Soleil, once exclusive headliners, now share the stage with the glare of arena floodlights and the intensity of sweat-drenched rivalries. The seeds of change were planted in the 90s when mega-resorts like Mandalay Bay and MGM Grand integrated boxing venues and championship fights, offering a glimpse into the broader appeal of sports. The 2000s saw luxury suites boasting in-room stadium views, dedicated sportsbooks, and state-of-the-art fan zones for the NBA Summer League and UFC championships. The rise of dedicated eSports arenas like the HyperX Arena at the Luxor cemented the growing popularity of competitive gaming. Sports have become a permanent fixture in the integrated resort experience, seamlessly blending into the entertainment roster. In retrospect, sports emerge as a natural constituent of the entertainment lineup, appealing to a broader demographic than traditional casino offerings and leveraging their dedicated fanbase. Beyond mere entertainment, sports events strategically fill calendar gaps and elevate resort occupancy.

Macau's sports entertainment landscape presents a fascinating dichotomy. While the iconic Macau Grand Prix remains a cornerstone event, predating even the

Stanley Ho era, the new concessionaires operating integrated resorts have shown lukewarm interest in a genre that doesn't align with their main customers' interests. Sports entertainment initiatives have been limited to occasional events like volleyball and snooker tournaments, alongside appearances by top sporting icons at resort events. For instance, David Beckham, global ambassador for Las Vegas Sands, attended the opening of their Londoner Macao hotel. This high-profile partnership extended to Beckham's venture developing dining, retail, and leisure concepts for their properties in Singapore and Macau.

Several factors contribute to the limited focus on sports entertainment in Macau's integrated resorts. Primarily, the concessionaires cater to mainland Chinese visitors, whose entertainment preferences often lean away from sports. Attracting international tourists with a strong interest in sports has been an uphill battle due to Macau's limited accessibility compared to regional hubs like Hong Kong and Singapore. Additionally, the small local population makes it difficult to achieve the critical mass needed for major sporting events to be financially viable. Finally, Macau previously lacked world-class sporting facilities. However, a recent development offers promise. The completion of the Galaxy Arena, a 16,000-seat multipurpose venue capable of hosting conferences, exhibitions, concerts, and sporting events, represents a major step forward. Signs of a growing sports focus are emerging. Notably, MGM China's successful hosting of the MGM Macau Tennis Masters exhibition featuring ATP and WTA players, and a partnership between Wynn Resorts and the Asian Tour bringing The International Series golf tournament to Macau, linked to LIV Golf, demonstrate this potential.

Arguably the crown jewel of Asian sporting pageantry, the Singapore Formula 1 night race transforms Marina Bay Sands literally into a front-row grandstand. V6 turbo-powered machines become luminous blurs under the floodlights, weaving their magic around the downtown street circuit. With over a quarter of a million spectators vying for a glimpse of the action, virtually every hotel is sold out during race weekend. This lucrative influx finds Singapore's integrated resorts basking in its glory, reaping significant rewards without needing to invest a single cent in organizing the event, or in Marina Bay Sands' case, hosting it for free right on their doorstep. Fueled by the electrifying atmosphere of the Grand Prix, a curious role reversal unfolds. High-rolling casino patrons, typically courted by VIP hosts, now find themselves lobbying for coveted access to the ultra-exclusive Paddock Club and pit walkabouts. Inspired by this ingenious strategy, Thai investors are exploring ambitious entertainment complexes featuring a dedicated Formula 1 circuit nestled within the resort grounds.

MGM Resorts boasts the most extensive sports partnerships among gaming operators, aligning itself with all four major professional leagues in the United States. This global reach extends to Asia, where its primary partner, ORIX Corporation, owns the Japanese baseball team ORIX Buffaloes. Such prestigious partnerships bode well for sports entertainment at the upcoming MGM Resorts Osaka. Similarly, Hard Rock International parlayed its close connections with the New York Yankees in their Hokkaido resort conceptual plan, incorporating a dedicated "Yankee experience" to capitalize on the tremendous Japanese baseball fandom. At their Florida home base, Hard Rock established a visible presence in Formula 1 as a founding partner of the inaugural Miami Grand Prix in 2022. This partnership deepened further with the circuit's strategic location adjacent to Hard Rock Stadium and their sponsorship of the Red Bull F1 team, cementing the brand's leading position in gaming within the motorsport world. Could Hard Rock also leverage the sport to the interest of its intended integrated resort bid in Hokkaido, Japan? F1 domestic attendance at the iconic but inaccessible Suzuka Circuit has witnessed sharp declines, with international spectators far surpassing domestic fans. A strategically developed Hokkaido Grand Prix, backed by Hard Rock's brand power, could potentially reignite local passion for the sport and land the company a coveted IR license.

By and large, the kind of sports featured in integrated resorts will be constrained by the physical playing environment they require. Just like average occupancy rate projection guides the number of keys for a hotel development, utilization rate is a critical consideration in planning all other facilities within an IR. Purpose-built venues, while ideal for long-running spectacles like Cirque du Soleil's Las Vegas productions, aren't always the most practical solution. Multi-purpose arenas offer greater versatility and optimize space utilization. Resort operators typically gravitate towards two broad categories of sports: Marquee events featuring top sports personalities, targeted at premium customers with high spending potential, and high-attendance sports aimed at maximizing visitor turnover. However, spectator capacity serves as a limiting factor for the latter category. The seating capacity of most resort facilities, typically limited to around 20,000, severely restricts their ability to host globally popular sports like football (soccer), where crowds often exceed several times that size. Or is this limitation truly set in stone? Football's global popularity, especially in Asia, makes it a tantalizing prospect for IRs. Top European clubs on off-season exhibition tours to Asia can easily draw crowds of 50,000 spectators or more. However, the considerable land footprint required for football stadiums is prohibitive for IRs operating in locations where land costs are high and its utility is limited, as these stadiums are difficult to repurpose for other uses when football events are not taking place. Exurban resorts, where land is generally more abundant and likely more affordable, might offer greater feasibility for such projects. The Wynn Golf Club in Las Vegas is a rare exception. Despite its prime location, with a high potential for alternative development, Wynn Resorts has retained the course as a premium amenity following unsuccessful attempts to replace it with a casino, hotel, and convention center.

Operating a major sports facility, such as a football stadium, would be a huge undertaking for an IR company, pushing it far outside its traditional comfort zone. In such a scenario, strategic partnerships could be a more compelling alternative. The Hard Rock Stadium in Miami, for example, has bolstered Hard Rock's brand equity through its $250 million, 18-year naming rights deal with the Miami Dolphins football team. While the stadium's distance from the Seminole Hard Rock Hollywood resort limits direct guest spillover, such partnerships can still be strategically beneficial. That said, I still believe that we could one day see a sports stadium designed and built specifically for an integrated resort. The concept of multi-use sports stadiums has come a long way, changing the traditional way they are operated and how they do business. A stadium currently under construction in the new city of Qiddiya in Saudi

Arabia is shattering the mold of traditional cocoon-shaped stadiums. Besides the retractable roof, its most novel feature is a massive LED wall that can transform the facility into different configurations within hours. The LED wall itself can be used for live event broadcasts, displaying high-definition videos, and even hosting laser shows. The wall can also "disappear" to expose one side of the stadium, revealing an opening that allows the stadium's three-sided seating to overlook the exterior of a 200-meter-high cliff that the stadium is built on. This "mode" is perfect for performances that place spectators at the center of the show and eliminates the limitations of typical fully-enclosed stadiums for such events. This innovative design transforms the stadium into a true multi-use mega facility, completely breaking away from the limitations of conventional stadium architecture. The exterior of the Qiddiya Stadium is clad with a matrix of modular multimedia cubes, creating a luminous silhouette that breaks architectural design boundaries and would be right at home in any modern integrated resort. An opportunity for a novel stadium design like this might just present itself in Thailand. The Rajamangala National Stadium is beginning to show its age, having turned 25 years old in 2023. Beset by operational issues, it recently suffered a major embarrassment that year when a sold-out international friendly football match between Tottenham Hotspur and Thai-owned Leicester City had to be canceled hours before kickoff due to heavy rain that made the pitch unplayable. Populous, the architectural firm behind the stadium in Qiddiya, might offer some innovative ideas for integrated resort developers to incorporate a genre-bending stadium concept into their Thai entertainment complex designs and solve the government's national stadium woes – a "killer" attraction to win a coveted gaming license in the kingdom.

thirteen
REJUVENATION

Amidst the hyper-connected and information-saturated reality of today, the human spirit yearns for sanctuary. Daily pressures, from demanding careers to social media anxieties, erode our well-being, sparking a desire for retreat and rejuvenation. This yearning has spawned a dynamic niche within the hospitality industry: wellness-centric havens dedicated to holistic well-being and personal renewal. Gone are the days of wellness being a luxury for the privileged few. The market has transcended its niche status, driven by a universal aspiration for escape, mindfulness, and holistic regeneration. Spa resorts, wellness retreats, and sanctuary getaways offer more than just opulent respite; they provide guests with a comprehensive embrace of serenity, bespoke wellness services, and opportunities to shed the burdens of daily life. The emphasis extends beyond standard hospitality offerings, encompassing mindfulness practices, highly-personalized wellness experiences, and a focus on the holistic well-being of body, mind, and spirit.

This burgeoning market has attracted mainstream hospitality players, once the exclusive domain of luxury brands like Six Senses, Aman Resorts, and Banyan Tree. In 2020, Hilton debuted Tempo by Hilton, a brand built around guided meditations, sustainable cuisine, premium non-alcoholic options, and cutting-edge fitness facilities. Hyatt followed suit in 2021, acquiring the Apple Leisure Group and its Zoëtry Wellness & Spa

Resorts portfolio. The global wellness market is projected to exceed $8 trillion by 2032, and integrated resort operators are well-positioned to capitalize on this rapidly growing trend. In Macau, the traditional saunas have given way to opulent wellness spas offering advanced treatments. Galaxy Macau features a Banyan Tree resort within its complex, while Marina Bay Sands in Singapore boasts a renowned Banyan Tree Spa. While no single integrated resort has yet fully harnessed the power of well-being as its core concept, the shift is underway, particularly with the emergence of new jurisdictions and resorts. Marina Bay Sands is doubling down on well-being in its $3.4 billion expansion, prioritizing guest wellness experience in the second phase of the resort's extensive makeover. It is crucial to recognize that while the wellness trend transcends age demographics and evolves into a lifestyle choice, its relevance remains particularly acute for the older generation. Japan, the world's fastest-aging society with a dominant demographic aged 65 and above, presents a fertile ground for wellness-focused integrated resorts. Similarly, Thailand's well-established reputation as a medical tourism hub positions it perfectly to integrate comprehensive wellness offerings into its future entertainment complexes. In this era where "health is wealth" takes center stage, integrated resorts are transforming into sanctuaries for holistic well-being, going beyond just leisure entertainment.

Beauty and wellness

Personal well-being is reshaping consumer trends. Revitalization now occupies top billing with the exhilaration of entertainment. Consumers invest as readily in rejuvenating retreats as they do in experiential escapades. This holistic pursuit encompasses health, beauty, and personal care, appealing to a broad demographic and driving considerable individual spending. And it's not just a woman's domain anymore. Men are increasingly joining the self-care party, breaking stereotypes and proving that well-being knows no gender. McKinsey's research confirms this shift, pinpointing six key wellness categories: health, fitness, nutrition, appearance, sleep, and mindfulness. A report by the Global Wellness Institute ranked Japan as the world's third-largest wellness tourism destination in 2022. Surprisingly, however, wellness was conspicuously absent as a central theme in most Japanese integrated resort proposals, except for Caesars Entertainment's IR concept for Osaka. This is particularly unexpected given the obvious synergy between wellness and the "exurban" focus of the Japan National Tourism Organization in promoting wellness-focused tourism in lesser-known destinations. Examples include stargazing and forest bathing in Misugi and the renowned natural hot springs of Beppu overlooking the ocean. In essence, a wellness-centric integrated resort plan for regional areas would appear to be perfectly aligned with the existing strategy for promoting wellness tourism in Japan, yet it remains largely unexplored within the context of Japanese IR development.

Central to the beauty and wellness industry is the over-the-counter market for cosmetic products. Japanese beauty products have historically dominated Asia, featuring globally popular brands such as Shiseido and Kanebo. However, the Japanese cosmetics market faced a formidable contender with the ascent of K-beauty in the late 1990s. K-beauty gained substantial traction, especially in Asia and increasingly globally, thanks to its innovative line of products that embraced unique ingredients and packaging inspired by natural sources, introducing trends like sheet masks and BB creams. This, coupled with affordability and more competitive pricing compared to Japanese brands, contributed to the rise of K-beauty. Additionally, the trendsetting influence of The Korean Wave played a key role in propelling the popularity of K-beauty products and trends. Data from 2023 indicates that Korean cosmetics now hold a larger market share than Japanese cosmetics in many countries, including China, Southeast Asia, and parts of Europe. This fact has not escaped the attention of the Mohegan owners of the Inspire Entertainment Resort, which opened in early 2024. With an overarching theme capitalizing on the Hallyu global phenomenon, there are plans in later phases of the Korean resort's development for a 4,500 square meter K-cosmetics and beauty hub. However, acting sooner rather than later might be prudent. While the Korean Wave holds strong, K-beauty faces a resurgent old foe. Buoyed by new brands like Three Cosmetics, MT Metatron, ReFa, and Sunohada, J-beauty is making a comeback, emphasizing sustainability and authenticity over fleeting trends. Meanwhile, a new player is shaking up the landscape: C-beauty. Chinese cosmetics are shedding their long-held image as "cheap substitutes" and rapidly gaining market share, both domestically and internationally. Brands like Winona, Perfect Diary, and Colorkey are leading the charge, with Chinese cosmetics imports into South Korea even doubling in 2023. This surge signals C-beauty's potential to shake up the established order and carve out a distinctive niche in the global beauty market. Macau's integrated resort operators could take a leaf out of the book of

Myeong-dong's K-beauty shopping streets in Seoul. These vibrant hubs offer a dream experience for beauty enthusiasts, immersing them in the latest trends and showcasing a diverse range of Korean brands. Introducing a dedicated C-beauty shopping street attraction could be a strategic move for Macau resorts, catering to the growing demand for Chinese beauty products and offering a unique local differentiator in the competitive landscape.

Thailand, long revered for its spiritual essence and verdant landscapes, is a global wellness tourism powerhouse. Renowned sanctuaries like Chiva-Som Hua Hin, Amanpuri Phuket, and Kamalaya Koh Samui stand as testaments to the kingdom's mastery in holistic well-being. It makes Thailand an exciting prospect for wellness-centric integrated resorts, seamlessly blending tranquility with culturally-rich entertainment experiences. Should the anticipated legislation regarding casino entertainment complexes come to fruition, Thailand, like Japan, possesses a wealth of exurban locales primed for such developments. The Koh Yao archipelago near Phuket, designated by the Public Health Ministry as a dedicated wellness district, exemplifies this untapped potential. The crux of success lies in navigating the intriguing duality of integration and isolation. Wellness spaces must harmoniously coexist within the integrated resort complex while maintaining their sacred aura of tranquility. This delicate balance can be achieved through strategic zoning, employing buffer areas to separate the vibrant energy of the casino and entertainment hubs from the serene havens dedicated to holistic rejuvenation. Imagine a haven where guests can transition from an adrenalin-filled night at the casino to a restorative morning meditation session, or where families can balance exhilarating water sports with enriching mindfulness workshops for their children. This holistic approach caters to diverse preferences while solidifying Thailand's position as a global leader in holistic well-being.

Medical tourism

Wellness tourism and medical tourism both share a focus on health and well-being and cater to distinct, yet sometimes overlapping, desires. Wellness tourism prioritizes preventative healthcare, holistic rejuvenation, and stress management with the goal of enhancing overall well-being, boosting energy levels, and cultivating a sense of inner peace. Medical tourism, on the other hand, seeks out medical procedures and treatments, often motivated by lower costs compared to the traveler's home country. Some are also drawn to the reputation for higher levels of reliability and expertise. This can range from dental care and cosmetic surgery to complex procedures like joint replacements and organ transplants. While medical tourists may also seek relaxation and recuperation, the primary motivation is for medical intervention.

With a 40% share of the global market, the Asia-Pacific region is already a dominant force in medical tourism. However, forward-thinking integrated resorts are redefining wellness experiences, venturing beyond traditional lifestyle offerings. By strategically integrating facets of medical tourism, these resort destinations can unlock a new level of growth and cater to a broader spectrum of guest needs. While complex procedures like oncology, orthopedics, and transplants remain the domain of specialized medical facilities, there's a burgeoning demand for accessible, high-quality medical services within the luxurious and convenient environment of an IR. Cosmetic surgery, weight management, dentistry, and fertility services are promising avenues for integration, enhancing the overall guest experience and diversifying revenue streams. In operating a dedicated wellness center in partnership with Bangkok Dusit Medical Services, Laguna Phuket, a non-gaming integrated resort in Thailand, stands as a trailblazer in this regard. This center offers a comprehensive suite of services, encompassing health check packages, IV therapies, personalized supplements, and even regenerative medicine programs, all naturally complemented by the resort's amenities. However, understanding the diverse landscape of medical tourism is crucial.

While Singapore, ranked second globally in the 2020-2021 Medical Tourism Index, excels in catering to the high-end segment seeking specialized care and complex procedures, the majority of the market prioritizes value and affordability. This segment finds its sweet spot in other Asian countries particularly in Malaysia, India, and Thailand, with the latter boasting an impressive network of over 60 internationally accredited medical facilities across hospitals, clinics, and wellness centers.

Singapore's specialized strength in top-tier medical tourism presents a unique opportunity to shape a distinct integrated resort experience focused on wellness and recovery should a new license become available. This concept aligns perfectly with some contemplations for a third resort to be developed on one of Singapore's southern islands which would be an ideal setting for a luxurious tropical retreat focused on preventative health and wellness like no other. Expanding offerings to include medical tourism alongside their established wellness programs, Thailand's entertainment complexes can create a more enriching and multi-faceted guest experience. By seamlessly integrating high-quality medical services within luxurious settings, these new complexes can strategically tap into both wellness and medical tourism markets, filling a gap in the offerings of current integrated resorts.

Rehabilitation

While integrated resorts increasingly offer some variety of wellness and medical facilities, extending these services to include on-site rehabilitation for substance abuse, mental health, and particularly for gambling addiction, can constitute a groundbreaking step. It might feel counterintuitive to offer such rehabilitative services in such close proximity to gambling-related facilities. However, such an initiative not only benefits individuals struggling with gambling addiction with readily accessible early intervention and integrated care, leading to higher recovery success rates but also helps reduce the burden on public healthcare systems. Furthermore, it serves as a powerful statement of an IR operator's commitment toward responsible gambling, reinforcing their corporate social responsibility to create a safe and supportive environment for patrons. By readily providing counseling and treatment services on-site, it demonstrates a genuine concern for the well-being of their guests and the community. Casino resorts that dare to chart a path by integrating rehabilitation services would represent an unprecedented positive step towards embracing responsible gambling practices, setting a positive example for the industry. By prioritizing the well-being of their patrons and the community, these operators not only make a positive impact but also encourage other industry players to adopt similar initiatives, fostering a more responsible and sustainable gaming environment for all. Rehabilitative facilities are particularly suited for exurban destination resorts set in therapeutic environments with somnolent, peaceful surroundings, free from distractions to promote relaxation and focus on recovery. For instance, the provinces of Saraburi and Nakhon Ratchasima in Thailand are home to many resorts located in conservation areas with nature access ideal for promoting mental and physical well-being, and their remoteness can ensure client privacy and confidentiality during treatment.

Shopping and dining

'A full stomach makes a happy heart,' this proverb about the basic need for sustenance and its connection to contentment rings even more true in the Asian context. For many Asians, the way to their hearts truly is through their stomachs. The diverse and rich culinary experiences of Asia play an important role in driving tourism. Travelers are drawn to explore unique flavors, local specialties, and the vibrant world of street food, making food an integral part of their cultural immersion. From sushi in Japan to curry in India, the culinary landscape becomes a gateway for tourists to connect with each country's history, traditions, and hospitality. This gastronomic adventure not only satisfies taste buds but also creates memorable travel experiences, encouraging repeat visits and positive word-of-mouth recommendations.

The melting pot of cultures in Singapore is vividly expressed through its diverse range of flavors and culinary traditions, solidifying its reputation as the food capital of the world. This characteristic contributes to Singapore's allure as a premier tourist destination and helps boost the popularity and success of integrated resorts like Marina Bay Sands and Resorts World

Sentosa. Some integrated resorts focus too much on Michelin-star restaurants and other fine dining to pamper their premium customers at the expense of broader market appeal. This overemphasis on exclusive establishments can inadvertently push guests to explore outside the resort in search of more varied, authentic, and budget-conscious options. While complete guest confinement isn't possible, particularly in urban locations, each minute spent off-site represents a missed opportunity for revenue generation and guest engagement. Today's increasingly discerning travelers seek experiences that cater to diverse palates and budgets. Moving beyond the tired model of the $2.99 buffet, resorts must adapt to this evolving demand. By offering a diverse selection of casual eateries and local street food alongside their upscale offerings, they can create an inclusive culinary landscape that appeals to a wider audience. Resorts World Sentosa's Malaysian Food Street is one such successful expression of this approach. It offers popular Malaysian dishes at accessible prices within an air-conditioned setting, catering perfectly to both the large numbers of Malaysian tourists and Singaporeans who share a common culinary heritage.

The Icon Siam mall in Bangkok took the paradigm in a novel twist with its offering of a captivating homage to Thailand's iconic floating markets. Sook Siam, an intricate rendition, features a canal network with charming wooden boats as stalls, all nestled amidst lush greenery and traditional architecture, transporting visitors to a bustling market scene. Complete with gentle lapping water and the murmur of vendors dressed in traditional garb calling out their wares, while the sizzle of cooking and the aroma of spices fill the air, it captures the original market's essence combined with modern comforts of air conditioning, comfortable seating, and the convenience of electronic payment. It's a perfect multi-sensory journey that still captures the heart and soul of Thailand's floating markets. This is a well-conceptualized rendition that the future Thai entertainment complexes could learn from to replicate authentic local food experiences. While Asian travelers are known for their passion for food, a surprising gap exists in the hospitality industry: the dearth of readily available all-inclusive resorts, a model thriving in other destinations. Unlike its widespread success in destinations like the Caribbean, Mexico, and the Maldives, this approach offering unlimited access to meals, drinks, activities, and amenities for a single price remains largely untapped in Asia. This presents an opportunity for new integrated resorts to carve out a unique niche. Asian travelers already seek such experiences on cruises, where the all-inclusive model is a key attraction. This translates well to exurban resorts, mirroring the isolated nature of a ship at sea. Imagine the appeal of an all-inclusive integrated resort nestled within the verdant landscapes of Hokkaido, Japan, or Chiang Mai, Thailand - a unique value proposition worth exploring.

Does retail therapy truly heal? The initial rush of endorphins and the tactile pleasure of new possessions are genuine, if fleeting. While true happiness cannot be bought in a store, the deeper truth lies in the therapeutic nature of the ritual, an escape from daily stressors. It's a self-care ritual, a way to reclaim control in a world that often feels chaotic. Shopping and dining are peas in a pod in a consumer experience, each seldom going without the other. Las Vegas, once solely known for its gambling scene, has embraced retail with open arms, creating a shopper's paradise alongside its vibrant entertainment offerings. This retail revolution can be traced back to 1981, with the grand opening of the 800,000-square-foot Fashion Show Mall on the Strip. This winning formula inspired other casino resorts to incorporate retail experiences into their own properties, transforming the Strip into a multifaceted destination. Today, visitors can indulge in retail therapy at the Forum Shops at Caesars Palace and the Grand Canal Shoppes at the Venetian, among many others. A pivotal moment came in 1999 when retail and attraction sales surpassed gaming revenue for the first time in Las Vegas' history. This marked a permanent shift in the city's identity, and the trend continued even after the COVID-19 pandemic. In fact, retail revenue led the recovery for integrated resorts not only in Las Vegas, but also in global gaming hubs like Macau, Singapore, and the Philippines. In 2022, Las Vegas non-gaming revenue soared, generating a whopping 69.8% of the total, more than double the amount of gaming revenue. The Fashion Show Mall, now a grand old dame at over 40 years old has expanded more than 2.5 times its original size, now boasting over 2 million square feet of retail space.

While retail can offer substantial benefits to an integrated resort by attracting more visitors and boosting revenue, it warrants careful planning in urban locations. Introducing shops and malls can detrimentally affect existing local businesses, especially if the resort's offerings aren't unique. In Singapore, the Marina Bay Sands Shoppes attracts tourist traffic away from nearby malls, which can potentially harm the wider retail landscape. However, a strategically chosen retail mix can create positive synergies with the local scene. It can compel existing retail operators to upgrade their offerings, fostering innovation and benefiting the entire ecosystem. Ultimately, the success of retail in urban integrated resorts hinges on striking a balance between attracting visitors and supporting the local economy. For exurban resorts, offering curated retail experiences can enhance the destination experience. However, attracting retailers can prove challenging due to the limited customer base because of the remote location. One solution lies in the concept of outlet malls. These shopping destinations, featuring popular brands with steep discounts, act as a magnet for bargain-hunting consumers willing to travel for exceptional deals. Simon Property Group is an industry leader in this space, renowned for its vast portfolio of successful outlet malls. Another example is Mitsui Fudosan Group, which has brought its "Japanese-styled outlet malls" beyond Japan, establishing them in Taiwan and Malaysia. While Genting Group has partnered with Simon Property to operate an outlet mall in Malaysia, the development exists independently of their casino resort. IR operators can leverage the expertise of such companies to attract major retailers and curate a tenant mix tailored to their guests' specific needs and preferences. This strategic collaboration creates a win-win situation, expanding an exurban resort's offerings while providing retailers access to a new, untapped market.

Live

The Marina Bay Sands integrated resort sits within the Singapore Bayfront development. This development features a mix of commercial, residential, and entertainment spaces, embodying the government's vision for a vibrant "work, live, and play" downtown precinct. While Las Vegas Sands benefited from the bold and successful urban master plan formulated by Singapore's city planners, some integrated resort developers are now designing mixed-use developments that incorporate both work and living elements, essentially creating integrated community environments. One such project is the redevelopment of the Treasury Casino and its surrounding buildings in Brisbane, Australia. Scheduled for completion in 2025, the ambitious Queens Wharf Brisbane integrated resort waterfront development encompasses the new Star Brisbane Casino, four hotels boasting a combined total of over 1,000 rooms, two residential towers featuring 2,000 apartments, an office tower, retail spaces, and the addition of a new bridge spanning the river. Notably, the development integrates nearly a dozen state-owned heritage sites, repurposed into vibrant community spaces. These areas will offer residents and visitors alike an enhanced experience with amenities like bike paths and riverfront walkways, contributing to the approximately 75,000 square meters of new public space.

A mixed-development integrated resort with a resident community brings several benefits. Selling residential units before or during construction generates early cash flow to offset construction costs. Residents become a reliable source of income, boosting sales and creating resilience against downturns. The vibrant resident community enhances the resort's image, attracting external guests and potentially justifying premium pricing. Resorts that integrate community and public spaces go beyond catering to guests. They create a welcoming environment that fosters a strong sense of belonging for residents. These spaces act as magnets, attracting residents and assuring lucrative revenue streams for both locals and tourists. This approach transcends the traditional resort model, transforming it into a vibrant community hub ensconced into the city's social, cultural, and economic fabric.

Developed economies with large middle-class populations, such as Japan, Singapore, and Thailand, present a unique opportunity for integrated resorts to incorporate residential elements designed for older adults, like retirement villages and assisted living facilities. This model capitalizes on the growing demand for high-quality senior living communities, while the resort can simultaneously tap into a key casino demographic: the senior generation. Why opt for bus programs when you can have these steady revenue generators living under the same roof?

fourteen
CONVENTION-AL WISDOM

The automated voice echoed through the packed subway car, its metallic timbre struggling to compete with the rhythmic rumble of the train and the screech of its brakes. The barely audible announcement roused many commuters from their pre-arrival reveries. Backpacks shifted, elbows nudged, and a subtle shuffle towards the exits began. With a hiss of pneumatic pressure, the doors slid open, and a wave of heat and the vibrant clamor of the platform washed in, as an eclectic crowd spilled out. Business suits mingled seamlessly with casual wear, forming a sea of bobbing heads that swarmed towards the escalators and lifts that would take them up two levels to the integrated resort. On the next floor, a fresh wave of tourists disembarked from buses, merging with the arriving commuters into a veritable human current flowing upwards. Stepping into the cool embrace of the resort's expansive foyer, the tangible energy was undeniable. The diverse crowd's animated murmur rose to a crescendo of multilingual conversation. Yet, amidst the apparent chaos, an orchestrated order prevailed. Those sporting scarlet and gold lanyards head towards the exhibition center's cavernous halls. A biennial technology exhibition, a magnet for 20,000 daily visitors, beckoned with its promise of innovation and networking. Less formally attired guests, meanwhile, made a beeline for the adjacent consumer fair, seeking bargains and the thrill of the hunt. Representatives from both events, strategically positioned along the path, distributed flyers and guide eager newcomers toward their booths. Still others stream in the direction of the long escalators that lead to the ballrooms and meeting suites above the exhibition halls. Up there, a contrasting scene unfolds within the grand ballroom. Intellectual electricity crackles as renowned finance titans hold court, captivating a capacity audience on the latest trends in the fintech space. Their eloquent presentations resonate through the opulent space, punctuated by the discreet rustle of note-taking and the gentle clinking of coffee cups. Across the wide aisle, hushed but intense strategic discussions emanate from a meeting suite, where a pharmaceutical company's leadership convenes for their annual management retreat. Further down the plush corridor, infectious laughter spills from a car distributor's appreciation banquet, the gleaming silhouette of their latest electric vehicle standing sentinel. One floor above, a quieter tempo prevailed. A government agency facilitates a knowledge exchange seminar, fostering dialogue between industry professionals. In another suite, a local business association convenes for its annual gathering. Adjacent, a religious group finds solace in their weekly prayer meeting, the space transformed into a haven of tranquility amidst the vibrant pulse below.

The landscape of the MICE (Meetings, Incentives, Conventions, and Exhibitions) industry has shifted dramatically from its hotel-centric past. While hotels remain key players in the smaller conference and seminar segment, their limitations in size and infrastructure necessitated the rise of dedicated convention centers. These behemoths, like the sprawling Hanover Messe in Germany with its 500,000 square meters of exhibition space, cater to large-scale trade shows and conventions with tens of thousands of delegates. MICE represents a valuable segment of the tourism market as conference travelers tend to spend more than leisure travelers. This is because they are often reimbursed for their travel expenses by their employers, and may also spend more on dining, entertainment, and shopping during their trips.

Studies have shown that conference travelers spend almost double what leisure travelers do. Compared to leisure travelers who might stay for a few days, conference attendees typically stay for a longer duration, sometimes even a week or more. This translates to more revenue for hotels, restaurants, and other businesses in the destination. And because many MICE events take place during the off-season for leisure travel, helping to fill hotels and resorts when occupancy might otherwise be low which helps to stabilize revenue flow and spread business throughout the year. Research has also shown that the MICE market is not as easily affected by economic fluctuations as the leisure tourism market.

These developments are welcome news for resort operators. Las Vegas, a pioneer in this transformation, embraced MICE early on, evolving from a casino hub to a world-class destination. This model has been successfully exported to Asia, with Marina Bay Sands demonstrating the invaluable contribution of MICE to creating the world's most profitable gaming property. Integrated resorts excel as MICE venues by strategically combining accommodation, entertainment, and dedicated MICE facilities under one roof. This seamless integration, with smooth transitions between meeting and exhibition spaces, entertainment areas, and retail outlets, fosters a sense of flow and convenience for attendees. However, broader factors influence MICE destination selection. Meeting the criteria set by conference organizers and participants is crucial for success. Beyond the scale and quality of MICE facilities and amenities, the host destination itself needs world-class infrastructure, seamless logistics, security, and a diverse array of attractions. Governments, therefore, have a strong vested interest in creating successful MICE destinations, as they generate significant economic impact beyond direct spending. Attendee spending ripples through various sectors like transportation, catering, and retail, benefiting businesses and creating jobs. Additionally, successfully hosting MICE events elevates a destination's image as a business hub, attracting further investment and boosting its overall brand identity. The two Singapore integrated resorts have boosted the event space in the country by 150,000 square meters and buoyed its MICE industry which contributes to almost 1% of the GDP. However, their true impact goes beyond mere venue size. It's the unique "hardware" and "software" of Singapore that truly invigorates the MICE industry.

Hardware

Excellent infrastructure and connectivity: The synergy between Singapore's transportation infrastructure and its financial center creates a frictionless environment for travel and business activity.

Tourism hub: From its futuristic cityscape to its past colonial charm, Singapore is a top regional tourism destination, a garden city with diverse culinary experiences, cultural festivals, attractions, and world-class sporting and entertainment events.

Hosting premier events: Singapore's ability to flawlessly host internationally renowned events, from the adrenaline-fueled Formula 1 Grand Prix (which inspired over twenty MICE events in 2022) to the logistically complex, sold-out Taylor Swift Eras Tour, showcases its capabilities as a world-class event destination.

Software

Business-friendly environment: Being headquarters to numerous large multinational corporations and ranked among the top Asian tourist destinations, Singapore offers a flourishing business climate.

Dedicated support: A dedicated MICE division within the Singapore Tourism Board (STB) proactively collaborates with industry players to attract and develop events.

Strategic partnerships: The STB executes strategic partnership initiatives with leading event organizers like Comexposium, bringing prestigious events to Singapore.

The integrated resorts represent just one element of a broader plan to achieve a $7 billion MICE market size by 2030. Singapore's success demonstrates how strong infrastructure and proactive initiatives can create a thriving MICE ecosystem.

Macau's pursuit of becoming a major MICE destination paints a contrasting picture compared to Singapore's established success. While its deregulated gaming industry in the early 2000s delivered impressive "hardware" – international hotels, convention centers, shopping malls, and world-class entertainment – fundamental issues still persist to hinder its progress. Seamless travel and logistics, crucial for MICE events, are hampered by limitations in connectivity and infrastructure. Additionally, Macau struggles to shed its persistent image as a "gambling haven" despite its external makeover. The disparity between Macau's reliance on casino revenue over its non-gaming offerings further reinforces this issue. Unlike Singapore, Macau lacks diverse attractions beyond its integrated resorts, placing the onus on concessionaires to fill the gap. The government, currently playing an ancillary role, could be more proactive in developing unique local experiences. Furthermore, "software" issues persist due to limited human capital that has a direct correlation to service quality. While Macau rivals Thailand in annual tourist arrivals during the pre-COVID-19 era, its visitors are predominantly leisure travelers from Guangdong Province and particularly the neighboring city of Zhuhai. Expanding the visitor base to include a significant segment of international visitors and business travelers necessitates diversification of offerings and marketing strategies. While the Macau government acknowledges these shortcomings and initiates countermeasures, achieving the status of a MICE destination requires a sustained, long-term commitment. The current situation limits growth opportunities for Macau's integrated resorts in the MICE segment. This discourages the development of new MICE spaces until broader economic challenges are overcome.

Japan views integrated resorts as the key to emulating Singapore's success in establishing a thriving MICE industry. Already Asia's fastest-growing leisure destination, Japan has set its sights on developing the lucrative MICE market. While Japan possesses "hardware" and "software" comparable to Singapore, even exceeding it in many aspects, major Japanese cities still rank behind Singapore, Bangkok, Hong Kong, and Kuala Lumpur in MICE standings. This stems from several factors. Japan lacks new, large-scale MICE facilities with the functionality offered by newer venues in other Asian capitals. Existing facilities struggle to compete for large-scale events with over 1,000 attendees. Most venue operators cater primarily to the domestic business market, with a dearth of planners proficient in attracting international conferences and exhibitions. The government's "unilateral criteria" for integrated resorts, mandating a minimum of 120,000 square meters of event space and 100,000 square meters of hotel space is unrealistic for non-metropolitan locations and ignores the diverse spectrum and needs of the MICE industry.

Success in MICE is not solely about size. Events range from small gatherings to large conventions, all contributing to the ecosystem. The Japanese IR framework, like its tourism strategy, suffers from an overemphasis on metropolitan attractions, which has led to over-tourism and social strain. It is the reason why Naomi Mano, Chairman of the Japan MICE Association, advocates for promoting MICE in non-urban areas through "modest convention, incentive, and meeting group sizes." These locations offer unique cultural experiences, natural beauty, and diverse cuisine, differentiating them from major cities. Rectifying the "one size fits all" fallacy is imperative before the Japanese government tenders its remaining integrated resort licenses. Every location has its own unique characteristics, including scale, form, and function, that necessitate a customized MICE template.

Just as Singapore is distinct from Macau, Macau is distinct from Japan, Osaka is distinct from Hokkaido, and Sentosa is distinct from Marina Bay, so too are their respective MICE environments. The market ecosystem, the key stakeholders involved, and the level of integration within the MICE supply chain all contribute to a destination's individuality.

Collaboration is essential for success in the MICE industry, even among competitors. By working together, stakeholders can create a positive cluster effect that benefits the entire ecosystem. The foundation of this collaboration is the destination itself, with the government serving as the cornerstone and primary stakeholder. Singapore's MICE industry flourishes due to the city's robust infrastructure and resources. The government plays a proactive role in stimulating the industry through partnerships with MICE supply chain organizations and sponsorships of major events like Formula 1. The Singapore EXPO, the first convention and exhibition facility in Singapore with over 100,000 square meters of event space, was funded by the trade ministry. Las Vegas Sands was awarded the Marina Bay integrated resort license in part due to its MICE expertise, which was instrumental in developing a thriving MICE cluster in downtown Singapore and enhancing the country's overall MICE capabilities and offerings. Singapore also possesses a conducive business environment essential for attracting MICE stakeholders such as conference planners, exhibition organizers, and associated businesses to establish their operations. The country had excelled in all of the key factors that contribute to MICE destination competitiveness, including accessibility, transportation, hotel inventory, attractions, business environment, safety, and security. This strong foundation allows Singapore to support a wide range of MICE events, from small meetings to large conventions and trade shows, and gain a reputation as an international MICE hub.

The success of MICE venues hinges on tailoring their strategy to the underlying software and hardware of their destination. This dictates the types and sizes of events they can successfully host. Therefore, exurban integrated resorts, lacking the necessary infrastructure and support systems for large-scale events, are not well-suited for a MICE-centric approach. This, unfortunately, hampered the success of regional integrated resorts in Japan. The government's imposition of large-scale MICE requirements, designed for metropolitan resorts, proved unsuitable for regional locations. Similarly, Macau presents a case where the government's vision for a MICE industry isn't adequately supported by sufficient action from its leaders. Further compounding these are its deeply ingrained infrastructural deficiencies.

Las Vegas companies have a strong track record in MICE due to their experience operating in America's convention capital. Among them, Las Vegas Sands stands out for its unmatched MICE pedigree. The company's late founder, instrumental in leading the highly successful COMDEX trade show, cemented their position as a MICE industry leader. Notably, Las Vegas Sands remains the only operator capable of facilitating large-scale events and providing a comprehensive suite of meeting, incentive, convention, and exhibition facilities across all its resorts. Ironically, the company opted out of the Japanese market despite being the only one fitting the criteria for experience in operating MICE facilities exceeding 120,000 square meters in scale.

Beyond Las Vegas Sands, other integrated resort companies primarily compete in the conventions, incentives, and meetings segments. In Asia, a few properties, such as Galaxy Macau, and Resorts World properties in Singapore and Malaysia, offer individual event spaces ranging from 5,000 to 10,000 square meters, suitable for smaller to medium-scale exhibitions and conventions with up to 10,000 attendees.

While modern integrated resorts boast stunning, iconic exteriors, architects face the conundrum of seamlessly integrating large MICE facilities that often require unappealing boxy structures. The Sands Expo at Marina Bay Sands hits the mark in successfully blending aesthetics and functionality in its convention and exhibition halls. The unique architectural design shatters the mold of conventional exhibition centers, featuring sweeping curved glass panels that define the facade with a sense of lightness and fluidity. Translucent fins add depth and texture, while intricate LED lighting transforms the exterior into a vibrant canvas at night. A large, canopy-like roof extends outwards, offering shade and drama, while skylights bathe the interior in natural light. This innovative design showcases how MICE facilities can be both visually striking and highly functional.

Functional is also the main operand under the roof where versatility is key for adapting the event space to purposes ranging from exhibitions to conferences, concerts, banquets, and seminars. Other critical design considerations include space utilization and customer experience. Operable walls and removable partitions facilitate the reconfiguration of space to be divided or expanded easily and quickly to serve different event requirements. The classic solution offers the ability to divide large spaces into smaller rooms or combine smaller rooms into one, and new advancements include motorized walls, curved systems for more dynamic layouts, and soundproof options for better acoustic separation. Modular pods can be added or removed based on event needs to provide temporary expansion or reconfiguration options. Automated, configurable bleachers allow for quick rearranging and creating different seating configurations or open layouts. Seats that can be hidden away or retracted into the floor allow for quick conversion between presentation and performance formats. Smart walls are integrated with interactive screens that can be used for presentations or information displays. There are even interactive floorings that can display information, respond to touch, and project images. Advances in building information modeling software technology and the use of structural technologies such as truss systems and beam and girder systems allow for the construction of large column-free spaces that offer the advantage of a large unobstructed span. Resorts World Sentosa has one of the largest column-free ballrooms among integrated resorts at 6,000 square meters.

An innovation that arose as a result of the COVID-19 pandemic is the hybridization of MICE events. Digital technologies like immersive holograms, avatar robots, and wearable tech have become invaluable tools, facilitating realistic experiences for both physical and virtual event attendees. Marina Bay Sands has spearheaded the trend with its cutting-edge hybrid event broadcast studio. Featuring a 3D stage with holographic capabilities, it caters to O2O2O (Online-to-Offline-to-Online) meeting needs seamlessly. Additionally, digital mapping tools can transform any surface into an interactive display, further enriching the experience. Even as the pandemic subsides, hybridization remains a promising solution for the MICE sector due to its inherent versatility. By incorporating a virtual component, events can attract wider audiences, including those unable to travel physically due to various constraints. They foster enhanced engagement through interactive elements like live Q&A, breakout rooms, and networking platforms, keeping attendees actively involved. Conferences can leverage hybridization to expand participation in keynote addresses, panel discussions, and workshops. Breakout sessions can cater to both physical and virtual audiences simultaneously. Similarly, exhibitions can benefit from virtual booths and product demonstrations alongside physical exhibits, while live streaming allows remote attendees to participate actively.

Sustainability is taking center stage in the MICE industry with an increased focus in the business sector on ESG (Environmental, Social, and Governance) considerations. Event organizers, attendees, and sponsors alike increasingly demand sustainable practices, giving preference to venues that minimize environmental footprint, prioritize green certifications, with energy-efficient infrastructure, and offer sustainable catering. For planners, travel and logistics are optimized through route planning, low-emission transportation, and embracing virtual participation where feasible. Event organizers are witnessing increased brand loyalty, attracting more engaged attendees, and securing sponsorships based on their sustainability commitments. In Singapore, the authorities have implemented numerous initiatives to help planners measure and reduce carbon impact and deliver greener events. Venue operators are also upping the ante. Marina Bay Sands is the first carbon-neutral business event venue in Singapore to adhere to green energy regulatory targets and investments in Renewable Energy Certificates. MICE venues are also increasingly incorporating biophilic design to inject sustainability features into their facilities. Strategic integration of natural light through skylights and atriums minimizes reliance on artificial lighting, lowering energy use. Vegetation strategically placed indoors can also provide natural cooling and shading, reducing dependence on air conditioning. Utilizing native, drought-resistant plants minimizes water requirements for landscaping, while rainwater harvesting systems can further reduce reliance on local water sources. The use of natural materials like wood, bamboo, and recycled content minimizes the use of energy-intensive and environmentally harmful materials like concrete and steel. Studies also show that incorporating nature into design spaces improves occupants' well-being, leading to increased productivity, reduced stress, and improved cognitive function.

To add more "cheese" for the MICE industry, the burgeoning "bleisure" trend, characterized by the merging of business travel with leisure activities, presents more opportunities for the sector and dovetails perfectly with the offerings of integrated resorts, which provide seamlessly blended business and leisure experiences within a single destination. Integrated resorts are perfectly placed to cater to the entirety of the travel experience. By strategically targeting this trend through targeted marketing, flexible package options, and bleisure activities, integrated resorts are poised to capitalize on this trend and solidify their position as the preferred destination for the modern MICE traveler.

Gamblers in Asia were once content with the bare essentials – a bed, a bath, and a proximity to the casino floor. Casino resorts responded in kind to these recidivist punters with basic accommodations. The landscape of gaming lodgings has blossomed far beyond its bare-bones origins, but vestiges of the old, casino-centric approach still linger. Step away from terra firma onto one of the many cruise ships plying the South China Sea, and you'll find hundreds of tiny, windowless cabins on the lower decks, not for the claustrophobic. You have to be Houdini's apprentice to use the cramped confines of the shower facility. For Asian cruise companies, the goal is to shepherd the maximum number of passengers onto the gangplank before setting sail. To achieve this, they optimize every available square inch of space to squeeze in as many bunks as possible. Bare comfort sufficed because the cabin is merely a pitstop to ultimately corral guests onto the casino deck, which generates over two-thirds of the ship's revenue. Atop the mountain range surrounding the Klang Valley in Malaysia sits the Resorts World Genting resort. It boasts the title of the world's largest hotel with the budget-class First World Hotel. However, this record capacity comes at the cost of space, with standard rooms compressed into tiny 16-square-meter boxes. Air-conditioning isn't an option, but you can open the window for some crisp mountain air.

The longstanding sales campaign in the casino business, even to this day, is offering free accommodations to customers. This marketing strategy leaves practitioners in the general hospitality industry bewildered. The room is the main asset in a hotelier's business, but for the casino operator, it's a commodity, a mere means to an end. The casino operator would provide their guest with a manger and some hay for the night if they could get away with it, and there's nothing divine about it; it's simply an awareness that what the customer seeks is materialistic fortune. The typical casino hotel operation has slimmer profit margins than general hotels, if any. Rooms are a cost center for the traditional casino business and are mostly comped to loyal patrons. However, casino resorts are significantly more profitable than hospitality businesses, and the casino revenue more than covers the free rooms given to customers. The transformation of Las Vegas over the last fifty years saw a shift in the conventional model as the gaming industry sought to attract more affluent customers and reach a wider demographic. Some bigger properties, like Wynn Resorts, the Venetian, and MGM Mirage, began to derive higher revenue from their non-gaming components than the casino. Their accommodations can command equivalent room rates to their 5-star-branded peers and still enjoy high occupancy despite having much bigger room inventories than the typical Hyatt or Hilton. The Asian market followed suit at the turn of the millennium, with rapid gaming deregulation creating an increasingly competitive environment.

Las Vegas Sands brought its luxury all-suite hotel concept to Macau and Singapore. The trio of Venetian, Palazzo, and Marina Bay Sands transcends mere marketing facades, embodying a vision of opulence targeted at an audience with discerning tastes. They cater to those seeking exclusivity and personalized services with grand interior spaces and sophisticated environments conducive to work and high-level meetings for discerning business travelers. The hotels boast a design ethos beyond mere decoration. Exquisite craftsmanship, high-end finishes, and elegant art collections elevate the ambiance to an artful opulence. Grand lobbies, expansive suites, and private terraces create a sense of unbound luxury and exclusivity, further enhanced by seamless technological integration for personalized control and effortless service. Highly trained staff anticipate and fulfill guest needs with discretion and personalized attention. Guests have exclusive access to fine dining with renowned chefs, bespoke spa treatments, and unique cultural events, culminating in unforgettable experiences. Private meeting spaces, business centers, and extensive shopping arcades more than fulfill diverse guest needs.

Faced with the success of Las Vegas Sands, Asian casino operators sought to emulate their winning formula. However, these nascent players lacked the established brand recognition and operational expertise of their American counterparts, particularly for large-scale resorts exceeding 1,000 rooms. Their solution: partner with established international hotel brands. Marriott, Hilton, IHG, Accor, Hyatt, and other renowned hospitality companies entered the picture, not only providing operational expertise but also lending their prestigious names to elevate the brand image of these new Asian casino resorts. Galaxy Macau leverages this strategy, providing guests with a curated selection of prestigious hotels, including JW Marriott, Andaz, Banyan Tree, Ritz-Carlton, Raffles, and Okura. Similarly, the City of Dreams Macau boasts a Grand Hyatt across the street. Even Las Vegas Sands deviated from its all-house-brand strategy in Macau, offering guests additional lodging variety with the Four Seasons, Conrad, Sheraton, and St. Regis brands. These partnerships go beyond brand enhancement. International hotel chains bring their vast loyalty programs, with some boasting over 100 million members, attracting additional clientele to the resorts. Despite these improvements in accommodation standards with the rise of integrated resorts, a fundamental issue persists: the prioritization of the casino over the hotel. In most cases, casino divisions control room inventory, relegating hotel managers to mere "paupers" compared to the "king" casino managers. Rooms are primarily used to entice and extend gambling sessions, with non-gaming guests receiving leftover inventory often released at the last minute and susceptible to being bumped for higher-spending casino patrons.

Viewing hotel rooms in integrated resorts as mere overnight stops solely measured by quantity is a grave misconception. This mentality belongs to bygone eras of hardcore, single-minded gambling establishments, a remnant of Macau's past under Stanley Ho. In reality, lodging considerations are critical partners to casinos and other facilities, forming the core of a successful integrated resort development. Undoubtedly, the casino floor generates the lion's share of revenue, justifying the resort's very existence. However, a recurring fallacy during planning stages is solely focusing on room count to match available casino positions. Beyond mere room key figures and typical type ratios, several variables come into play. These accommodations are intrinsically linked to the specific business strategy and target demographic of the resort.

A comparative glance at the two Singapore integrated resorts reveals their contrasting approaches to customer focus. Marina Bay Sands (MBS), strategically located in the heart of the downtown bay area, boasts nearly 1,000 more rooms than Resorts World Sentosa (RWS). Despite occupying less real estate, MBS prioritizes spaciousness and quality. Its three towers offer larger rooms with higher-quality fittings, catering to a white-collar clientele. To further solidify its grip on the premium market, MBS plans to triple its suite count compared to RWS. Capitalizing on its expansive space, RWS takes a distinct segmentation approach. Boasting six distinct hotels, each designed as a unique haven for a specific clientele, the resort caters to every visitor's individual desires, guaranteeing a perfect fit. The Ora Hotel, formerly Festive Hotel, resonates with the Asian preference for family travel and multi-generational trips. Its family-sized rooms with connecting accommodations offer the perfect setting for large family groups. However, the lack of kitchens, catering to the Asian passion for home-cooked meals, proved problematic, leading to unwanted culinary adventures in guest rooms. Meanwhile, the former Hard Rock Hotel and other lodging options cater to a diverse blend of holidaymakers, business travelers, and high rollers, offering a departure from the spartan, budget-oriented rooms found at the other Resorts World property across the Causeway in Malaysia.

Integrated resorts are much more than just gambling destinations; they offer a complete entertainment experience. Hotels play a crucial role in this ecosystem, not just as places to sleep but also as key revenue generators and strategic customer acquisition tools. Operators utilize various methods to maximize hotel yield, from timeshare schemes (though sometimes controversial) to sale-and-leaseback agreements, unlocking critical cash flow for construction, and optimizing asset holdings. This aligns with the industry's shift towards lighter models, as exemplified by the growing trend of major US casino companies spinning off their real estate into gaming REITs. VICI Properties, a spinoff of Caesars Entertainment, stands as a success story. Through acquiring MGM Resorts' REIT counterpart, VICI now boasts 50 properties and nearly 60,000 rooms, demonstrating the "best-of-both-worlds" scenario: full control of the hotel experience without direct capital investment. Similarly, timeshares can create repeat customers by funneling them back to the resort. This strategy was likely a key component of the ambitious CityCenter Las Vegas plan. More than just an integrated resort, CityCenter is a large mixed-use development encompassing a mall, casino, entertainment venues, hotels, and even owner-occupied condominiums. Over 2,000 of these condos provided a guaranteed stream of resident customers, helping offset the project's massive cost. The visionary behind CityCenter, James Murren, envisioned it as a vibrant urban microcosm inspired by New York's East Village. However, Murren's vision was marred by unforeseen circumstances. The 2008 financial crisis strained finances, leading to construction delays, cost escalation, and legal disputes. Investment ballooned to nearly $10 billion, necessitating a major restructuring. Despite these hurdles, the CityCenter masterplan was eventually launched, albeit with multiple new owners. Today, MGM Resorts manages the Aria hotel, casino, and condo-tel, while the Blackstone Group owns the underlying real estate. These components, known as the Aria Campus, are physically integrated but lack full functional cohesion due to the complex ownership structure.

Upcoming integrated resorts have the opportunity to draw inspiration from the broader hospitality industry. As they navigate a landscape marked by swift consolidation and the entrance of new brands into the market, these resorts are pushing the envelope beyond interior design concepts and cookie-cutter amenities. Marriott took a fascinating detour from its traditional four-wall hospitality experience when the hotel chain teamed up with Coachella, the iconic Californian music festival, to offer a unique glamping experience for festival-goers seeking luxury amidst the desert heat. Eight distinct tents, inspired by various Marriott brands like Aloft and Autograph Collection, dotted the festival grounds. Each tent was fully air-conditioned with high-quality linens and all the high-end amenities expected of a Marriott—electricity, reliable Wi-Fi, and premium toiletries. They all came with VIP perks such as access to private viewing areas, hospitality tents, private bathrooms and showers, and golf cart shuttles within the festival grounds.

Hilton and the PGA Tour have teamed up to offer a unique and immersive experience for golf enthusiasts – pop-up hotels nestled right on the golf course. This partnership, named 'Hilton on the Green,' debuted in 2022 and has since become a fan favorite, offering a luxurious stay with unparalleled views and access to the action. Guests wake up with a stunning view of the fairway, just steps away from the tee box with each pop-up hotel strategically placed for optimal access to the tournament while maintaining privacy. The package includes gourmet room service meals, dedicated relaxation areas, and pre-game pep talks from expert analysts. The collaboration goes beyond providing luxurious accommodations to create unforgettable memories for the guests. Such novel initiatives help Hilton to attract new customers, strengthen its brand image among golf enthusiasts, and showcase its commitment to unique and immersive experiences.

Singapore's Boat Quay Hotel broke new ground with a unique take on pop-up experiences—transforming select rooms into immersive tributes to artist Simone Legno's *tokidoki* pop culture for eight months. This innovative approach demonstrates how integrated resorts can also leverage their multi-use spaces, activating them as pop-up accommodations. Such concepts offer practical benefits for seasonal or promotional alignment, where the pop-up rooms can complement specific events or campaigns, drawing targeted audiences and enhancing engagement. During high-demand periods, temporary room conversions can maximize occupancy and revenue.

Luxury hotel group Four Seasons is diving headfirst into uncharted waters with its venture into luxury yacht accommodations. It promises to redefine the yachting experience by combining the personalized service and luxurious amenities of Four Seasons hotels with the freedom and adventure of the open seas. The inaugural Four Seasons yacht is scheduled to set sail in 2025 with suites ranging from 85 to 3,800 square feet and featuring private terraces, plunge pools, and even in-suite spas. Everything expected in a Four Seasons will be found on board, including multiple restaurants, bars, lounges, a spa, a fitness center, and a pool deck. Itineraries will focus on exploring unique and off-the-beaten-path destinations with first sailings beginning in the Mediterranean.

Imagine waking up to a new view each morning, not by changing rooms, but through the gentle rotation of your luxurious hotel suite. This vision will become a reality at the Eco-Floating Hotel in Qatar, a marvel of engineering and sustainability designed to redefine the hospitality experience. This innovative hotel features a doughnut-shaped structure that slowly rotates on its axis, completing a full revolution every twenty-four hours. The gentle revolution not only offers guests panoramic vistas of the Arabian Gulf as they relax on their private balconies but also serves a crucial purpose: generating clean energy. The circular design incorporates cleverly positioned vertical-axis wind turbines and even utilizes the umbrella-like shape of the rotating structure to harness wind power and generate 25 kW of electricity, contributing to the hotel's sustainability goals. A vortex-shaped roof collects rainwater for irrigation and purification, and solar panels further contribute to its renewable energy needs. With 152 luxurious rooms, the hotel boasts all the expected amenities of a five-star establishment, including indoor and outdoor pools, a spa, a gym, and even a mini-golf course.

And if you're seeking an experience that's truly out of this world, Hilton Hotel has partnered with Orbital Assembly, a company specializing in the design and construction of space stations, to pioneer the world's first "space hotel" in the Earth's stratosphere. Targeted for a 2025 opening, it will boast a futuristic rotating design that generates artificial gravity, mimicking Earth-like comfort. Picture a high-end resort orbiting Earth, featuring plush accommodations, gourmet restaurants, bars, entertainment venues, and fitness facilities - all while experiencing weightlessness or the familiar feeling of gravity within the rotating sections. Major Tom, you are home.

sixteen

PRIMUM NON NOCERE

Communities are cohesive social units, united by common interests and characteristics, which generally embrace diverse viewpoints and values to varying degrees. They are often protective of their social fabric and strive to maintain the status quo. When faced with disruptions or perceived threats to their social equilibrium, communities often push back collectively This resistance often embodies a "free-rider" mentality, where they seek to enjoy the benefits and resources offered by a system without fully participating or contributing equitably. This persistent behavior of insular groups inclined to accept benefits without accompanying compromise or inconvenience is aptly encapsulated in the widely recognized acronym "NIMBY," standing for "not in my backyard." NIMBY has reared its territorial head in scenarios that are familiar to many:

While communities readily welcome investments that bring jobs through traditional industries like factories or manufacturing plants, they often turn cautious and even oppose developments like chemical plants, *fracking, or nuclear facilities* due to concerns over potential health risks and community safety.

Though the concept of *eldercare facilities* garners general support, opposition flares when residents face the prospect of one near their homes. This can be attributed to various factors, including the negative perception associated with illness, decline, and death, leading to a desire for distance. Furthermore, concerns about stigma and its negative impact on property values fuel opposition.

There's a curious inconsistency we often see when it comes to *transportation infrastructure*. People tend to appreciate the convenience of a new highway, rapid transit line, or airport when it's located at a comfortable distance. Public support for infrastructure projects can wane when they are proposed close to residential areas. Concerns about noise pollution, potential air quality degradation, vibrations, visual blight, and safety hazards often lead to vocal opposition.

Communities are generally uncomfortable having a *cemetery or columbarium* in their neighborhood. This stems from a complex interplay of psychological, cultural, and practical factors. The proximity to death can be unsettling for many people, triggering feelings of fear, sadness, and mortality salience. They are often associated with darkness, gloom, and the supernatural in popular culture and certain religious or cultural beliefs might view them as impure or inauspicious, leading to opposition based on these deeply held convictions.

In Singapore, residents of a neighborhood raised an outcry when *dormitories for migrant workers* were built in their immediate vicinity. While people generally recognize the valuable contributions migrant workers make, many residents have prejudices about increased crime or safety hazards associated with large dormitories.

Casino developments are frequent targets of the NIMBY syndrome, and understandably so. While the allure of economic benefits and job creation attracts many, the prospect of a nearby casino often sparks fierce opposition.

Residents raise valid concerns, ranging from anxieties about increased crime and noise pollution to worries about the social impact of gambling addiction and the erosion of community values. In Singapore, when the government contemplated deregulating casinos in 2005, a powerful voice emerged: Families Against the Casino Threat in Singapore (FACTS). This civil society group opposed the proliferation of casinos, seeing them as a threat to the city-state's social fabric and individual well-being. They actively engaged in advocacy and public awareness campaigns, urging policymakers to consider the negative consequences of casinos. Through outreach to communities and fostering open discussions, they highlighted the dangers to families, such as addiction, debt, and crime, and the broader impact on Singaporean society. Public feedback also clearly indicated substantial opposition and religious organizations weighed in against the plan. Faced with such broad concerns, the government took several measures to reassure the public and address anxieties. A detailed white paper outlining the rationale for casinos, the benefits and risks, and the proposed regulatory framework was released for public feedback. Extensive public consultations and forums were held to gather and address feedback from citizens, community groups, and religious organizations. Additionally, independent studies on the social and economic impacts of casinos were commissioned. A national framework to address problem gambling was developed, including the establishment of a National Council on Problem Gambling and programs to counsel and treat problem and pathological gamblers. This transparency and engagement with civil society and the public played a pivotal role in shaping Singapore's approach to casinos. Today, Singapore boasts some of the most stringent regulations in the global gaming industry, recognized for their effectiveness in mitigating the negative social and economic impacts often associated with casinos.

Japan's foray into casino legalization has been nothing short of tumultuous. Despite being a predominantly Shinto-Buddhist nation with deep cultural reservations about gambling, the government pushed through a law authorizing up to ten integrated resorts. This decision came after decades of public opposition, evident in overwhelming votes against casinos in national polls. Notably, the law's passage happened during the late Prime Minister Abe's final term, wielding his party's parliamentary majority despite strong disapproval from the political opposition and citizens alike. The public remained unconvinced by government assurances that Japanese resorts would follow the successful model of Singapore, with its strict regulations and limited access for locals. Skepticism reigned around claims of reduced gambling addiction there, particularly given the lack of open debate in Singapore compared to Japan's free press and culture of expression. The Japanese media played a crucial role in voicing critiques and concerns. Despite these oppositional forces, the lack of a unified national civil society movement ultimately allowed the legislation to pass. However, it's crucial to understand the nuances of Japanese civil society. While it might lack resources for large-scale campaigns, it thrives at the local level. Neighborhood associations are strong, fostering active civic participation in immediate communities. This suggests that the Japanese casino debate might take a different shape with local-level activism playing a key role in shaping outcomes.

When authorities in Yokohama, Osaka, Nagasaki, Wakayama, and Hokkaido proposed integrated resort developments, they were met with fierce resistance from local citizens, who took their protests to the streets with picket lines. The relentless public outcry eventually forced Hokkaido and Wakayama leaders to reconsider, fearing electoral consequences and dwindling public support. Conversely, some local governments downplayed the dissenting voices, dismissing them as a minority within the population. Particularly resolute in advocating for the nation's first IR project was the mayor of Yokohama, Japan's second-largest city. Envisioned along the pristine Yokohama Bay, this project was backed by then-Prime Minister Yoshihide Suga, a Yokohama native. The municipality presented a persuasive vision for the IR's development, emphasizing its positive economic impact: revitalizing industrial bay areas, unlocking real estate value, and creating a vibrant work-live-leisure hub spanning Minatomirai to Yamashita-cho. The integrated resort was envisioned as a pivotal and iconic feature, poised to rejuvenate tourism and elevate Yokohama's status beyond its current shadow of Tokyo. Additionally, the development promised tens of thousands of new jobs, supporting local businesses and fostering economic growth. The plan's ambition seemed justified by overwhelming interest from the local business community and major international casino companies, who were eager to invest – proposed investments exceeded a staggering ten billion dollars, more than double the city's annual budget. It seemed like a win-win situation, so what went wrong?

Integrated resort developments promise a business boom, with local chambers of commerce salivating at the prospect of lucrative contracts and opportunities.

Local politicians, dependent on private sector support, readily aligned themselves with this vision of economic security. However, a large part of the population remained uneasy with the gambling aspect. Municipal authorities, echoing the national government's rhetoric, emphasized the financial benefits while downplaying potential social issues. This reductive strategy failed to resonate, generating tepid support in national polls and leaving residents' concerns unaddressed. For residents, the stakes were even higher. The casino's proximity triggered the NIMBY syndrome, sparking anxieties about increased crime, addiction, and community disruption. Residents weren't appeased by the social safeguards, including a 6,000-yen entry fee for Japanese citizens, and restrictions limiting them to three visits per week and ten per month. However, the law lacked specifics on critical areas like problem gambling prevention, treatment, public education, and feedback mechanisms. Instead, these responsibilities were delegated to local governments, creating a patchwork of inconsistent policies across prefectures. While Japan adopted many of Singapore's social safeguards, it crucially missed the mark by not establishing a national problem gambling advisory body. Yokohama residents took to the streets, chanting "Casi-NO!" and forming civic groups to force a referendum. They gathered enough signatures to trigger a plebiscite, but the ruling party's dominance in the local legislative assembly rendered their petition toothless. As expected, the referendum was crushed. Then came the unexpected savior: the COVID-19 pandemic. The global shutdown caused a delay in the IR application schedule, extending it beyond the mayor's current term. In 2021, residents effectively turned the mayoral election into a casino referendum, electing a leader who pledged to scrap the IR plans.

The resounding "No!" by residents to the Yokohama integrated resort plans sent shockwaves through the Japanese government, shattering their carefully constructed plans and forcing pro-casino lawmakers to scramble. This grassroots victory resonated far beyond Yokohama, inspiring similar opposition movements in other prefectures planning for IR developments. In a swift turn of events, integrated resorts transformed from economic boons into political liabilities. The most immediate casualty was former Prime Minister Yoshihide Suga, whose resignation mere months after the failed Yokohama IR push coincided with the ruling Liberal Democratic Party (LDP) losing control of the city to the opposition. Fearing a similar fate, the Wakayama prefectural assembly, initially rejecting calls for a referendum, eventually caved to public pressure and shelved its IR plans entirely. However, Osaka proved to be a different story. Leaders there remained determined to establish an IR on a man-made island in Osaka Bay, despite facing similar civic action as Yokohama and Wakayama. While they survived local elections despite resident opposition, the Ishin To government continues to grapple with anti-casino sentiment, casting a shadow over the slow-progressing Yumeshima IR project. Meanwhile, the national government seems to have put its plans for issuing two more IR licenses on hold indefinitely, further fueled by the rejection of Nagasaki's application due to concerns about financial feasibility. These developments highlight the sharp shift in the power dynamic within Japan's casino debate.

Legislating casinos can be a political tightrope walk, potentially leading to self-inflicted electoral wounds.

Rushing into it without a strong mandate can spell disaster. A stable government with robust public support is crucial for navigating this potentially treacherous political terrain. Singapore serves as a prime example of successful casino implementation. The PAP ruling party's long-standing dominance and a transparent legislative process allowed them to introduce casinos relatively smoothly. However, recent electoral losses, which reduced their overall majority, have put any thoughts of additional integrated resort licenses on hold, highlighting the vulnerability of casino policies to political shifts. South Korea, with its sizable middle class and known gambling affinity, presents a tantalizing market for integrated resorts. Currently, only one state-owned casino resort permits Koreans to gamble. The Kangwon Land Casino, with its substantial turnover, surpasses the combined revenue of all the other dozen or more foreigner-only casinos in the country. However, frequent political upheaval and corruption scandals create a major deterrent to liberalization. Korean leaders have become increasingly cautious, particularly after witnessing the negative impact of the Japanese integrated resort legislation on the once all-powerful Liberal Democratic Party ruling government in Japan. While Koreans' proclivity for gambling could drive casino success, it also raises social concerns about addiction and its impact on individuals and families. This creates a complex equation for policymakers, who must weigh the economic benefits against social costs.

Over the years, the Thai government has conducted multiple studies and feasibility assessments on legal casinos as a means to counter illegal gambling, but public and civil society opposition and internal disagreements among lawmakers have stalled progress. The opposition centers around concerns about increases in crime, addiction, and social ills associated with gambling, highlighting its predatory nature. Families and communities are particularly worried about their negative impact. Critics argue that casinos promote materialism and greed, undermining Thai values and culture. Some see it as catering to wealthy foreigners, exacerbating social inequalities. There is also wide distrust in the government's ability to effectively regulate and distribute casino-generated revenue fairly and transparently. Thailand leaders have good cause to tread carefully and consider how civil society might react to any plans to advance the casino agenda. Civil society in Thailand operates in a complex and often-restrictive environment, but despite facing numerous challenges, has demonstrably wielded considerable power in shaping the country's political landscape. They have played a crucial role in twice overthrowing military dictatorships and successfully pressured governments to implement policy changes, such as the introduction of healthcare schemes and minimum wage hikes. Their strengths lie in extensive grassroots support through regional networks and community engagement and utilization of diverse tactics like protests, petitions, social media campaigns, and legal action to further their causes.

Following the recent legalization of casino gambling in several Asian neighbors, including Japan, Thai lawmakers have shown renewed interest in pursuing a similar path. Two parliamentary committees, convened by consecutive governments, considered legislation for "entertainment complexes," a Thai interpretation of integrated resorts. Lawmakers overwhelmingly supported the initiative, with the previous administration's committee recommending up to five such complexes with casinos in the kingdom. This would overturn the 1935 law prohibiting all forms of betting except the National Lottery and horse racing. However, a key takeaway from the committee report emphasizes the need for further studies on the social impact, public health and safety, and public opinion. Additionally, developing legislation and policies with public confidence and support is crucial. The law must clearly outline preventive safeguards to mitigate negative social and security issues that could disrupt public order. This element is ultimately the most critical factor for successfully legalizing casino gambling in Thailand. Thai political parties stand united in their support for casino legalization, unlike their counterparts in South Korea and Japan who faced significant opposition. However, securing the backing of civil society is the key hurdle they must overcome.

Emerging gaming jurisdictions like Thailand can glean crucial insights from Japan's rollercoaster casino rollout, particularly the case of Yokohama. The crux lies in genuinely addressing citizen concerns and crafting a well-balanced framework that assuages public anxieties. It demands unwavering candor, ensuring actions align with pronouncements, leaving no room for Potemkin's pretense. Firstly, it's vital to acknowledge the potential downsides of casinos on society. Openly discussing these negative impacts builds trust and fosters constructive dialogue. Secondly, active collaboration with civil society is essential. Engaging communities through meaningful conversations helps identify concerns and craft solutions aligned with public interests. Finally, empowering the electorate through a casino referendum offers a valuable gauge of public sentiment. While opposition is expected, this direct approach provides a transparent measure of support and allows the government to adapt its plans accordingly. Had Japan embraced such an approach, focusing less on downplaying negatives and more on genuine engagement, their journey could have been smoother.

Unlike their flamboyant counterparts in Las Vegas, Singapore's integrated resorts intentionally minimize the casino element. While the two Singaporean casinos rival their American counterparts in size, their profile is vastly different. In Las Vegas, the casino floor reigns supreme, with guests often forced to navigate a gauntlet of slot machines to reach their rooms. Restaurants intermingle with the casino, and even minors are allowed limited access. However, Singapore's deeply rooted cultural taboo towards gambling relegates the casinos to the periphery. At Marina Bay Sands, even glimpses are rare, except for fleeting views at casino entrances. Resorts World Sentosa takes it further, completely hiding the casino from sight, other than a somewhat contradictory huge "CASINO" sign at the entrance to the casino. Despite this lack of visual enticement, both Singaporean casinos thrive, with Marina Bay Sands even holding the title of the world's most profitable casino property. This success offers valuable lessons for Japan's upcoming Osaka resort, set to boast the largest casino in Asia. By following Singapore's lead and visually shielding the casino from non-gamers, Japan can ensure a smoother transition for its more conservative society. Conversely, Manila's integrated resorts, reflecting the Philippines' more liberal culture, embrace the Western model. As Thailand drafts its casino legislation, it should consider Singapore's approach, prioritizing cultural sensitivity and minimizing negative societal impacts in consideration of its conservative society.

The Singapore government led an admirable initiative in crafting the integrated resort model, a strategy that shifts focus away from the casino while enriching other attractions and entertainment options to create a comprehensive experience, appealing to more conservative Asian cultures. However, the effectiveness of the model surpasses merely relegating the casino to the background; establishing physical barriers is insufficient without the adoption of best practices in responsible gambling by both the government and operators. It's akin to the difference between sweeping the casino under the rug and taking a proactive approach to addressing the need for responsible gambling by regularly lifting it up and vacuuming it to ensure proper attention and care. To build trust, emerging jurisdictions pursuing integrated resorts should be courageous and transparent. This means openly acknowledging that casinos are an inherent part of the integrated resort vision, while also admitting the potential social problems they can create and that casinos will exact their pound of flesh. Therefore, the primary focus should be on developing a plan to mitigate these issues to a minimum before emphasizing the myriad benefits that an integrated resort can offer. Singapore's Prime Minister has been forthcoming about the downsides even as he rationalized the decision for the integrated resort, saying, "The social impact is not negligible. By making gaming more accessible and even glamorous, it could encourage more gambling and increase the risk of gaming addiction. A casino could also lead to undesirable activities like money laundering, illegal money lending, and organized crime." Tackling the bull by the horns, he added, "We must also address the non-economic issues—tangible minuses like an increase in problem gambling and broken families, and intangible losses like the impact on Singapore's brand name and social values." He could not have been more candid in admitting, "We must assume that the IRs will increase the amount of gambling in Singapore. More gambling will mean more problem gamblers." Acknowledging anything less is quixotic and socially irresponsible.

seventeen

INTEGRATED

One of the defining features of Singapore's integrated resort model is its deliberate effort to keep the casino out of the spotlight, coupled with a robust responsible gaming regime upheld by a strict set of social safeguard rules.

"The IRs will have all kinds of amenities: hotels, restaurants, shopping, convention space, even theaters, museums, and theme parks. They attract hundreds of thousands of visitors per year. The great majority will not be there to gamble. They may be tourists, executives, or businessmen, who go to enjoy the resort or attend conventions or conferences. But within this large development and slew of activities, there is one small but essential part which offers gaming and which helps make the entire project financially viable," said Singapore's prime minister, Lee Hsien Loong, in 2005 when he explained the government's plans to legalize casino gambling where gaming facilities will occupy less than 5% of the total integrated resort area. These social components of the framework have bolstered the reputation of the Singapore integrated resort industry, earning it recognition as a safe and secure destination for gaming and entertainment and undoubtedly contributed to the industry's success. However, the true driver of economic success for integrated resorts, propelling the Singapore duopoly to the world's top ten most profitable gaming destinations, lies in how faithfully they deliver on the essence of their "integrated" label.

Combining diverse attractions under one roof does not define an "integrated" resort. True integration seamlessly harmonizes hotels, ballrooms, theaters, casinos, retail, dining, and the surrounding destination into a cohesive customer experience. This unleashes the synergy between each element, maximizing revenue across all property aspects. Failing to achieve true integration leads to missed opportunities and subpar returns. Unlocking an integrated resort's full economic potential demands more than just mastering internal harmony. The *sine qua non* of success is two-fold: integration within the venue and the development of a symbiotic relationship with the surrounding environment. Achieving this optimum integration transcends the resort and the capabilities of the operator. It requires a carefully constructed interplay with the vision and implementation of the broader marketplace. Achieving a fully-integrated resort necessitates top-to-bottom integration at every stage, from envisioning the concept to executing daily operational tasks:

Industry Vision & Goals: Ensure the resort fulfills the shared vision and objectives of the industry and destination.

Industry Structure: Adhere to the industry framework and contribute to the overall masterplan.

IR Specifications: Design and deliver the resort in accordance with the established template and vision.

Business Plan: Develop a sound business plan, financially modeled and aligned with the overall IR concept.

Business Operations: Execute daily operations seamlessly following the outlined strategy.

Industry vision and goals

The rise of integrated resorts in Singapore and Japan stemmed from a common need to address their declining market share in regional tourism during the early 2000s. In Singapore, various ambitious projects were launched to enhance their allure. One such initiative was the transformation of the business district into a buzzing downtown area. The Marina Bay masterplan envisioned a vibrant work-live-play district anchored by an integrated resort (Marina Bay Sands), stunning Gardens by the Bay park, and electrifying international events like the Singapore Formula 1 night race. This holistic approach aimed to elevate Singapore's global image and attract diverse travelers. Concurrently, Sentosa Island was envisioned as a tropical leisure haven for families. Resorts World Sentosa, a family-oriented integrated resort, was built to offer diverse attractions and entertainment, positioning Singapore as a premier family-friendly destination. There's a unanimous consensus that Singapore's two integrated resorts have not only met but surpassed the government's initial vision. Following its 2010 opening, Singapore witnessed double-digit growth in both tourist arrivals and tourism receipts. There's no doubt that Universal Studios Singapore's draw extends to countless leisure and family tourists, and Marina Bay Sands, complete with its iconic SkyPark, has become a must-visit landmark on every visitor's itinerary.

Japan sought to emulate the success of Singapore's integrated resort industry. However, the vision had to be adjusted as the Japanese tourism industry experienced a remarkable turnaround, fueled by the surge in Chinese outbound travelers. Japanese lawmakers then shifted the mission to adapt the IR legislation to prioritize the development of the MICE tourism market over general tourism. Amidst political complexities and volatility in the regional market, the consortium of ORIX Corporation and MGM Resorts has secured the first Japanese IR license to develop an integrated resort in Osaka, scheduled for completion in the fall of 2030. The world eagerly awaits the realization of this $8 billion vision – a project with the potential to reshape Osaka's future.

Industry structure

Singapore's integrated resort industry operates under a duopoly structure, providing two distinct resort experiences embodied by Marina Bay Sands and Resorts World Sentosa. A tiered casino tax system incentivizes the operators to prioritize premium gamblers. It imposes a higher tax rate on revenue generated from mass market gaming, a segment more vulnerable to financial problems and susceptible to addictive behavior. It is one facet of a comprehensive social safeguard framework that effectively reduces issues like problem gambling, crime, and money laundering. Stringent regulations dissuade both customers and operators by imposing severe penalties, including imprisonment and fines, for breaches of established rules. This framework is further strengthened by robust regulatory oversight, which continuously monitors the industry and refines the rules to enhance IR operators' diligence in responsible gaming practices and adherence to ethical codes, thereby combating illegal gambling practices.

Singapore's IR structure operates efficiently, bordering on excessively so. The casino industry's duopoly structure has undeniably benefited the operators, generating substantial profits. However, the government has taken steps to moderate this exclusivity through increased casino taxes and mandated multi-billion-dollar investments in upgrades and expansions. These measures suggest a possible longer-term shift towards opening the market to more operators. However, careful evaluation of the social impact of additional casinos is essential before proceeding.

Japan adopted an IR structure bearing a striking resemblance to Singapore's successful model, to the extent of replicating its oligopolistic market, which will effectively create regional market monopolies for their three planned integrated resorts. However, where the Japanese government grossly erred was in its execution. Firstly, it did not comprehensively address the negative social impacts as Singapore did, and secondly, in the manner in which the integrated resort sites and operators were chosen. The cumbersome selection process proved frustrating for many operators, leading to numerous withdrawals and admitting many less qualified bidders. It ultimately resulted in only one approved resort in Osaka. In contrast, Singapore's rigorous selection and probity process ensures that only high-quality shortlisted bidders have a seat at the table.

The mistakes in Japan's initial foray into integrated resorts could be rectified by adopting a more streamlined approach modeled after Singapore's success. This would involve implementing a pre-qualification process that ensures potential IR operators meet strict criteria, including financial stability, a proven track record in developing and managing IRs, and a commitment to responsible gambling practices. Following this, a methodical selection process should be conducted, evaluating each proposal one at a time to ensure a good fit between the operator and the specific IR location. In addition, they can group the integrated resorts into geographically defined regional clusters, thereby creating a more competitive market environment.

IR specifications

The Request for Proposals for the Marina Bay integrated resort site in Singapore specified "a large-scale iconic lifestyle destination with a compelling mix of convention and exhibition facilities, themed attractions, entertainment and performance venues, casino, recreation facilities, hotels, and retail uses." It was envisaged as a key component of the vision for the new Marina Bay downtown area to "become an international business and financial hub." The RFP further articulated the desired design style of the resort and requirements for the provision of facilities such as museums, art galleries, and the inclusion of public amenities along the waterfront. The envisioned IR on Sentosa was to be "a large-scale iconic development and a must-visit attraction for visitors. The requirements call for "a world-class tropical resort that offers the whole family a fun and memorable leisure experience" that will "broaden Singapore's tourism and entertainment options, complement existing tourist attractions as well as catalyze new tourism investments" and become a part of an "enthralling mix of island resort recreational and entertainment facilities." The stipulation was for an IR design that "reflect and respect the local context of the site, specifically its tropical island nature with its lush natural greenery and marine coastal frontage." A visitor arrival center and public promenades along the waterfront were specified in the RFP.

Official IR specifications establish the groundwork for developers, outlining key technical, design, architectural, and operational aspects. These serve as a baseline for crafting proposals that align with jurisdictional goals and community integration. While these templates differ for each jurisdiction, IR specifications typically define broad parameters without micromanaging design or architecture. They may set the broad strokes to ensure the concepts blend seamlessly with their surroundings and adhere to urban master plans, leaving developers to leverage their expertise and vision to shape solutions that integrate well within these parameters. The level of detail within specifications often reflects the government's primary motivations. When the focus is purely economic (maximizing tax revenue), specifications tend to be less concise due to the lack of a broader vision. However, overly detailed specifications can stifle creativity and innovation, potentially leading to scenarios that don't fit with market dynamics. This can impact business feasibility and risk turning away prospective bidders. Finding the right balance is crucial. While some level of detail is necessary to ensure alignment with government objectives, excessive regulations risk hindering long-term benefits. Particularly, authorities should not interfere in technical aspects such as the physical characteristics of a resort, which are driven by the underlying business plan and should be exclusively the purview of the operator.

Japan's IR specifications, with absolute space requirements for hotel areas and MICE facilities, arguably overstepped boundaries, potentially hindering business flexibility and innovation to the detriment of regional integrated resort business propositions. Social considerations might necessitate specific requirements such as limits on gaming areas, responsible gambling practices, or environmental sustainability measures. Singapore's integrated resort RFPs limited gaming areas to 15,000 square meters and capped slot machines per casino at 2,500.

Not all IR specifications are encapsulated within master plans like that of Singapore. In such cases, IR developers have to ensure that their resort design is integrated with its surroundings. This integration goes beyond aesthetics, encompassing crucial factors such as logistical planning. If an IR site is not designated, developers should preferably avoid choosing locations in close proximity to resident communities, schools, and religious institutions to minimize social disruption. Carefully analyzing projected visitor numbers and existing traffic patterns is crucial to prevent congestion. Additionally, the resort's offerings should avoid directly competing with local businesses in the vicinity. One example of a master plan that didn't fully consider the logistical aspects was the integrated resort plan for Yokohama in Japan. The chosen site was a wharf, whose conventional fan or finger-shaped design is optimized for accessibility, ease of navigation for docking vessels, and maximizing the number of berths. However, the characteristic narrow landward end of the pier, designed for security and efficient cargo flow, becomes a bottleneck when repurposed to channel tens of thousands of daily resort visitors. A similar conundrum exists for Yumeshima Island, where the MGM Resorts Osaka will be built. The island currently has only two roadway access points with limited lanes, as they presently serve a container terminal and a few small industrial facilities. One route to access the island is via a bridge from the adjacent man-made island of Maishima, while the other requires passing through a narrow tunnel connected to the reclaimed island of Sakishima. A new subway line is under construction in anticipation of the Osaka Expo in 2025. Despite discussions, plans for a railway line into the island remain unconfirmed. Keihan Railways, the train operator, has delayed its decision regarding the rail extension until an exit clause in the agreement between the IR consortium and the Osaka prefectural government expires in September 2026.

Proposals that demonstrate the best integration with the main premises outlined in the IR specifications are more likely to succeed. This is usually articulated in the evaluation parameters for the IR tender. For example, the Singapore IR evaluation criteria focused on four key areas: tourism appeal and contribution, development investment level, architectural and urban design excellence, and the strength of the consortium and partners' track record.

Business plan

Modern integrated resorts shatter conventional expectations with audacious design and architecture. Towering pyramids, intricate replicas, and larger-than-life themes dominate the landscape, often pushing boundaries with sheer scale. Many incorporate dynamic elements like erupting volcanoes and dancing fountains, adding a layer of visual grandeur that breathes life into the complex. Iconic examples include Caesars Palace, the Bellagio, the Venetian in Las Vegas, and Marina Bay Sands' spectacular triptych in Singapore. However, stunning visuals are just the first act. Successful integrated resorts go beyond the shimmering facades. In Singapore, while architectural concept and design play a crucial role, they only constitute 25-30% of the assessment score for an integrated resort proposal. While the visual impact of the outward form is undeniably crucial, it needs to be balanced by functionality, which serves as the engine of a truly "integrated" experience.

Behind the walls of the integrated resort, meticulous planning is required to blend form and function into the design and layout of every facility. This intricate process begins with insights from business operations, strategically determining the placement and proximity of each element. Integrated resorts prioritize both exceptional customer experiences and operational efficiency. However, their competitive advantage stems from their ability to cater to a wide range of demographics. Within the same venue, one must meet the specific needs of each segment. The biggest hurdle? Maintaining exclusivity for premium guests while serving the mass market. Achieving a luxurious, high-end experience for some guests while simultaneously catering to a broader, general audience within the same resort presents a unique paradox. This requires a strategic approach that balances exclusivity with inclusivity, employing a touch of artful differentiation rather than complete separation. Though Universal Studios Singapore, nestled within the Resorts World Sentosa integrated resort, welcomes families and minors with open arms, the operator has to carefully manage the proximity to the casino environment. Larger resorts with ample space have the advantage of creating physical separation and buffer zones, simplifying the task of catering to diverse demographics. Conversely, this becomes inherently more difficult for resorts with a smaller footprint.

Accommodations and attractions should be designed with a range of price points to cater to the diverse budgets of each target demographic. The strategic curation and management of attractions and amenities must align with the resort's business strategy and be consistent with its revenue model. Ideally, every major component should be established as a profit center.

Business operation

If functionality defines the engine of an integrated resort, "flow" constitutes the heartbeat of its operation. Integration in action is embodied by seamless flow in every aspect of resort operations. Inadequate transportation infrastructure for the Osaka integrated resort, which is currently not equipped to handle the expected 30 million annual visitors, will hand the operator a mammoth task of efficiently handling the massive daily footfalls within the resort.

Managing the immense volume of people within an integrated resort presents a logistical nightmare analogous to that of a busy airport handling tens of thousands of passengers daily. Both environments rely heavily on efficient traffic and people movement for smooth operation. Optimal flow management offers substantial benefits, including improved efficiency by streamlining movement and allocating resources effectively, enhanced customer experience through minimized congestion and real-time information, and ensured safety by proactively identifying and mitigating congestion and security risks. Airports often employ radial design layouts to facilitate natural flow. Additionally, they leverage a network of sensors and cameras to gather real-time data on passenger flow, queue lengths, and resource utilization. This data is analyzed to identify bottlenecks, predict congestion, and optimize resource allocation. Real-time information on routes, wait times, and personalized suggestions are provided through digital signage, mobile apps, and dynamic staffing adjustments based on current data. This comprehensive approach minimizes wait times at key points like security checkpoints and baggage claim. Furthermore, intelligent baggage handling systems streamline routing and tracking, reducing delays and lost luggage incidents. Integrated security systems provide real-time situational awareness to security personnel, enabling informed decision-making. Real-time crowd monitoring strengthens safety measures by detecting possible dangerous situations and allowing for a faster response in emergency situations.

A well-defined resort master plan establishes the foundation for a smooth and seamless guest movement within the resort. However, flow encompasses more than just arrival, departure, and guests navigating the resort. A major bottleneck in resort flow often occurs during check-in and check-out processes. For large resorts with thousands of rooms, these formalities can be anything but routine, especially during peak seasons. It's not uncommon for arriving guests to endure ten-hour wait times for registration and room assignments. Furthermore, overbooking of hotels and ticketed attractions disrupts the flow, highlighting inefficiencies in resort processes. Long queues at the breakfast buffet are a common frustration for many guests. Lost in the resort or unable to find your car in the vast parking garage? These inconveniences, along with the need to visit multiple counters or undergo different procedures for various attractions, contribute to a fragmented guest experience.

Many resort experiences continue to be plagued by these seemingly straightforward issues. The absence of seamless customer experiences often arises from inefficiencies within the back-of-the-house operations at resorts. Large-scale resorts employing thousands of staff frequently encounter unnecessary hierarchies and bureaucratic obstacles in their organizational structures, hindering decision-making processes and diminishing efficiency. Internal competition often restricts the sharing of resources and drives up operating expenses. Additionally, top-down management approaches can severely stifle productivity. In large organizations, delegating responsibilities and empowering employees is crucial for optimal productivity.

Oligopolistic markets, with their potential for easy profits, can breed complacency among operators, hindering the optimization of business operations. However, market leaders prioritize operational excellence regardless of market dynamics. They consistently lead the industry in average occupation rate, average daily rate (ADR), revenue per available room (RevPAR), and top quartile gaming performance in average daily revenue per gaming position, net contribution per player visit, and gaming position utilization ratios. These top operators iteratively curate their products and services, continuously fine-tuning them to adapt to changing market conditions and customer preferences. Employing tools such as automation and yield management technologies, they strike a balance between "high-tech" solutions and personalized "high-touch" service to streamline operations and elevate the customer experience. Integration is not a static process but an ever-evolving endeavor.

Can the real integrated resort please stand up? Not if it operates in a jurisdiction with strict regulations without enforcement. Not if it espouses the industry vision only long enough to secure an operating license. Not when the resort is less than the sum of its parts, which reveals outward form without function. Not when the business model focuses mainly on casino gaming. Not when responsible gaming is a rule, not a credo. Not when the concept of an "integrated resort" exists in name only.

eighteen
TILL…DO US PART

Building an integrated resort is a complex financial undertaking, a high-risk, high-reward endeavor. With costs often exceeding the billion-dollar mark, only a handful of casino companies have the financial muscle to venture solo. Strong cash flow, ample liquidity, and minimal debt are the hallmarks of success in this high-stakes game. Even industry titans can find themselves teetering on the edge. During the construction of Marina Bay Sands in Singapore, Las Vegas Sands was caught in the crossfire of the 2007 global financial crisis, triggered by the U.S. subprime mortgage debacle. This cash shortage threatened to derail the project, and only through a personal financial lifeline from the then-owner, Sheldon Adelson, was default averted. The Sands' close call offers valuable lessons for operators and governments alike. Even the "king of the hill" can be brought low by the sheer magnitude of an IR undertaking. Unfortunately, the industry landscape is littered with echoes of this story: projects that never materialized, faced crippling delays, or worse, were abandoned mid-construction, leaving behind a trail of wasted resources and unrealized dreams. This harsh reality necessitates a measured approach to IR development. Thorough financial planning, a diversified funding strategy, and robust risk mitigation measures are paramount for navigating the treacherous financial terrain of these large-scale ventures. Only by acknowledging the inherent challenges and adopting a cautious yet ambitious approach can companies hope to achieve sustainable success in the seductive, yet perilous, world of integrated resorts.

Two recent developments highlight the critical role of thorough vetting and industry expertise in the risky world of integrated resort development. In Japan, Nagasaki prefecture's chosen developer stumbled at the financial hurdle, failing to secure funding during licensing reviews. Similarly, Caesars Entertainment's South Korean IR plans faced years of inactivity and partner changes before ultimately being abandoned due to insufficient funding. These cases echo the plight of an ongoing project in the central Philippines, where the local developer's debt burden forced them to seek a bailout. These failures underscore the importance of experience beyond mere financial resources. Aspiring novice operators, even with ample cash, can face operational obstacles once the doors open for business. A recent example is a Jeju island resort built by a wealthy Chinese entrepreneur, currently struggling to deliver financial performance. The industry has moved beyond the "golden age" of Macau, where unqualified entrants could make mistakes and still capitalize on a booming market.

Choosing the right integrated resort developer is a crucial and complex decision, fraught with risks as well as rewards. For regulators, it's akin to entering into a long-term, strategic partnership with an investor – a partnership that can unlock immense economic benefits and propel regional development, or conversely, jeopardize financial stability and cast a shadow over the industry's reputation. Similar to how individuals scrupulously vet potential marriage partners, ensuring compatibility and shared values, a rigorous and transparent selection process is essential for regulators.

This process must not only assess the financial muscle of the developer, but also delve deeper into their corporate governance practices, operational expertise, and alignment with the jurisdiction's envisioned development goals. Financial strength is undoubtedly a critical factor, ensuring the developer can shoulder the high investment costs and navigate unforeseen financial problems as evidenced by the tale of Nagasaki prefecture and their chosen developer's inability to secure funding during licensing reviews. However, relying solely on financial clout can be a dangerous gamble, as evidenced by Wakayama Prefecture's experience with the SunCity Group. While they boasted financial strength, the group's chairman was later arrested for running an illegal gambling operation, highlighting the importance of looking beyond mere financial resources. The conviction of Alvin Chau, whose junket empire masked illegal activities, underscores the necessity of scrutinizing the developer's reputation and past conduct. A lack of transparency in financial reporting, prior legal issues, or a history of involvement in ethically questionable business activities should all be cause for thorough due diligence.

The Singapore government spared no effort in its probity process to vet the actors in its integrated resort industry. Its vigilance served to keep every single Chinese junket operator outside its jurisdiction, with none able to meet its minutiae of transparency and disclosure requirements. In contrast, the previously highly regarded Australian state casino regulatory agencies suffered a major fall from grace after gross shortcomings in their oversight of the local industry resulted in rampant infiltration by organized crime elements and pervasive money laundering. Singapore also has a pre-qualifying Request for Concepts stage in its IR tendering process that other jurisdictions don't have. The lack of such a pre-vetting step in Japan was what primarily led to many dubious actors seeping through the cracks, which allowed the likes of SunCity and a litany of unknown business entities to cast themselves as bona fide contenders for the Japanese IR licenses.

Proper probity encompasses more than just whether an investor possesses a deep enough pocket to foot the multi-billion-dollar IR development bill. It is a thorough inquest into their suitability in terms of the bearings of the companies and their top officers to ensure that not a single bad actor is in their midst. The comprehensive checklist scrutinizes their experience in the integrated resort business and puts their standing and business practices under a microscope to examine if they conform to what a regulator desires for its market. Not every operator that is already regulated in other jurisdictions has a mission statement and corporate vision that necessarily fit with the industry ideals of a new jurisdiction. It can delve into the personal characters of the primary shareholders and C-suite executives at a level of disclosure even more intrusive than a bride-to-be's mother's inquisition of a would-be son-in-law. No stone should be left unturned; otherwise, as they say, you are resigned to forever holding your peace.

Those in high public office and bureaucrats who wield influence, hold decision powers or are privy to confidential information should be made to adhere to a high standard of decorum in the espousal of incorruptibility. The flesh can be weak when there are billions of dollars at stake. There is always a cadre of agents and proxies willing to broker on behalf of willing parties on either side of the divide. Rank-and-file public servants earning pittances can all too easily waver at the offer of a large payday in return for providing some "harmless" information or making a preferential evaluation. The pressure to secure a casino concession, coupled with the potential for huge bonuses, may push company executives and brokers towards unscrupulous tactics. Strict protocols should be instilled to lessen the possibility of any impropriety. Informal exchanges between regulators and bidders should not be permitted or discouraged in and around the license bidding period. Formal meetings require the creation of official minutes. It is important to create an environment that is transparent and beyond reproach. In Japan, a certain governor was said to have private breakfast tête-à-têtes at his favorite hotel with his favored casino developers. Shady brokers in suits offer face time with key lawmakers in return for monetary benefits. Government-appointed consultants cavort and party openly with executives of the companies they were supposed to assess. Large business blocs and powerful corporate heads possess more than a symbiotic relationship with government leaders. It all came to a head when a vice minister was convicted for accepting bribes from a Chinese lottery company seeking an IR license in Hokkaido. The Japanese authorities then belatedly imposed rules to govern meetings between public officials and the bidders.

Integrated resorts are synonymous with massive-scale facilities, attracting large visitor numbers, generating significant revenue turnover, and necessitating major investments often exceeding $1 billion. Las Vegas Sands stands alone as the only company that has consistently ventured on its own in all of its casino resort investments. Malaysia's Genting Group also predominantly kept operations within the "family," except in instances necessitated by specific jurisdictional requirements. For example, in the case of the Philippines, foreign companies can only hold up to 40% equity in land ownership, prompting casino developers to seek local business partners. In most instances, there is also a tacit belief in the necessity of having a local joint-venture partner. A local partner understands the intricacies of doing business in the area, possesses greater knowledge of local customer preferences, and may possess a unique bond with government officials and lawmakers, which can provide a critical advantage in competitive licensing situations. By and large, companies join consortiums in developing integrated resorts, not only to share substantial investment costs but also driven by various strategic motivations beyond financial considerations.

The development and operation of integrated resorts, encompassing diverse attractions like casinos, hotels, and entertainment venues, hinges on a symphony of collaboration between various entities. While formal consortiums offer a structured approach, partnerships can flourish in a multitude of forms, each contributing their unique strengths and expertise.

1. Core Partners

These entities act as the pillars upon which the entire venture rests. Holding a substantial equity stake (typically a significant percentage of the total investment), they play a central role in driving the resort's success by contributing:

Local knowledge and network: A proven track record in navigating the complexities of regulatory processes or securing licenses in the region, sometimes bolstered by established governmental relationships or a profound understanding of local cultural nuances. This can help tip the scales in a consortium's favor during competitive casino license tenders.

"Killer Content": Introducing iconic elements that become the signature attractions of the resort, setting it apart from the competition. This could include world-class theme parks, renowned museums housing prestigious collections, or exclusive theatrical productions featuring award-winning luminaries. These "killer content" attractions not only elevate the resort's prestige but also act as powerful drawcards for visitors, generating excitement and encouraging them to choose a particular destination over others. Such content can take many forms:

Iconic attractions: Theme parks, Formula 1 racing circuits, or other world-renowned attractions.

Cultural monuments: Collaborations with prestigious museums like the Guggenheim or MoMA, offering unique cultural experiences.

Exclusive entertainment: Partnerships with renowned figures like Lin-Manuel Miranda or Andrew Lloyd Webber to create original Broadway or West End productions, drawing in theatre enthusiasts.

2. Strategic Partners

Sharing many characteristics with Core Partners, these entities possess valuable strategic expertise that can take diverse forms, acting as powerhouse collaborators who fill specific gaps in the consortium's skillset:

Marketing & Branding: Expertise in crafting compelling marketing campaigns and establishing a strong brand identity for the resort, leveraging their established media connections or deep understanding of target demographics. This expertise is crucial for attracting a wider audience and ensuring the resort resonates with its intended guests.

Architectural & Engineering Services: Renowned architectural or engineering firms lend their expertise in designing and constructing the resort, ensuring it meets the highest standards of safety, functionality, and aesthetics. Their cutting-edge designs and focus on sustainability can not only enhance the guest experience but also contribute to the resort's long-term viability.

Financial Expertise: Bringing in partners with a strong grasp of financial management, risk assessment, and capital acquisition is crucial for securing funding, managing operational costs, and ensuring the financial viability of the venture. Their expertise can help the consortium navigate complex financial landscapes and make sound economic decisions throughout the development and operation phases.

In some cases, Strategic Partners may be granted equity in exchange for their contributions, particularly if their expertise is deemed crucial for the project's success. This incentivizes them to remain invested in the long-term prosperity of the resort and fosters a sense of shared ownership in its success.

3. *Equity-Only Partners*

Equity partners play a crucial role in supporting ventures by providing substantial financial investment. In exchange for their capital, they receive an equity stake in the company. Unlike venture capitalists who often take a more active role in management, equity partners typically focus on the venture's long-term success and the potential for a strong return on their investment. Although they may not be involved in the daily operations, equity partners offer financial stability and the resources needed to bring the project to life and ensure its continued economic viability. It's important to note that there are also activist equity partners. These partners, while still financially motivated, may also push for specific changes within the venture to improve its performance or align it with a particular social or environmental cause. Their involvement can be beneficial, bringing fresh perspectives and potentially accelerating growth. However, it's crucial to carefully assess an activist partner's goals and ensure they align with the venture's long-term vision.

4. Content Partners

Content partners play a vital role in enriching and broadening the experience for visitors by providing non-financial resources:

Entertainment Powerhouses: Integrated resorts leverage partnerships with renowned entertainment companies like Cirque du Soleil to elevate the guest experience by offering bespoke performances or unique shows. These collaborations not only inject a distinctive flavor into the resort's offerings, setting it apart from the competition, but also capitalize on the existing brand recognition of the entertainment partner. This recognition attracts visitors, particularly those seeking a specific type of entertainment experience that aligns with the partner's reputation. While technically considered vendors or suppliers, these entertainment companies often transcend these labels due to the palpable and immersive nature of their offerings. This is especially true for partners who develop bespoke content tailored specifically for the resort, fostering a deeper connection between the entertainment and the resort's overall brand identity.

Luxury Hospitality Brands: Partnering with established names like Waldorf Astoria, Peninsula or Raffles elevates a resort's prestige and brand recognition, attracting discerning travelers seeking consistent service and world-class hospitality standards. Featuring these luxury brands leverages their existing reputation and guest expectations, ensuring a seamless and luxurious experience for high-end clientele. When the Macau casino industry opened up in the early 2000s, the nascent home-grown concessionaires were unknown quantities. Including established hospitality brands was essential to luring travelers, especially the discerning ones who seek consistent service and quality standards during their stay.

Dining: Integrated resorts recognize the importance of catering to diverse palates and budgets, crafting a symphony of gastronomic experiences that resonates with every guest. This strategic approach ensures a satisfying and memorable dining experience, solidifying the resort's position as a premier destination. For discerning travelers and high rollers seeking an unrivaled culinary adventure, integrated resorts often feature Michelin-starred dining establishments. These restaurants, adorned with prestigious accolades, offer exquisite dining experiences that are both exclusive and unforgettable. For guests of Caesars Palace, the renowned Nobu restaurant is an integral part of the property's identity. Michelin-starred restaurants have become almost de rigueur for prestigious resorts, elevating the overall dining experience and aligning with the resort's image of luxury and exclusivity, much like Resorts World Sentosa in Singapore, featuring the Joël Robuchon Restaurant. Some resorts take the culinary experience a step further by partnering with renowned chefs or restaurateurs to curate bespoke dining experiences. These unique offerings, tailored specifically to the resort's location, theme, or target audience, add an extra layer of intrigue and exclusivity.

5. Development Partners

Construction and design companies bring multifaceted expertise to the table, their synergy extending far beyond optimizing a resort's design conceptualization and civil construction services.

Technical Knowledge: They possess in-depth knowledge of construction methodologies, materials, and building codes, ensuring projects meet all technical and regulatory requirements.

Project Management: They have extensive experience in planning, scheduling, budgeting, and managing complex construction projects, mitigating risks, and keeping projects on time and within budget.

Subcontractor and Supplier Relationships: They have established relationships with reliable subcontractors and suppliers, ensuring access to necessary resources and competitive pricing on materials and labor.

Construction Equipment: They may own or have access to a fleet of specialized construction equipment, reducing the need for expensive rentals and ensuring efficient execution of tasks.

Supply Chain Management: Their expertise in coordinating and managing the supply chain ensures timely delivery of materials and equipment, minimizing delays and disruptions.

By partnering with an experienced construction company, IR consortiums can leverage these synergies to reinforce the depth of the consortium and to have a reputable local partner on the team. In Japan's construction industry, Shimizu Corporation, Kajima Corporation, Obayashi Corporation, Takenaka Corporation, and Taisei Corporation are the major players, known for their landmark projects and engineering prowess. These giants actively lobby to influence government policies and infrastructure investments. Shimizu's century-long legacy and strategic alliances ensure its voice resonates in policy decisions. Obayashi's expertise in mega-projects is complemented by its adept navigation of regulatory complexities, forging close ties with government officials. Taisei, renowned for earthquake-resistant building techniques, actively engages policymakers and industry associations to shape policies that advance its business interests. Together, the five firms form the backbone of Japan's infrastructure development. Their symbiotic relationship with the government offers bidders a distinct advantage in the IR licensing sweepstakes, as they bring more than just their construction capabilities to a consortium and also unlock access to the corridors of power within the government.

Partners in an IR consortium bring diverse capacities and play distinct roles. For example, content partners are primarily brought in to enhance and broaden the experiential dimension of an integrated resort. These are more transient than the core offerings, serving as attractions that can be easily refreshed to maintain visitor interest. Content relationships are purely commercial and term-based, contrasting with the more enduring nature of core and strategic partnerships. While content partnerships naturally end after their contractual period, dissolving a core or strategic partnership is much trickier and messier, often resembling acrimonious divorces with prolonged legal battles and severe financial repercussions. Therefore, it is prudent to carefully vet and deliberate on the choice of a core or strategic partner, similar to choosing a spouse, as compatibility extends beyond mere agreement on terms to establishing rapport both on and off the negotiating table. Powerful personalities like Sheldon Adelson, Steve Wynn, and Kazuo Okada – known for their volatile nature – might not always collaborate easily. This is exemplified by the major rift between former partners Wynn and Okada, and the historical rivalry between Adelson and Wynn. Such acrimony is common, even among family-run businesses like Genting Group, which experienced several breakups, including the dissolution of joint ventures in South Korea and the Philippines.

A failed partnership in an integrated resort project, with its high capital investment and complex regulations, poses substantial risks and can have far-reaching repercussions on reputation and other business interests. To mitigate this risk, a rigorous 360-degree review of prospective partners is imperative. The gravity of this task cannot be overstated; every facet of a partnership should be thoroughly evaluated. One effective approach is the methodical vetting process based on the Balanced Scorecard framework. This widely-used framework translates an organization's vision and strategy into actionable objectives and measurable performance metrics across various perspectives. The IR Balanced Scorecard, specifically designed for this context, can assess prospective partners using a comprehensive set of financial and non-financial indicators, encompassing both qualitative and quantitative measures. By aligning objectives and measures across these perspectives, the IR Balanced Scorecard facilitates an unbiased evaluation, allowing an IR consortium to determine whether a partner possesses the requisite capabilities and compatibility to contribute to the project's long-term success...for better, not for poorer.

nineteen
THE "MATCHMAKER"

I first introduced the IR Balanced Scorecard methodology in my previous book, Japan Casino Uprising, which was published in 2022. This tool arose from witnessing the unsystematic approach employed by Japanese authorities and regional governments in evaluating the eligibility of IR consortiums. The private sector wasn't blameless either, with some consortiums formed haphazardly. This lack of rigor stemmed, in part, from the limited experience of many gaming companies in forming consortiums and the novelty of Japanese companies partnering with foreign entities. These factors collectively contributed to the stalling of the Japanese IR industry, resulting in only one successful consortium being chosen for the three available licenses. The last chapter underscored the vital importance of both a rigorous assessment when selecting business partners to form an integrated resort consortium and a comprehensive evaluation process when choosing the right consortium for an integrated resort development. Financial gain is a primary driver for member companies in an IR consortium, but their ideal fit extends beyond just financial metrics. Similarly, for governments awarding IR licenses, the selection process of a concessionaire extends far beyond purely economic considerations. They must carefully assess a wide range of social and political factors to identify the most suitable candidate for this high-stakes, multi-billion-dollar gamble. A mismatched partnership in this complex environment can have irreversible consequences, highlighting the need for thorough evaluation on all fronts.

Forming and assessing successful integrated resort consortiums demands a holistic approach that goes beyond a purely logical framework. Every tangible aspect, regardless of perceived significance, must be carefully evaluated. Making the right decision requires considering a multitude of interconnected variables, each with its own unique influence. The challenge lies in the heterogeneity of these variables. While some parameters can be addressed deterministically through factual analysis and historical precedent, others are inherently probabilistic, requiring a measured leap of faith based on expert insights and forward-looking analysis.

The Balanced Scorecard (BSC), a groundbreaking framework incorporating non-financial metrics into corporate strategic planning, was developed at Harvard University by David Norton and Robert Kaplan. Its success extended beyond the business domain, fostering adoption within the non-profit and governmental sectors. This adaptability solidified its value as a tool for deciphering the intricate landscape of integrated resorts. The BSC employs a four-perspective approach to monitor and measure organizational performance. The IR Balanced Scorecard (IR-BSC) adopts this framework, tailoring it to the specific factors and criteria in the IR development domain. Unlike the BSC's focus on evaluating past performance, the IR-BSC serves as a forward-looking analytical tool, balancing environmental variables against predefined goals for a new IR project. Governments can use the IR-BSC to establish a clear baseline. This can inform the development of IR masterplans and the creation of detailed tender specifications. Without such a structured approach, formulating IR development plans can be akin to an unguided, ineffective process. The IR-BSC mandates a comprehensive and rigorous process, ensuring all stakeholders' concerns are addressed, making it an indispensable tool for new jurisdictions embarking on a new IR industry. Within fledgling IR consortiums, the IR-BSC facilitates the identification of potential partners who possess complementary skillsets, share a common vision, and are aligned in their objectives. The tool extends its analysis beyond simply identifying strengths. It also conducts a critical examination of potential risks, including non-compliance with regulations, financial vulnerabilities, questionable past performance, inadequate governance structures, and any underlying cultural conflicts. Selecting IR partners goes beyond industry ranking. A successful approach considers factors like a company's specific expertise, experience with similar projects, and cultural fit.

The IR-BSC framework departs from traditional, financially-driven partner selection methods by incorporating a multifaceted partnership "equity" assessment. This comprehensive approach emphasizes a diverse range of parameters, extending beyond mere financial metrics. It fosters a balanced evaluation, aligning with the well-known proverb, "True wealth goes beyond material possessions." A prominent Japanese conglomerate discovered the true value of the IR-BSC when its application revealed a surprisingly different picture of the suitability of various casino operators for their IR consortium. By employing the IR-BSC, the conglomerate gained a nuanced understanding of all of its suitors, encompassing factors like operational expertise, cultural compatibility, and brand reputation.

This in-depth analysis proved invaluable, mitigating the known pitfalls associated with the Dunning-Kruger effect. The Dunning-Kruger effect refers to a cognitive bias where individuals with limited knowledge in a specific domain overestimate their expertise. The IR-BSC, through its comprehensive approach, acted as a safeguard against this bias, mitigating overconfidence and promoting informed partner selection.

The IR-BSC goes beyond simply profiling prospective partners by employing a comprehensive set of assessment parameters. It delves into both internal and external factors, encompassing both micro and macro elements. A crucial step involves assigning weighting factors to each parameter, reflecting its relative importance in determining partner suitability. These weights are ideally established through collaborative sprint workshops with diverse team members across departments.

The initial data collection stage is critical for the IR-BSC process. Data granularity directly impacts the accuracy of the final scores. This research phase involves gathering and organizing information into a central data pool used to populate the scorecard. Evaluating foreign casino operators presents a significant hurdle for the Japanese: the limited availability of information in Japanese. This language barrier acts as a major roadblock, significantly extending the data collection process. The lack of readily available information in the local language can tempt some to compromise on the comprehensiveness of their evaluation, potentially overlooking crucial details. Recognizing these specific challenges, I developed the IR-BSC (Integrated Resort Balanced Scorecard) specifically for the Japanese IR market. This framework functions as a comprehensive evaluation tool, structured around eight critical parameters:

1. Brand
2. Market
3. Financial
4. Solution
5. Political
6. Partnership
7. Eligibility
8. Legacy

Each parameter within the IR-BSC is further broken down into its intrinsic characteristics. Each of these characteristics is then individually scored based on its relevance to the partnership.

The second stage of the IR-BSC process involves a series of interactive workshops. During workshops, participants engage in discussions to determine the relative importance of each characteristic within a specific parameter. This collaborative effort ensures a comprehensive evaluation by considering various viewpoints. Following these discussions, participants assign proportionate weights to each characteristic, reflecting their significance within the parameter. To calculate a weighted score for each characteristic, the system multiplies its raw score by the weight factor assigned during the workshops. This weighted score reflects the importance of that specific characteristic within the overall assessment. Finally, the weighted scores for all characteristics within a parameter are aggregated and normalized to obtain the final parameter score.

Brand Parameter

The characteristics that comprise the Brand parameter are crucial elements that shape and distinguish a company's brand identity and perception in the marketplace. These characteristics serve as pillars upon which a brand's reputation, visibility, and success are built, influencing consumer behavior and brand loyalty. These characteristics encompass:

Brand Awareness: This measures how easily consumers can recognize a brand, even if they don't have detailed knowledge or experience with it.

Perceived Quality: A consumer's personal judgment on how good or exceptional a product or service is compared to its competitors. This judgment is influenced by factors like brand reputation, performance, features, and value for price.

Brand Association: The mental links and impressions consumers form about a brand. These associations can be positive, negative, or neutral, and are influenced by various factors like product features, benefits, evoked emotions, brand values, and personal experiences.

Brand Loyalty: A customer's tendency to consistently choose a specific brand within a product category over competitors. This behavior stems from a combination of factors like positive experiences, satisfaction, emotional connection, or perceived value.

Brand Assets: The tangible and intangible resources owned by a brand that contribute to its unique identity, market position, and overall value. These assets encompass elements like intellectual property (trademarks, patents), reputation, customer base, and brand equity.

Several Las Vegas gaming brands exemplify companies scoring highly on many of the listed brand characteristics. Their brand awareness is substantial, with Las Vegas Sands achieving global recognition due to the success of Marina Bay Sands in Singapore and their Venetian resorts.

Wynn, known for its premium offerings, resonates strongly in the luxury gaming space. Sands, in particular, fosters strong customer loyalty through consistent quality across their properties. Caesars Entertainment, with its diverse brand assets, possesses the versatility to cater to different markets and customer demographics. However, Macau casino brands remain heavily associated with gambling due to the market's historical focus. While they offer diverse amenities, these only marginally soften the image. The Macau government actively seeks to address this perception by incorporating non-gaming development requirements within renewed casino concessions, aiming to diversify offerings and move beyond the enclave's legacy "gritty casino" image.

Market Parameter

This metric assesses a company's commitment to a specific market, evaluating both their investment in building relationships and establishing a local presence, as well as their capacity to successfully develop the market. The IR-BSC further extrapolates this parameter into five salient characteristics:

Operational Experience: This refers to the company's experience in conducting and managing business activities within the local market. Not all operators start fresh in a new jurisdiction. Seminole Hard Rock, for example, leveraged its over 30 years of experience in Japan, even though it wasn't directly in the gaming sector. Similarly, some gaming companies might have marketing offices in a region, catering to local clientele for their properties elsewhere. This existing presence demonstrates a level of familiarity with the market and can be a stepping stone for further ventures. Establishing a consortium with a reputable local company is a strategic way to quickly gain local operating experience and market insights.

Client Experience: This focuses on the company's knowledge of local customer preferences and cultural nuances, gained through serving and marketing to customers in the region.

Time Invested: This reflects the duration of the company's active involvement in the specific jurisdiction.

Resource Investment: This measures the strength and capability of the company's local team.

Delivery Capacity: This evaluates the company's readiness and accessibility of resources to meet the requirements of developing and operating an integrated resort.

The first two characteristics signify a company's comprehensive market experience within a specific jurisdiction or region. For instance, Genting's long history in the Southeast Asian market provides them with a substantial advantage. This grants them a "home ground" edge in the race for the two Singapore IR licenses. In contrast, American operators, apart from those holding concessions in Macau, typically have limited market knowledge, often being restricted to the sales territories where they maintain some presence with sales and marketing offices

However, Asia is not a homogenous region, and in insular Japan, Asian operators may not fare better than Western companies, as demonstrated by the success of MGM Resorts in clinching the only IR license in Japan. But MGM's success was also due to their dedication to devoting considerable time and resources in Japan over the lengthy gestation period of the gaming legislative process.

The final characteristic illustrates the extent of a company's financial and human resources, indicating its capability to manage both current and future development projects. While it is easy to present a flawless facade during a bidding war, this does not guarantee a company's ability to fulfill its commitments. Even Las Vegas Sands had faced a delivery hiccup halfway through the construction period of Marina Bay Sands. This highlights that no company is immune to such problems.

Financial Parameter

While a company's profitability is important, it's not the sole indicator of financial health. The IR-BSC probes deeper, analyzing six key financial ratios and metrics to yield a comprehensive assessment of a company's financial well-being. This approach ensures a better understanding of a company's ability to finance and manage complex integrated resort projects.

Revenue: The total income generated by a company from its normal business operations.

EBITDA: Stands for Earnings Before Interest, Taxes, Depreciation, and Amortization. It is a measure of a company's operating performance, calculated by adding back interest, taxes, depreciation, and amortization expenses to net income.

Debt: The amount of money that a company owes to creditors. It includes loans, bonds, and other financial obligations that must be repaid over time.

Debt-to-Equity Ratio: A financial ratio that compares a company's total debt to its shareholders' equity. It is calculated by dividing total debt by shareholders' equity and is used to evaluate a company's financial leverage and risk.

Financial Leverage: Refers to the use of debt to increase the return on investment. It allows a company to finance its operations with borrowed funds, which can amplify profits but also increase the risk of financial distress if not managed properly.

Interest Coverage: A ratio that measures a company's ability to pay interest expenses on its outstanding debt. It is calculated by dividing a company's earnings before interest and taxes (EBIT) by its interest expenses. A higher interest coverage ratio indicates a company's ability to meet its interest obligations comfortably.

Enterprises like Seminole Hard Rock and the Genting Group stand out with robust liquidity, dwarfing the debt-heavy profile of American counterparts such as Caesars Entertainment, Las Vegas Sands, MGM Resorts, and Wynn Resorts, each grappling with long-term debts exceeding $10 billion. However, a company's financial strength should not be measured purely on its debt burden and it's important to analyze its ability to manage this debt. Analyzing ratios further illuminates financial health; for instance, Sands and MGM exhibit stronger debt-servicing capacity with interest coverage ratios between 4 and 5, in contrast to Caesars and Wynn hovering at 1 or lower. Genting Hong Kong's downfall, fueled by a nearly 80% debt-to-equity ratio, stands as a stark reminder of the systemic risks associated with unchecked financial imbalances. Wynn Resorts has negative shareholder equity, which means they owe more to creditors than their assets are worth. This is likely due to a combination of borrowing money and paying out dividends to shareholders. However, they still appear financially stable because they have a good amount of working capital (cash readily available) and strong earnings before interest, taxes, depreciation, and amortization (EBITDA). This strong cash flow helps them cover their debt obligations and allows them to invest in the company's future.

Solution Parameter

The Solution parameter serves as the benchmark for meeting the comprehensive criteria outlined in a legislative framework for integrated resorts. For instance, the Singaporean government delineated four primary criteria in the Request for Proposals for its two integrated resorts, assigning varying weight factors to the criteria for each site.

Criteria	Marina Bay	Sentosa
Tourism appeal and contribution	40%	45%
Level of development investment	30%	25%
Architectural design and concept excellence	20%	20%
Strength of consortium and track record	10%	10%

Japan had similarly outlined four general objectives for its integrated resort vision:

1. Delivering world-class entertainment experiences.
2. Providing premium facilities for Meetings, Incentives, Conferences, and Exhibitions (MICE).
3. Offering a variety of accommodation options.
4. Functioning as gateways to attract tourism to Japan as a whole.

However, the Japanese government had not disclosed the relative weighting of these criteria in the bidding process. This lack of transparency hindered bidders from fully understanding the relative importance of each objective.

Political Parameter

This parameter assesses the potential political risks and benefits a company faces based on its political affiliations and lobbying activities. It considers both the advantages gained from political influence and the potential drawbacks. The significance of this parameter varies based on the extent to which local or geopolitical factors influence decisions regarding the legalization of casino gambling and the selection of operators, which varies across different regions. In jurisdictions with transparent and unbiased selection processes, such as Singapore, political sway is minimal.

Conversely, countries like Japan and Thailand are heavily influenced by politics, with the political aspect carrying substantial weight. Foreign policy considerations are especially important in Japan, where a company's country of origin can significantly affect its success. Any political influence, whether positive or negative, linked to a company and its activities necessitates thorough scrutiny and evaluation. The intricate nature of the political landscape in Japan prompted the IR-BSC to devise six characteristics for a comprehensive analysis of the political parameter:

Pre-award: This characteristic examines the political landscape before a project is awarded, considering factors like government stability and the impact of any changes in regulations.

Decision: This characteristic focuses on the decision-making process for awarding IR licenses, including the level of transparency and extent of political influence.

Operations: This characteristic evaluates any political factors that may impact the business operations of an IR, such as regulatory changes or public opposition.

National polity: This characteristic analyzes the national political environment and its pre- and post-legislation impact on the IR plans.

Prefectural polity: This characteristic assesses the political landscape at the regional level, considering the influence of local governments.

Municipal polity: This characteristic evaluates the political environment at the city or town level, where the IR is planned to be located.

Partnership Parameter

Just like a perfect match on paper doesn't guarantee a successful relationship, a company meeting all the desired quantitative criteria (financial wherewithal, industry experience, IR-BSC scores) might still fall short. This is because quantitative factors don't fully capture the crucial qualitative element of shared vision and alignment. Imagine a matchmaking scenario where two individuals match perfectly on their profiles but lack any chemistry in person. Similarly, a potential partner might seem ideal on paper, but in-person interactions could reveal mismatched priorities or incompatible operating styles. Therefore, direct face-to-face engagement with prospective partners is an indispensable aspect of assessing mutual compatibility. This process moves beyond financial metrics to examine shared values, goals, and potential areas of conflict. By engaging in open and transparent dialogue, a company can ensure they're not just choosing a partner on paper, but also a true collaborator with whom they can achieve shared success.

The IR-BSC framework empowers a systematic approach to evaluating an entity's suitability for partnerships which is particularly critical when choosing core partners.

It achieves this by analyzing past collaborative efforts, compatibility in management styles, and alignment of organizational structures. This assessment hinges on the following key characteristics:

Partnership Experience: Experience in navigating business collaborations in the jurisdiction in question and diverse cultural and business environments.

Success Record: Past collaboration history indicates a company's capability to manage partnerships effectively.

Business Philosophy: Alignment in core values, work ethic, and decision-making styles.

Partnership Structure: Level of flexibility in discussing and negotiating partnership structure and responsibilities.

The gaming industry's history of failed core partnerships underscores the importance of careful partner selection. Cases like Las Vegas Sands and Galaxy Entertainment's dissolved Macau partnership, or Genting Singapore and Landing International's failed South Korean venture, highlight the risks involved. The high-profile breakups between Steve Wynn and Kazuo Okada, or the dissolution of Lawrence Ho and James Packer's Macau venture further emphasize these potential pitfalls.

Eligibility Parameter

The stereotype of the casino industry as a haven for crime and vice is outdated and inaccurate. In reality, the industry is subject to extensive regulations that ensure responsible operations and prioritize public safety. These regulations can, in some aspects, be even more rigorous than those governing the financial services market. Nevada, New Jersey, and Singapore are globally recognized for their stringent regulatory frameworks in the gaming industry. These frameworks entail thorough licensing procedures, involving careful due diligence on all stakeholders, ranging from shareholders and executives to frontline staff. Operating companies and their affiliates must adhere to strict standards of integrity and compliance to retain their licenses. Hence, it is crucial to conduct thorough investigations when selecting a business partner to ensure they comply with the regulatory requirements of the jurisdiction, encompassing the company itself and its key office holders:

Company: Financial stability, reputation, licensing history, compliance programs.

Shareholders: Background checks, financial interests, potential conflicts of interest.

Executives: Experience, qualifications, integrity checks, regulatory compliance history.

Legacy Parameter

When evaluating a potential business partner, the legacy parameter scrutinizes both its succession planning and the company's historical record, crucial factors for fostering long-lasting partnerships. A robust succession plan signifies proactive measures to ensure stability and continuity amid leadership transitions, instilling confidence in partners reliant on sustained commitments. A well-defined succession plan is key to minimizing risks from personnel changes, especially in an industry like gaming, where leadership transitions in major companies are frequent.

Understanding a company's legacy offers insights into its values, culture, and overarching vision, which are foundational for establishing well-aligned partnerships. A positive legacy reflects reliability, integrity, and past successes, attributes that partners seek for mutual growth and success. Mergers and acquisitions create a volatile industry landscape. They disrupt succession plans and dilute legacies as companies grapple with unpredictable restructuring and cultural integration. These dynamics introduce uncertainty, particularly regarding leadership continuity and strategic direction, potentially impacting existing partnerships. The IR-BSC evaluates the legacy question by examining three primary characteristics:

Leadership Succession: This aspect assesses whether the company has a comprehensive plan in place to ensure smooth transitions in leadership roles.

Mergers and Acquisitions: Evaluating a company's history of mergers and acquisitions is important, considering how its broader strategic direction through these deals might affect its legacy and existing business partnerships.

Gaming vs. Entertainment: This characteristic focuses on distinguishing gaming activities as a form of entertainment from their role within the broader casino industry, especially in the context of the integrated resort model.

All parameter scores can then be populated into a dedicated Excel spreadsheet and assigned weights according to their relative importance. The sum average of the weighted scores produces the assessed company's IR-BSC score.

The IR-BSC tool's in-depth methodology leads to unique and distinct conclusions for each user – conclusions that wouldn't be revealed by a superficial analysis. This means two different companies are likely to arrive at different results when evaluating the same potential

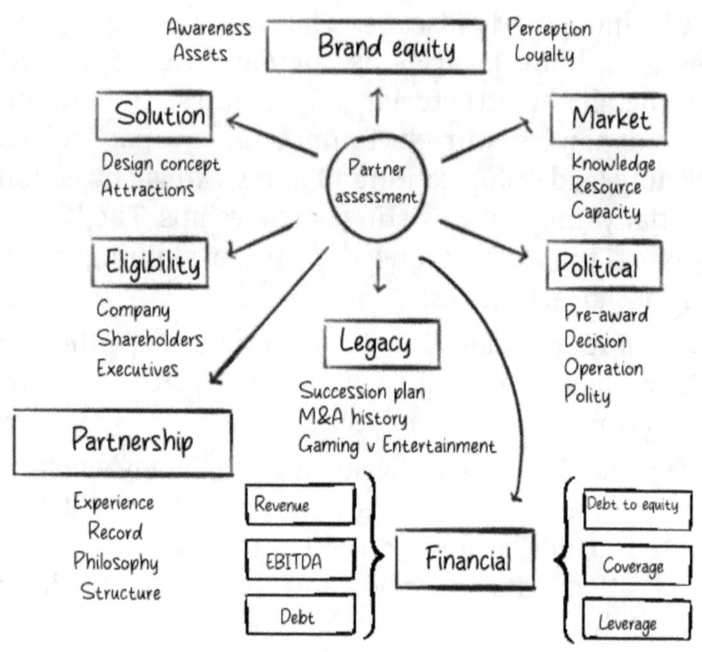

IR Balanced Scorecard

Model for Japan consortium partner selection

partner, as the scoring and weighting process considers the appraising company's own perspective. Interestingly, the IR-BSC can also be used for self-assessment, allowing companies to evaluate their suitability and attractiveness as partners. Compared to traditional evaluation methods, the IR-BSC tool can deliver surprisingly different outcomes. Its parametric model synthesizes diverse data into a manageable format, clearly outlining each criterion. Ultimately, the IR-BSC serves as a data-driven and transparent rubric, guiding investors toward ideal partners for their business ventures and jurisdictions seeking the most suitable integrated resort solution.

INDEX

A

Absolute Poker. *See* online
gambling
accessibility, 33, 76, 77, 82, 87, 88,
91, 93, 96, 102, 103, 104, 116,
123, 145, 170, 176, 204, 239,
267
connectivity, 58, 77, 79, 83, 87,
91, 94, 97, 102, 103, 148,
200, 201
Acres, 137
Acropolis. *See* museum
addiction, 25, 96, 143, 189, 221,
222, 224, 226, 227, 230
addictive, 96, 235
early intervention, 189
rehabilitation, 189
Adele, 126
Alain Ducasse. *See* Michelin
Alexander Osterwalder. *See*
Harvard
Aloft. *See* Marriott
Alvin Chau. *See* SunCity
Aman Resorts, 182
Amanpuri, 186
American Gaming Association,
151
AMLA. *See* money laundering
Andaz. *See* Hyatt
Andrew Lloyd Webber, 252
Anthony Bourdain. *See* Michelin
Aomi. *See* Japan
Apollo Global, 5
Apple, 40
architecture, 36, 121, 122, 127,
180, 191, 238, 240

Aria. *See* CityCenter
artificial land. *See* reclamation
ArtScience Museum. *See* museum
Atlantis, 112
augmented reality, 158, 174
Australia, 11, 99, 195
authentic, 118, 144, 169, 191,
192
Authenticity, 169
Autograph Collection. *See*
Marriott
average daily rate, 244
Ayutthaya. *See* Thailand

B

Baby Boomers, 137
baccarat. *See* casino games
Background checks. *See* due
diligence
Bahamas, 97, 112
Bally, 137
Bangkok. *See* Thailand
Banyan Tree, 182, 212
Barriere Group, 141
Beckham, 176
Beijing, 52, 114, 136
Bellagio. *See* MGM Resorts
Beppu. *See* Japan
Bergin Inquiry, 12
BetMGM. *See* MGM Resorts
big data, 137
Black Friday. *See* online gambling
Blackstone, 5, 162, 215
Merlin Entertainment, 162
bleisure, 209
Blue Man Group, 165
Boat Quay Hotel, 217

Bob Igor. *See* Disney
Boyd Gaming, 112
brand identity, 43, 200, 252, 254, 264
    brand image, 43, 212, 217
Bruno Mars, 124, 175
bus programs, 137, 147, 196

C

Caesars, 24, 38, 41, 46, 111, 139, 144, 154, 165, 184, 215, 247, 266, 269
    Caesars Palace, 39, 41, 126, 128, 193, 240, 255
    Caesars Rewards, 135
    Eldorado Resorts, 112, 128
    Forum Shops, 193
    Harrah's, 140, 165
    Horseshoe, 128, 140
    LINQ, 154, 155
    Park Place, 41
    Silver Legacy, 140
Cambodia, 26, 59, 97, 99, 135
    Phnom Penh, 53
carbon. *See* ESG
Casino Austria, 141
Casino Control Act. *See* Singapore
casino games, 153, 157
    baccarat, 152, 154
    Electronic table games, 153
    Linked progressive jackpots, 137
    Multiplayer, 153
    table games, 69, 137, 148, 154, 155
C-beauty, 185
    Colorkey, 185
    Perfect Diary, 185
    Winona, 185
Celine Dion, 124
Chakri Dynasty. *See* Thailand
Changi International Airport. *See* Singapore
Charlie and the Chocolate Factory, 166
Chiang Mai. *See* Thailand

China, 23, 26, 42, 51, 52, 59, 72, 96, 98, 114, 115, 136, 163, 165, 176, 185
    Guangdong, 51, 53, 202
    Hengqin Island, 114
    Zhuhai, 165, 202
Chiva-Som, 186
Cirque du Soleil, 65, 158, 165, 167, 175, 178, 254
    'O', 65, 167
    Mystère, 167
City of Dreams Macau. *See* Melco Entertainment
City of Dreams Manila. *See* Melco Entertainment
CityCenter, 112, 215
    Aria, 215
civil society, 13, 221, 222, 226, 228
    civic groups, 224
Clark. *See* Philippines
Clay Christensen. *See* Harvard
Club Med, 110, 111, 112
cluster, 51, 55, 57, 97, 204
Coachella, 216
collectivistic, 85
Coloane. *See* Macau
Colorkey. *See* C-beauty
COMDEX, 205
Comexposium, 201
community engagement, 76, 84, 227
Como, 128
Connecticut, 24, 149
connectivity. *See* accessibility
Conor McGregor. *See* UFC
Conrad. *See* Hilton
corruption, 2, 15, 98, 108, 132, 226
Cotai. *See* Macau
COVID-19. *See* pandemic
Creative Technology, 43
Cryptologic. *See* online gambling
Cyprus, 47

D

Danang. *See* Vietnam
David Norton. *See* Harvard
David Thompson. *See* Michelin
Delaware, 149
Disney, 127, 161
  Bob Igor, 162
  ESPN, 162
  Lion King, 159
  Lucasfilm, 161
  Star Wars, 161
Dominican Republic, 112
Don King, 125
Don Mueang. *See* Thailand
due diligence, 6, 15, 21, 107, 132,
  248, 274
  Background checks, 274
Dunes, 39
Dunning-Kruger effect, 263
duopoly. *See* oligopoly

E

early intervention. *See* addiction
Eastern Economic Corridor. *See*
  Thailand
Echelon Place, 112
Eco-Floating Hotel, 218
economic rejuvenation, 6, 33, 56
  gentrification, 115
  revitalization, 5, 28, 87, 93,
    101, 106, 115, 118
El Rancho, 112
Eldorado Resorts. *See* Caesars
Electronic table games. *See*
  casino games
Encore Las Vegas. *See* Wynn
  Resorts
Engelbert Humperdinck, 166
Entertainment City. *See*
  Philippines
entertainment complex. *See*
  Thailand
entry fee (casino), 34, 135, 224
  minimum age, 34, 73

environmental, 11, 13, 76, 77, 82,
  83, 88, 95, 103, 105, 144, 208,
  239, 254, 261
escrow accounts, 14
ESG, 208
  carbon, 95, 208
  Renewable Energy
    Certificates, 208
ESPN. *See* Disney
eSports, 175
experiential, 66, 124, 183, 257
exurban. *See* rural

F

Families Against the Casino
  Threat. *See* Singapore
Fashion Show Mall, 193
Fertittas. *See* Red Rock Resorts
Financial Action Task Force, 23,
  98, 142
  FATF, 23, 98
Flamingo, 39
Florida, 7, 9, 161, 177
  Miami, 179
Floyd Mayweather, 126
foreigner-only casinos, 226
Forest of Mirrors, 159
Formula 1, 28, 177, 178, 200,
  204, 252
  Miami Grand Prix, 178
  Red Bull F1, 178
  Singapore Formula 1, 234
  Suzuka Circuit, 178
Forum Shops. *See* Caesars
Four Seasons, 213, 217
Foxwoods, 141
Fukuoka. *See* Japan
Full Tilt Poker. *See* online
  gambling
Fumiko Hayashi, 7
functional, 76, 124, 206, 215

G

Galaxy Entertainment, 24, 42, 46,
  47, 133, 136, 140, 273

Galaxy Arena, 176
Galaxy Macau, 183, 205, 212
GamingPlay, 157
Gardens by the Bay. *See* Singapore
Genting Group, 4, 39, 42, 46, 55, 65, 66, 114, 134, 136, 137, 140, 152, 161, 166, 194, 250, 258, 267, 269
    Genting Hong Kong, 269
    Lim Keong Hui, 66, 129
    Malaysian Food Street, 191
    Resorts World brand, 42, 46, 129
    Resorts World Genting, 55, 59, 112, 210, 214
    Resorts World Las Vegas, 157
    Resorts World Sentosa, 46, 50, 59, 79, 134, 138, 148, 160, 191, 207, 214, 229, 234, 235, 241, 255
    Star Cruises, 43
Genting Highlands. *See* Malaysia
gentrification. *See* economic rejuvenation
Global Wellness Institute, 184
Golden Nugget, 39
Gordon Ramsay. *See* Michelin
Grand Canal Shoppes. *See* Las Vegas Sands
Groupe Partouche, 141
Guangdong. *See* China
Guggenheim. *See* museum

H

Hakkasan, 129
Hallyu. *See* soft power
Hamilton. *See* Lin-Manuel Miranda
Hanover Messe, 198
Hard Rock, 9, 24, 38, 65, 125, 134, 144, 177, 179, 266, 269
    Hard Rock Live, 134, 140
    Hard Rock Punta Cana, 112
    Hard Rock Stadium, 178, 179
Harrah's. *See* Caesars

Harry Potter World, 162
Harvard, 145, 261
    Alexander Osterwalder, 145
    Clay Christensen, 145
    David Norton, 261
    Robert Kaplan, 261
Hengqin Island. *See* China
high-rollers, 24, 89
high-speed rail, 87, 101, 102
Hilton, 182, 211, 212, 216, 218
    Conrad, 213
    Tempo, 182
Hoiana, 89, 99
Hokkaido. *See* Japan
holographic, 154, 207
Horseshoe. *See* Caesars
House of Nod, 159
Hua Hin. *See* Thailand
Hunger Games. *See* Lionsgate
Hyatt, 182, 211, 212
    Andaz, 212
    Zoëtry, 182
HyperX Arena. *See* Luxor

I

I.M. Pei, 79
Icon Siam, 191
IHG, 212
Inclusivity, 145
Indochina, 38, 139
Inspire Entertainment Resort. *See* Mohegan Gaming
iPort. *See* Thinkwell
IR Balanced Scorecard, 48, 258, 260, 261
    IR-BSC, 261, 262, 263, 264, 266, 268, 271, 272, 275, 276, 277

J

James Cameron, 165
James Murren, 215
James Packer, 273
Japan
    Aomi, 118

Beppu, 184
Fukuoka, 25, 83
Hokkaido, 9, 25, 33, 83, 95, 104, 116, 177, 178, 192, 203, 223, 250
IR Basic Policy, 35, 169
IR Bill, 6, 10, 12, 15, 25, 28, 33, 35
Japan MICE Association, 203
Japan National Tourism Organization, 184
Kabuki, 170, 171
Koto, 118
Marina City, 83
Meiji Restoration, 163
Misugi, 184
Nagasaki, 74, 75, 83, 94, 116, 223, 225, 247, 248
Nagoya, 25
New Chitose International Airport, 94
Odaiba, 118
Osaka, 15, 24, 32, 45, 54, 69, 70, 71, 73, 82, 83, 84, 89, 94, 95, 100, 116, 130, 145, 159, 171, 174, 177, 184, 203, 223, 225, 229, 235, 236, 239, 240, 242
Osaka Commerce University, 3
Osaka Expo, 95
Sasebo, 83, 94
Tokyo, 25, 33, 83, 118, 119, 155, 161, 162, 223
Tomakomai, 83, 94
Wakayama, 83, 84, 97, 223, 225, 248
Yokohama, 4, 7, 13, 46, 83, 84, 116, 123, 223, 224, 225, 228, 239
Yumeshima, 94, 225, 239
Japan Casino Uprising, 260
J-beauty, 185
Kanebo, 184
MT Metatron, 185
ReFa, 185
Shiseido, 184
Sunohada, 185
Three Cosmetics, 185
Jeju. *See* Korea
Jersey Boys, 159
Jimmy Kimmel, 154
Joël Robuchon. *See* Michelin
junk bond, 4
junket. *See* VIP room

K

Kajima, 257
Kamalaya, 186
Kanebo. *See* J-beauty
Kangwon Land, 33, 96, 226
K-beauty, 184
K-cosmetics, 185
Keihan Railways, 240
Khon Kaen. *See* Thailand
Kimono Roboto. *See* Melco Entertainment
Kinmen. *See* Taiwan
Koh Samui. *See* Thailand
Koh Yao. *See* Thailand
Korea
Jeju, 247
Myeong-dong, 186
Korean Wave. *See* soft power
Koto. *See* Japan
Krabi. *See* Thailand

L

Laguna Lang Co, 112
Laguna Phuket, 188
Landing International, 273
Las Vegas
Las Vegas Strip, 51, 57
Nevada, 22, 46, 111, 125, 149, 151, 273
Las Vegas Sands, 3, 14, 18, 24, 38, 41, 43, 45, 72, 89, 96, 114, 128, 134, 136, 138, 139, 165, 176, 195, 204, 205, 211, 212, 246, 250, 265, 268, 269, 273
Grand Canal Shoppes, 193
Londoner Macao, 176

Marina Bay Sands, 14, 18, 44,
    50, 51, 59, 62, 79, 94, 95,
    121, 122, 127, 128, 130,
    140, 148, 157, 166, 173,
    177, 183, 190, 193, 194,
    199, 206, 207, 208, 211,
    214, 229, 234, 235, 240,
    246, 265, 268
  Paiza Club, 45
  Palazzo, 211
  Parisian Macau, 122
  Sands China, 44, 46
  Sands Expo, 206
  Sheldon Adelson, 20, 39, 41,
    65, 89, 246, 258
  Venetian, 39, 65, 128, 129,
    148, 193, 211, 240, 265
Lawrence Ho. *See* Melco
  Entertainment
Lee Hsien Loong, 232
Liberace, 124, 165
Liberal Democratic Party, 225,
  226
Light & Wonder, 137
Lim Keong Hui. *See* Genting
  Group
Linked progressive jackpots. *See*
  casino games
Lin-Manuel Miranda, 166, 252
  Hamilton, 166
LINQ. *See* Caesars
Lion King. *See* Disney
Lionsgate, 165
  Hunger Games, 165
  Twilight, 165
Lisboa. *See* SJM
live streaming, 152, 208
Londoner Macao. *See* Las Vegas
  Sands
Louvre. *See* museum
Lucasfilm. *See* Disney
Luxor, 175
  HyperX Arena, 175

M

Macau

Coloane, 80
  Cotai, 51, 80, 81, 113
  Cotai Strip, 51, 55, 58, 80, 81,
    127
  Macau Grand Prix, 175
  Pearl River Delta, 122
  Taipa, 80
Madame Tussaud's, 159
Malaysia, 53, 66, 140, 166, 194,
  210
  Genting Highlands, 46, 55, 59,
    137
Malaysian Food Street. *See*
  Genting Group
Manny Pacquiao, 126
Marcos, 23, 98, 142
Marina Bay Sands. *See* Las Vegas
  Sands
Marina City. *See* Japan
Marquee, 129, 178
Marriott, 212, 216
  Aloft, 216
  Autograph Collection, 216
  Ritz-Carlton, 212
  Sheraton, 213
  St. Regis, 213
Marvin Hagler, 126
Matsu. *See* Taiwan
McKinsey, 184
medical tourism, 145, 183, 187,
  188
Meiji Restoration. *See* Japan
Melco Entertainment, 42, 46, 47,
  66, 112, 133, 136, 155
  City of Dreams Macau, 212
  City of Dreams Manila, 123,
    151
  Kimono Roboto, 155
  Lawrence Ho, 66, 155, 273
Merlin Entertainment. *See*
  Blackstone
MGM Resorts, 8, 15, 24, 38, 43,
    45, 65, 89, 130, 134, 136, 156,
    171, 174, 177, 215, 235, 239,
    267, 269
  Bellagio, 39, 123, 128, 148,
    167, 240

BetMGM, 156
MGM Osaka, 45
MGM Resorts Osaka, 177
MGM Rewards, 156, 157
mySTRIP, 156
myVEGAS, 156
Miami Grand Prix. *See* Formula 1
MICE, 28, 29, 58, 134, 135, 136,
  140, 198, 199, 200, 201, 202,
  203, 204, 205, 206, 207, 208,
  209, 235, 238, 270
Michelin, 118, 191, 255
  Alain Ducasse, 128
  Anthony Bourdain, 128
  David Thompson, 128
  Gordon Ramsay, 128, 129
  Joël Robuchon, 255
Michigan, 149
Microgaming. *See* online
  gambling
millennials, 137, 140, 166
minimum age. *See* entry fee
  (casino)
Misugi. *See* Japan
Mitsui Fudosan Group, 194
Mohegan Gaming, 24, 141
  Inspire Entertainment Resort,
    162, 170, 185
MoMA. *See* museum
Money laundering, 12, 23, 25, 53,
  89, 98, 132, 141, 142, 149,
  152, 231, 235, 248
  AMLA, 11, 98
monopoly. *See* oligopoly
Moshe Safdie, 121
MSG Sphere, 111
MT Metatron. *See* J-beauty
Multiplayer. *See* casino games
multiplier effect, 29
museum, 160, 164, 169, 172, 173,
  174
  Acropolis, 172
  ArtScience Museum, 173, 174
  Guggenheim, 62, 172, 174, 252
  Louvre, 62, 121, 172
  MoMA, 175

National Museum of China,
  172
  Smithsonian Institution, 172
Myeong-dong. *See* Korea
Mystère. *See* Cirque du Soleil
mySTRIP. *See* MGM Resorts
myVEGAS. *See* MGM Resorts

N

Nagacorp, 48
Nagasaki. *See* Japan
Nagoya. *See* Japan
nahm, 128
Nakhon Ratchasima. *See* Thailand
National Council on Problem
  Gambling. *See* Singapore
National Museum of China. *See*
  museum
Native American, 7, 24, 92
NBA Summer League, 175
net contribution per player visit,
  244
Nevada. *See* Las Vegas
New Chitose International
  Airport. *See* Japan
New York, 4, 215
New York Yankees, 177
Nobu, 255
Norwegian Cruise Lines, 144

O

O2O2O, 207
Obayashi, 4, 257
Odaiba. *See* Japan
Okada, 258, 273
Okada Manila, 123
Okura, 212
oligopoly, 50, 54, 236
  duopoly, 21, 50, 113, 114, 232,
    235
  monopoly, 7, 11, 50, 53, 54, 55,
    59, 96, 113, 133, 161, 236
Omni, 129
online gambling, 23, 149, 150,
  151

Absolute Poker, 149
Black Friday, 149
Cryptologic, 148
Full Tilt Poker, 149
Microgaming, 148
online casino, 97, 156
online operators, 97, 149, 150
PartyGaming, 149
PIGO, 97, 150, 151
Pinnacle Sports, 149
POGO, 98, 151
Pokerstars, 149
UIGEA, 149
Wire Act, 149
Orbital Assembly, 218
ORIX, 4, 8, 15, 32, 54, 177, 235
Osaka. *See* Japan
Osaka Commerce University. *See* Japan
Osaka Expo. *See* Japan
outlet mall, 194

P

PAGCOR. *See* Philippines
Paiza Club. *See* Las Vegas Sands
Palazzo. *See* Las Vegas Sands
pandemic, 70, 113, 144, 193, 207, 224
    COVID-19, 70, 113, 144, 193, 202, 207, 224
Paramount, 162
Parisian Macau. *See* Las Vegas Sands
Park Place. *See* Caesars
PartyGaming. *See* online gambling
Pattaya. *See* Thailand
PayPal, 157
Pearl River Delta. *See* Macau
Penghu. *See* Taiwan
Penn Entertainment, 162
Pennsylvania, 149
Perfect Diary. *See* C-beauty
personalize, 138
PGA Tour, 216
Phangnga. *See* Thailand

Philippines, 21, 22, 23, 30, 38, 40, 46, 53, 59, 81, 82, 85, 91, 92, 93, 97, 98, 99, 107, 116, 135, 136, 139, 142, 150, 151, 152, 193, 229, 247, 251, 258
    Clark, 93
    Entertainment City, 38, 81, 82, 86, 91, 92, 97
    PAGCOR, 22, 23, 92, 98
Phnom Penh. *See* Cambodia
Phuket. *See* Thailand
PIGO. *See* online gambling
Pinnacle Sports. *See* online gambling
plebiscite. *See* referendum
POGO. *See* online gambling
Pokerstars. *See* online gambling
political factors, 260, 271
political landscape, 85, 227, 271, 272
political shifts, 72, 226
Populous, 180
pop-up, 216, 217
probity, 142, 236, 248, 249
Proto, 154
Proxy gambling, 22, 152
Puy du Fou, 162

Q

Qatar, 218
Qiddiya. *See* Saudi Arabia
Queens Wharf Brisbane, 195

R

racino, 4
Raffles, 212, 255
Rajamangala National Stadium. *See* Thailand
Rayong. *See* Thailand
reclamation, 79, 82
    artificial land, 95
    reclaimed, 80, 81, 91, 94, 118, 122, 240
Red Bull F1. *See* Formula 1
Red Rock Resorts, 126

Fertittas, 126
ReFa. *See* J-beauty
referendum, 84, 86, 161, 224,
 225, 229
 plebiscite, 84, 224
rehabilitation. *See* addiction
REIT, 5, 215
 VICI Properties, 215
religious, 13, 86, 88, 198, 220,
 221, 239
Renewable Energy Certificates.
 See ESG
Request for Concepts, 6, 63, 249
Request for Proposals, 237, 270
Resorts World Genting. *See*
 Genting Group
Resorts World Las Vegas. *See*
 Genting Group
Resorts World Sentosa. *See*
 Genting Group
responsible gambling, 34, 96,
 143, 189, 230, 236, 238
 responsible gaming, 53, 108,
 138, 139, 143, 155, 157,
 232, 235, 245
revenue per available room, 244
revenue per gaming position, 244
revitalization. *See* economic
 rejuvenation
ring study, 73
Ritz-Carlton. *See* Marriott
Robert Kaplan. *See* Harvard
Rod Stewart, 126
Rodrigo Duterte, 23
rural, 33, 56, 57, 58, 82, 113, 115,
 116
 exurban, 94, 101, 102, 104,
 106, 116, 119, 165, 184,
 186, 190, 192, 194, 205

S

Salina Turda, 164
Sands China. *See* Las Vegas Sands
Sands Expo. *See* Las Vegas Sands
Saraburi. *See* Thailand
Sasebo. *See* Japan

Saudi Arabia, 180
 Qiddiya, 179, 180
SeaWorld, 162
segmentation, 138, 139, 214
Seminole Tribe of Florida, 9, 24,
 38, 66, 134, 161, 179, 266, 269
Sentosa. *See* Singapore
Sheldon Adelson. *See* Las Vegas
 Sands
Sheraton. *See* Marriott
Shimizu, 257
Shinzo Abe, 169
Shiseido. *See* J-beauty
Siegfried and Roy, 124
Silver Legacy. *See* Caesars
Simon Property, 194
Simone Legno, 217
 tokidoki, 217
Sinatra, 124, 165
Singapore
 Casino Control Act, 12
 Changi International Airport,
 80
 Families Against the Casino
 Threat, 221
 Gardens by the Bay, 234
 National Council on Problem
 Gambling, 221
 National Master Plan, 77
 Sentosa, 14, 50, 78, 80, 161,
 169, 203, 234, 237, 270
 Singapore EXPO, 204
 Southern Islands, 78, 79
Singapore Formula 1. *See*
 Formula 1
Six Flags, 162
Six Senses, 182
SJM, 42, 55, 65
 Lisboa, 42, 123
 Stanley Ho, 66, 176, 213
Smithsonian Institution. *See*
 museum
social fabric, 30, 57, 77, 104, 117,
 219, 221
 Social considerations, 238
 social impact, 144, 221, 228,
 230, 236

soft power, 24, 88
    Hallyu, 23, 28, 170, 185
    Korean Wave, 185
Southeast Asia, 23, 97, 128, 185
space utilization, 178, 206
Spectrum Gaming, 3
sports betting, 125, 149, 150
    sportsbook, 125, 154, 162
sprint workshops, 263
St. Regis. *See* Marriott
Stanley Ho. *See* SJM
Star Brisbane Casino, 195
Star Cruises. *See* Genting Group
Star Wars. *See* Disney
Stardust, 128
Steve Wynn. *See* Wynn Resorts
Sukhothai. *See* Thailand
SunCity, 41, 48, 99, 248, 249
    Alvin Chau, 99, 152, 248
Sunohada. *See* J-beauty
supply chain, 76, 91, 203, 204,
    256
Suvarnabhumi Airport. *See*
    Thailand
Suzuka Circuit. *See* Formula 1

T

table games. *See* casino games
Taipa. *See* Macau
Taisei Corporation, 257
Taiwan, 5, 96, 194
    Kinmen, 96
    Matsu, 96
    Penghu, 96
Takenaka, 4, 257
Tao, 129
tax, 11, 21, 26, 27, 36, 49, 52, 135,
    235, 236, 238
Taylor Swift, 28, 126, 201
Tempo. *See* Hilton
Thailand
    Ayutthaya, 119, 163
    Bangkok, 56, 57, 88, 100, 101,
        102, 103, 106, 119, 128,
        159, 165, 175, 188, 191,
        202
    Chakri Dynasty, 163
    Chiang Mai, 101, 102, 192
    Don Mueang, 100
    Eastern Economic Corridor,
        57, 119
    entertainment complex, 56,
        57, 59, 86, 87, 88, 100, 101,
        102, 103, 104, 106, 107,
        108, 109, 119, 142, 151,
        163, 165, 175, 177, 180,
        183, 186, 188, 192, 227
    Hua Hin, 186
    Khon Kaen, 102
    Koh Samui, 186
    Koh Yao, 186
    Krabi, 101, 119
    Nakhon Ratchasima, 102, 190
    Pattaya, 56, 57
    Phangnga, 101, 119
    Phuket, 56, 101, 119, 186, 188
    Rajamangala National
        Stadium, 180
    Rayong, 57
    Saraburi, 190
    Sukhothai, 163
    Suvarnabhumi, 100, 101
    Udon Thani, 102
Thinkwell, 165
    iPort, 165
Thomas Hearns, 126
Three Cosmetics. *See* J-beauty
tokidoki. *See* Simone Legno
Tokyo. *See* Japan
Tomakomai. *See* Japan
TPG Group, 5
transparency, 22, 32, 105, 106,
    107, 144, 221, 248, 270, 271
transportation, 29, 56, 57, 58, 73,
    76, 80, 83, 88, 91, 99, 101, 102,
    103, 147, 200, 204, 208, 220,
    242
Treasure Island, 167
Treasury Casino, 195
Twilight. *See* Lionsgate

U

Udon Thani. *See* Thailand
UFC, 126, 175
    Conor McGregor, 126
UIGEA. *See* online gambling
Universal Studios, 46, 134, 158,
    160, 170, 234, 241
utilities, 56, 57, 88, 104

V

Venetian. *See* Las Vegas Sands
VICI Properties. *See* REIT
Vietnam, 38, 59, 89, 97, 99, 112,
    135
    Danang, 97
VIP room, 42
    junket, 15, 22, 23, 24, 38, 41,
        42, 45, 53, 82, 99, 113, 116,
        133, 139, 142, 152, 248
virtual audience, 208
virtual reality, 158
    VR, 154, 158, 159
Vladivostok, 46, 94

W

Wakayama. *See* Japan
Warner Bros, 162
Weidner (William), 96
West Virginia, 149

Wicked, 166
Wind Creek, 139
Winona. *See* C-beauty
Wire Act. *See* online gambling
Wynn Resorts, 38, 39, 41, 43, 44,
    45, 47, 61, 128, 136, 143, 176,
    179, 211, 266, 269
    Encore Las Vegas, 61
    Steve Wynn, 20, 39, 40, 41, 61,
        65, 258, 273
    Wynn Golf Club, 179
    Wynn Las Vegas, 61

X

Xcaret, 164
XS, 129

Y

yield management, 244
Yokohama. *See* Japan
Yoshihide Suga, 7, 223, 225
Yumeshima. *See* Japan

Z

Zhuhai. *See* China
Zoëtry. *See* Hyatt
zoning, 11, 76, 77, 79, 82, 92, 186
Zouk, 129

Also by Daniel Cheng

THE RAINBOW UPOPO
AN AINU NOVEL

JAPAN CASINO UPRISING